THE BIOLOGY OF LOVE

ALSO BY DR. ARTHUR JANOV

The Primal Scream

The Anatomy of Mental Illness

Prisoners of Pain

The Feeling Child

Primal Man

Imprints

Why You Get Sick and How You Get Well

The New Primal Scream

THE
BIOLOGY OF LOVE

DR. ARTHUR JANOV

Author of the International Bestseller *The Primal Scream*

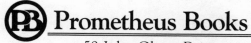

Prometheus Books

59 John Glenn Drive
Amherst, New York 14228-2197

Published 2000 by Prometheus Books

Inquiries should be addressed to
Prometheus Books, 59 John Glenn Drive, Amherst, New York 14228–2197.
VOICE: 716–691–0133, ext. 207.
FAX: 716–564–2711.
WWW.PROMETHEUSBOOKS.COM

04 03 02 01 00   5 4 3 2 1

Library of Congress Cataloging-in-Publication Data

Janov, Arthur.
    The biology of love / Arthur Janov.
        p.   cm.
    Includes bibliographical references and index.
    ISBN 1–57392–829–1
    1. Emotions in infants. 2. Affect (Psychology) 3. Love. 4. Love—
Physiological aspects. 5. Infants (Newborn)—Psychology. 6. Prenatal influences.
7. Infants (Newborn)—Wounds and injuries. I. Title.

Printed in the United States of America on acid-free paper

For my France

Remember, if you take the wrong train, every stop you make is wrong. That train gets its start very early in life, including gestational life. The train starts out in the dark and once the rails are set, we move on them inexorably to the end of our lives.

—Paraphrased from Saul Bellow

It is the task of History to establish the truth.

—Karl Marx

It is the appeal to history that establishes our inner truths.

—Arthur Janov

CONTENTS

7

ACKNOWLEDGMENTS

This book was years in the making. All along the way there were people who helped make it what it is. There is my research assistant, David Lassoff, and my science consultant, Dr. Jonathan Christie. I want to thank Professor Frank Wood of Wake Forest University Medical Center, who edited much of the neurology for me. If there are any discrepancies left, they are my responsibility. My thanks to Dianne Woo, who edited the book in terms of English and organization, and finally to my wife, France, doctoral candidate and codirector of the Primal Center in Venice, California, who made sure that my notions of the current practice of Primal Therapy are concordant with her clinical experience. She spent months helping out on this work. I am indebted to the work of Dr. Paul MacLean of the National Institute for Mental Health for all of his vast knowledge of the brain; we all sit at his feet. It is not only I who feel indebted to Dr. MacLean. All of us in the field recognize that without him brain science would not have advanced to where we are today. I am indebted, as well, to Dr. Allan Schore, who has written what is for me the bible of modern neuropsychology. Dr. Michael Odent, author of *The Nature of Birth and Breastfeeding* and *Birth Reborn*, offered many helpful suggestions regarding childbirth. Thanks to Carol Donner, who illustrated the brain so as to make some of my concepts easier to comprehend. Finally, thanks to my patients, from whom I learn more every day, and to my staff, who endure years of training to learn a most difficult craft because they know of its importance in saving lives.

Dr. Arthur Janov
The Primal Center
Venice, California

e-mail: primalctr@ earthlink.net

INTRODUCTION

L et me begin by explaining what *The Biology of Love* is about and what it is not about. It is about how parental love in the early stages of life influences each of us, how it literally shapes the brain and affects us for a lifetime. What it is not about is academic neurobiology. Given the exciting new discoveries that have been made in this field of brain science, there is a need to merge what we know about neurology with what we observe in clinical practice, and to present it in a nontechnical manner.

This book is written for the layperson who wishes to learn how feelings and emotions—the "motions" we make when we feel—direct our lives. In these pages I take facts culled from up-to-date research and place them into a frame of reference that cohesively brings together widely disparate results.

Much new work has been accomplished on studies of the brain that makes it possible to join the fields of dynamic psychology and neurology. We can use all of the new research to understand why we don't sleep, why we have nightmares, why we are so driven, why we often can neither get along with others nor sustain relationships, why we can't love, why we take alcohol and drugs and what these do to the brain, where pain goes after we experience it, what happens to our feelings when they are driven into the unconscious mind, how our feelings are repressed, what lies in the unconscious, and many more aspects of the human condition. These discoveries are important only if, finally, they help us feel better and lead a decent life. We will see how a mother's love translates directly into the biochemistry of her child and how that love sculpts the brain into new forms. The "loved" brain is different.

If we have a good idea about how emotional pain changes the brain we can perhaps measure the treatment for that pain in terms of neurologic changes. Where are obsessions formed, for example, and why are they formed in the first place? I think we know why, having treated dozens of cases of obsessional rituals. How can we resolve emotional problems such as phobias, sexual deviations, and impulsive behavior? What exactly is "crazy"? Where in the brain might we find this craziness if, indeed, there is a place where it exists? I also will discuss the several currently prescribed tranquilizers and how they work to calm us. What are they really calming?

Although it is the usual professional conceit—or lack of it—that we somehow never know enough to make definitive statements about the sources of mental and emotional problems, I believe we now know enough to arrive at some answers, and to a fuller understanding without resorting to "psychologese" or technical jargon. We are never going to know enough to make an absolute final judgment on any subject, but that shouldn't prevent us from trying to make some sense of a field where the diagnostic manual is thicker than the Manhattan telephone book.

In my work in Primal Therapy, I have delved into the deep unconscious of thousands of patients. For the past thirty years I have steadfastly maintained a belief in the effects of the prebirth and birth trauma experiences in later life. Now research is catching up. There is documentation of this everywhere we look.

When there is no scientific basis for theory and psychotherapy and when observations are colored by preconceived notions, the result is such phenomena as rebirthing therapy, in which patients are instructed to scream and pound the walls in order to "release their pain." This is not "therapy" at all and is deleterious. People must be allowed to work their way down the levels of the brain gradually to reach and connect with their deepest level of the unconscious. In order to do that we must know what lies down in the brain and work within its structures. Without that understanding it is every man for himself, immersed in a sea of approaches unanchored in science. One notion alone, the concept of the imprint, would, in my estimation, change the practice of existing psychotherapy. That is why I will spend time discussing it. We have spent too much time investigating current sources of stress in order to understand the appearance of anxiety, stomach disorders, high blood pressure, heart palpitations, depression, etc., because we have left out the central ingredient of many disorders—history . . . imprinted pain.

Though I had been in the practice of psychoanalytic therapy for seventeen years, I witnessed deep feelings for the first time in 1967, and spent decades trying to figure it out. They were feelings I had never seen before. Yes, my previous patients cried and sobbed but almost never rolled on the floor in agony, screaming out their pain. For those not in pain every day of their lives, this notion might seem aberrant. It is not.

In 1971, when professors in the Department of Neurology at UCLA told me that the storage of birth memories was impossible, it set back my work for years. Eventually I learned that storage is not only possible but highly directive of our later life. Our work at the UCLA Pulmonary Laboratory advanced the research, particularly as it relates to birth trauma. We were discussing gating even before the gate theory emerged in the current literature. In my 1971 book, *The Anatomy of Mental Illness*, I discussed the role of serotonin in mental illness years before the research caught up. I say this not for bragging rights, but to show that we must not be closed-minded to new approaches. It is comfortable to hold onto our past notions, sometimes too comfortable; they become a catechism we perform each day.

The Biology of Love takes a look at how the first weeks and months of life, not just social life, but presocial womblife, change our brains; how feelings and memories are stamped into the brain, and how and why they endure for the rest of our lives. It addresses why nothing in adult life can radically alter what happened to us as infants and even before birth. If a trauma or lack of love happened to us during a critical period, nothing in adult life can change it because the changes that took place at the time were imprinted in the neurobiologic system permanently. Don't be discouraged, though; there are solutions, which I will address in this book.

We will look at life in the womb and its effect on us as adults. We know, for example, that administering heavy anesthesia to the mother during childbirth shuts down the baby's system, causing lifelong effects that range from low libido to passive, phlegmatic character traits. We know that a woman who takes tranquilizers and/or consumes significant amounts of alcohol during pregnancy is already affecting the neurotransmitter levels of her offspring, possibly leading to anxiety or depression in the child's later life. When the pregnant mother's inhibitory brain chemicals become deficient, so do those of her baby. When a mother loves her infant, the hormones of love (such as oxytocin, vasopressin, and seratonin) become stronger in the baby for a lifetime. He will grow up to be a better parent to his own children. He will have a different physiology than that of someone not loved in early infancy . . . and a different brain.

Prebirth trauma causes changes in neurotransmitter output and in the number of their receptors. Neurotransmitters are the chemical vehicles that transport our feelings throughout the nervous system, or stop those feelings in their tracks. Too much pain, too prolonged an early lack of love, can shut the gates against feeling. Diabolically and dialectically, early pain can weaken the "gates" that our brain system erects to block that very trauma. A baby born to a heroin-addicted mother is literally miserable. Her endorphin receptors have been downsized to accommodate the mother's drug habit. A happy, well-nourished pregnant woman, on the other hand, sufficiently equips her fetus to face the potential hurdles of birth and of obstacles later in life. That baby will be loaded with antianxiety and antipain chemicals so as to surmount obstacles and adversity.

I also examine the effects of the love by caregivers—the mother and father—on our biology and how the lack of love very early on changes our "thinking" cortex and "feeling" limbic system. When there is little emotional rapport between mother and newborn, for instance, nerve cells in certain brain structures do not develop properly. The prefrontal cortex—the planning, thinking, logical, integrating outer layer of brain cells—is impaired by a lack of early love and will not function to full capacity later in life. This deprivation leads to less control over one's impulses and a reduced ability to think abstractly, as well as impaired coordination and a diminished ability to plan ahead.

During the first months of life, if a mother or father does not look into a baby's eyes with love and warmth, does not caress her, talk to her, and feel love for her, that lack of feeling determines the growth rate of cortical nerve cells, or neurons, in the child's brain. Loving the child is loving his brain. All else being equal, a loved brain is a normal one.

The description of key structures of the brain in this work is not meant to be a definitive model. In later chapters I explore in more detail the role specific brain structures play in emotions and feelings, as well as how they translate love or lack thereof into physical symptoms.

What's love got to do with it? More than we can imagine. Love is not simply a word uttered to a child, but an act of feeling that, ironically, most often requires no words. If we hug and kiss our child and adore her, she will get the message and her life will be utterly different. If we don't, words won't help.

In the *Biology of Love*, I shall offer the reader a new concept of love, one more in keeping with information about the brain and psychology. We will see how concrete love actually is, not just each person's idea of what it is. We will discover how love ultimately determines how we think, feel, perceive, and act as adults. It determines how long we live and what illnesses we will fall prey to later in life. It is no exaggeration to say that very early lack of love already sets the limits on how long we will live and how happy our lives will be. The secondary defenses of smoking, drinking, overeating, and drug taking to push down our early deprivation will eventually help to create premature deaths. We usually don't die of overweight. We die from the lack of love that makes us overeat. The same for smoking and drinking. Above all, early love, being cherished and adored as a child, will determine how much we love life later on. Lack of that love leaves us with the constant feeling of not getting much out of life, not caring very much if we live or die, because we can't feel the life we're living. So many individuals seem indifferent to their own death because life holds so little for them. I think we know enough to explain why that is.

I explore how our intolerance and inhumanity toward others, even to our own children, is connected to brain function, and how a change in brain function can make us more "human." Why are drugs and alcohol so important to some people? What do they do to the brain, and why do some people have such a hard time kicking the habit? Are the twelve-step programs important? Only if you don't address the origins of the pain.

Let us prepare to sail into uncharted waters, to take an extraordinary trip into the depths of the unconscious. Once there, we'll find it to be a place full of light, insight, and peace. All those hidden demons—those painful memories lodged in the brain that caused a shutdown in the baby and adult—will be liberated. We call them demons but they are not. They are precise needs and memories that are imprinted and surge forth in a constant effort to find their way out of the unconscious. The cortical apparatus necessary even to begin understanding and controlling our pain is not developed until age two, and it will be years later that we have the complete capacity to integrate what lies in the unconscious. In the meantime, early lack of love and other traumas may damage this cortical, inhibitory apparatus, leaving the child hyperactive, manic, anxious, and tense. It is not a state that we grow out of. It is an aberration.

Simply put, unexpressed feelings can drive us "crazy," or at the very least make us agitated and uncomfortable. Expressing these feelings can help us regain our sanity and stability.

To embark on this journey, we must have a rudimentary understanding of the brain and how it works.

Part I

THE STRUCTURE OF THE BRAIN

1

THE STRUCTURE OF THE BRAIN

The brain mirrors our evolutionary history. From the reptilian brain, which governs instinct, to the limbic system, which processes feelings, to the frontal cortex, which governs understanding and reasoning, the brain is a map to our own origins. This remarkable, self-constructed organ has been in development for hundreds of millions of years.

Ideas lie in the intellectual realm, feelings in the emotional realm. If a person says, "I feel inferior," she is speaking from two levels. The *idea* of inferiority is a top-level cortical brain event. The *feeling* of inferiority is a lower-level brain event. It is the limbic system that offers us the feeling of feeling. Herein lies the first major point: it is not enough to think about feelings. It is essential to feel them so as to gain the ability to feel. Feelings *are* our humanity.

If we are not loved and adored but rather treated with indifference and neglect in our childhood, we may well feel "not good enough . . . not good enough to be loved." That becomes an imprint. It endures. If this kind of parental treatment goes on throughout childhood, then the imprint will be locked in. That means that all the encouragement in the world at age twenty will not erase that feeling. Encouragement—"You are wonderful, you know"—is an idea; ideas cannot change feelings.

Only feelings can. This seemingly simple notion has profound implications. For if we are trying to regain our humanity, we need to regain our feelings; and we cannot do that through the mode of ideas alone.

To regain feeling one must fully experience all of the hurt blocking it, and bring the pain to conscious-awareness. Then an "idea" can make changes, when it flows out of feelings. Conscious-awareness strips the unconscious of its power to direct behavior. Ideas and feelings reside in different places in the brain. We must not try to make one level do the work of another level. We must not attempt to use ideas to replace feelings. The feeling of feeling involves specific structures in the brain such as the hippocampus and amygdala. Ideas about those feelings are processed in the top-level cortex, specifically the left hemisphere, forward part of the brain. If we use the frontal cortex alone to feel, we are in trouble. The most we can expect is a crying "about," an adult looking back at childhood, instead of a child actually feeling her hurts.

The forces driving our behavior are located largely in three different brain systems: (1) the cortex, which operates conscious-awareness; (2) the limbic system, which drives feeling; and (3) the brainstem, which processes instincts and survival functions. Imprints take place in different parts of the brain depending on their force and when they occurred. Very early developments, prebirth and birth, will impact the most competent nervous system at the time—the brainstem. Traumas in early childhood will affect the brainstem and limbic system. Later, as the neocortex develops, thinking processes will be involved. The brainstem is a three-inch-long stalk that joins the brain with the spinal column and is composed of three main parts: the *medulla, pons,* and *midbrain.* Among its other structures are the *reticular activating system* (groups of nerve cells that alert the higher levels of the brain to stimuli) and the *locus ceruleus* (a collection of neurons, or nerve cells, that activate the nervous system in response to pain and sometimes pleasure as well).[1]

First, the brain is divided horizontally into two hemispheres, each with its own specific functions. The right hemisphere, which is larger than the left, is the site of feelings and emotions and of holistic, global thinking. Thoughts, planning, and concepts are the domain of the left hemisphere. The right brain is largely mature at the second year of life; the left brain is only beginning its maturation at that time. Feelings predate thoughts. In terms of evolution we are feeling beings long before we are thinking ones. If we want to go back in time in our brains we must travel on the appropriate vehicle. Ideas are the wrong train. We must time travel with the brain that was involved with the imprint at the time, so that a birth trauma may be lodged far below ideas and even below feelings; engraved in the brainstem, which is the most primitive aspect of our nervous system. This imprint can only be "explained" in terms of salamander movements, writhing and turning without the use of limbs. This is the language of the brainstem. Later it will help to understand what we went through, but we cannot skip evolutionary steps and expect change. This is my second major point: we cannot defy evolution in the understanding and treatment of problems. The brain won't allow it.

The brainstem speaks the language of high blood pressure, palpitations, and angina; the silent killers expressed quietly. It contains the secrets of our birth and of our lives before birth in the womb. If we want to know what kind of birth we had it will tell us in its own way. It will be precise and unmistakable. Its wonderful quality is that it cannot and will not lie. If the memory included a heart rate of 180 beats per minute, then in the reliving there will be exactly 180 beats per minute. It is one way we verify memory.

The last structure to know anything about ourselves is the left frontal cortex. Events early in life can be processed by the right-feeling hemisphere without the left side being aware. It must guess about feelings and is often wrong. Hence, misperceptions and misinterpretations. The paradox is that the most evolved part of our brains often knows the least about the rest of ourself and of others. I will endeavor to show how using the frontal cortex alone cannot make profound changes in anyone; this means that insights into behavior and symptoms is a vain exercise. Understanding is sometimes helpful but is not the sine qua non of personal development. It is possible to "get well" on a cortical level and yet remain "sick" below it. This is why dream analysis, ideas about feelings, is unhelpful. The best kind of dream analysis is to feel the feeling inside the dream, and all of its symbolism will become apparent.

The brain consists of three distinctive areas. The lowest level is known as the *brainstem*, or reptilian brain. Above the brainstem is the *feeling*, or limbic, brain. The limbic system translates instincts into feel-

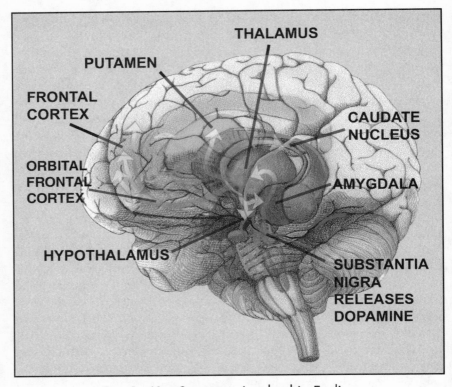

Fig. 1. Key Structures Involved in Feeling

ings and sends the combination to the frontal cortex, the area at the top front of the brain. The newest part of the brain is the *neocortex* (meaning "new cortex"), the covering of the brain.

The brainstem controls basic, automatic functions such as eye reflexes, heart rate, digestion, breathing, and vomiting. It harbors most of our instincts and survival mechanisms. It contains our hard-wired needs. The brainstem produces the drive that energizes feeling. It adds the "punch" to feelings. Unadulterated rage and fear can originate in the brainstem and can move to the limbic system for focus or to find outlets in artistic expression such as violent images or stories, for example.

The medulla contains groups of nerve cells involved in regulating heart rate, blood pressure, digestion, and breathing. The pons sits above the medulla and is connected by nerve fibers to the *cerebellum*, which is a separate organ attached to the back of the brainstem. Sensory information from the ears, face, and teeth is relayed by the pons. Above the pons is the *midbrain*, which is the smallest part of the brainstem and handles eye movements, pupil dilation, and the coordination of limb movements.

Ideally, the brainstem, limbic system, and neocortex bring our instincts, feelings, and thoughts together harmoniously. Much of the time, though, the three levels are kept apart, crushing our feelings in a blizzard of ideas, for example. We will see how early trauma produces a blockage from one level to another so as to keep other levels from being overwhelmed by input. Very often, the limbic system and brainstem produce their own inhibitory chemicals to keep the message of pain out of the hands of the frontal interpretive cortex. This allows the cortex to think, plan, and go on about its business without too much interference from below. Sometimes, however, the lower-level imprints are so powerful that they break through the protective barrier; it is then that we suffer anxiety, panic, phobias, and obsessions. It is then that we cannot sleep, as impulses rush forward provoking the frontal area to race ahead to keep the demons at bay. The diabolic aspect of this is that the very same traumas, even in the womb, that require high levels of inhibitory neurohormones are the ones that diminish those levels. That is, the traumas are of such a magnitude that they damage the repressive system for life.

The lower imprints are constantly trying to inform conscious-awareness of things it doesn't want to know about. It wants to tell the cortex that it feels unloved and hurts, but the cortex is too busy trying to get love to listen to the message. It doesn't even know it feels unloved, yet acts it out every day. The cerebral switchboard redirects the message of "unlove" elsewhere; to the heart for palpitations, to the head for migraine, to the blood vessels for hypertension. They accept the message and translate it into their own language. If we learn the code of the brain we can retranslate the symptom back to the real information, thus extirpating the pain from its lodgings on lower brain levels. It means "breaking the code." That means acknowledging the imprint, the coded memory that may date back to birth. That is why the concept of the imprint is so crucial. Without it, we are adrift, unable to understand the origins of things or even that there are origins lying in the antipodes of the brain. We are then forced to place everything in current context. Yet we are historical beings, and the truth of ourselves lies in the history; and that history lies in the brain. It is knowable.

THE FRONTAL CORTEX AND FEELINGS

The front part of the cortex sits at the level of the orbs of the eyes and is the top layer of the brain. Called the *orbitofrontal cortex* (OBFC), it processes outside information with memory and personal history to produce awareness, not to be confused with consciousness. Consciousness is defined as all three levels of brain activity functioning in harmony. When there is proper access between the frontal cortex and lower centers it is called "conscious-awareness." The prefrontal cortex, located behind the forehead, and the OBFC first play an active role at about age two, handling comprehension and reflection. Because few of us will be performing brain surgery in the near future, I am going to take literary license and refer to the OBFC and prefrontal cortex as simply the frontal area, or frontal cortex. The OBFC is largely the "stop" mechanism to inhibit impulses. When there is severe damage to this area we find restlessness, lack of inhibition, hyperactivity, and distractibility. This can happen without a blow on the head but with developmental impairment due to a lack of love very early in life.[2] The cortex changes dramatically when there is early deprivation. In its place is a different kind of brain that has fewer cells to do its work.

THE LIMBIC SYSTEM

The limbic system, made up of several structures, is largely developed by the age of twenty months. The hippocampus of this system is fairly mature at age two, but new evidence indicates that with intellectual stimulation new hippocampal cells can be created in late adulthood. The brain can grow new cells, possibly for the rest of our lives.

The amygdalae are a pair of almond-shaped structures on the inner surface of the temporal lobes, adjacent to the hippocampus. They act as a kind of crossroads in the brain. Writes researcher Joseph LeDoux: "The amygdala has direct and extensive connections with all the sensory systems of the cortex . . . also communicates with the thalamus. . . . The same part of the amygdala on which sensory inputs converge sends fibers deeper into the brain to the hypothalamus, which is thought to be the ultimate source of emotional responses."[3] The amygdala seems to be the focal point of feeling, sending and receiving messages to organ systems via the hypothalamus. It also transmits emotional information, suffering, to the thalamus which then translates it for the frontal cortex, making us aware of what we are feeling.

Recent evidence shows that the amygdalae develop long before the neocortex does, both in personal development (ontogenetic) and in our long history from animals to human beings (phylogenetic). It is one of the most ancient structures of the brain, a site close to the hippocampus, also ancient but not as old as the amygdala. The amygdala is dominant in processing emotional information up to the middle of the first year of life. To learn what the unconscious holds we need to access this structure. It can be done.

The amygdalae seem to "grow" their own opium. They secrete opiates, which suppress pain and keep painful information out of conscious-awareness. I find it astounding that this piece of jellylike material we call a brain can tell itself to release a poppy derivative to take away the perception of pain. Moreover, it tells itself exactly how much to release and when, and also when to stop. Actually, it is not all that surprising when we consider that many plants that need sun to produce energy for their growth (oxygen-giving photosynthesis) tend to shut down when there is too much exposure to sunlight. The concept of overload and shutdown, in short, is something we can trace to plant life.[4] For some plants, persistent and unrelenting sunlight becomes dangerous because it causes decreases in the rate of photosynthesis. Here is what two plant researchers say: "If the protective processes are overwhelmed, photo*inhibition* [my emphasis] will decrease the efficiency and capacity of photosynthesis."[5] The leaf damage is tantamount to a sunburn. Perhaps to labor the point: they found that extremely intense sunlight activates a signaling system that "warns" regions of the plant not yet exposed to the light of impending danger. It closes down and literally "won't let the light in," something that we might extrapolate to human beings. The key principle here is overload and shutdown.

OVERLOAD AND SHUTDOWN: HOW WE REPRESS

Our brains can reach back in evolution to plant life to construct protective devices. In the plant paradigm there may be clues to how our brains work. There are a number of studies on nerve cells showing that when there is a barrage of input the cells become "silent"; they fail to respond further. This is another way of demonstrating how overload produces shutdown. If it happens in a nuclear plant bells and alarms go off. If it happens to the human system nothing happens. At least nothing overt. Below decks there is a constant flurry of activity as hormones spill into the system: body heat goes up, white cells scurry to and fro, and brain cells are recruiting supporting cells in the service of repression. Alas, the alarm is silent and no one is there to hear it. The alarm chimes and screams yet we are deaf. The guts are screaming while we go around with a beatific smile as if all were right with the world, or we are so busy with business deals that we ignore a disaster in the making. That disaster can spell the end of our lives.

THE HIPPOCAMPUS

Behind the amygdalae, the hippocampus forms the tip of the ram's horn; the word means "sea horse," which this structure resembles. An ancient structure of the brain, the hippocampus is apparently responsible for "declarative memory," the context and circumstances of an event as opposed to its emotional content, which is the province of the amygdalae.

Located at the junction of the ram's-horn shape of the limbic system, the hypothalamus is about the size of a cherry. It is situated behind the eyes and beneath the thalamus and is connected to other regions of the nervous system. The hypothalamus regulates hormone production and stimulates the immune system via the pituitary gland, which lies just beneath it. It also helps regulate vital functions, including blood pressure, heart rate, and body temperature. The hypothalamus governs both the parasympathetic nervous system and the sympathetic nervous system, which make up the autonomic nervous system. The autonomic nervous system controls internal organ function. We shall see how important this system is.

We have taken a cursory look at some key brain structures involved in feeling. In the next chapter we will examine how those structures interact and send messages to each other, and how information is encouraged or blocked in neural highways known as "pathways." We will see how the unconscious becomes the "unconscious." We will discover what happens to our feelings when we can't access our higher centers where awareness lies. In chapter 7 I will introduce two new notions: the imprint, and critical periods. We will find out how events outside of us—a look, a scowl, or a harsh word—become imprinted inside our brains for a lifetime. And we will discover how there are crucial times when outside impact has the greatest influence on us, altering the development of the brain.

There are periods before birth and soon after when the brain is developing at an incredibly rapid clip. These periods are when nerve cells of the brain—neurons—are developing their connections to other neurons to form nerve circuits. Serious trauma during these periods—a mother anxious or depressed, or a mother who drinks or smokes heavily—can deviate the brain permanently.

MESSENGERS OF THE BRAIN

Altogether, the nervous system consists of billions of neurons that interconnect. These nerve cells receive signals, or information, from the body's sense organs and transmit them to the central nervous system. Each neuron consists of a cell body and branches called dendrites. Signals travel between neurons via conducting fibers called axons, which branch at the end to form axon terminals. The gap between an axon terminal and the receiving nerve cell is called a synapse. Signals traverse this gap with the help of chemicals called neurotransmitters. The number of synapses changes with early trauma and thereby produces a different kind of brain. When we are not loved early on (and it is always very early in life that I am discussing, prebirth and the first eighteen months after birth) in a sense, we do not have "all of our marbles" to enter life's fray. Those marbles, inter alia, are the synaptic junctions. It is where the chemical messengers are dumped that either hold back information or improve its capacity to communicate, particularly to higher levels that could make sense out of it all. Tranquilizers most often work in these gaps to impede the message, a very old one . . . "no one cares about me." The brain, limbic system, and brainstem are loaded with messages such as this.

The spiderlike branches leading from a nerve cell to other neurons are called dendrites; they provide information to other nerve cells. When love is missing, the dendrites suffer. There is less branching, and the result is a different—and permanently different—brain. The stress hormone receptors (corticosteroids) are also reduced, so there are likely to be more free-floating stress hormones in the brain.[6] What is left is a toxic brain environment with fewer synapses, particularly in the limbic-feeling centers, to carry information from one region to another. This may explain why a person is not sympathetic to others and is not sensitive to their pain, being insensitive to himself. His feeling centers are impaired.

Many different chemicals serve as these messengers. They help pass lower-level information to higher areas. Serotonin, for example, aids in the inhibition of pain and also deals with satiety, thus having a positive side to it. However, I shall concentrate on its repressive components since it is basically an inhibitory neurotransmitter.

Acetylcholine passes information between the brain and spinal cord. Norepinephrine controls heart rate and stress response. It is associated with reward. Dopamine helps coordinate body movements and helps stimulate us and our cortex to make us vigilant and is associated with goal seeking. Too much dopamine, though, can overstimulate the cortex and literally "drive us crazy." The endorphins play a major role in controlling sensitivity to pain. These neurotransmitters are further discussed in later chapters but for now we need to be aware, as most of us are already, that the brain produces its own painkillers. At times I will focus on certain transmitters as they relate to emotional upset, keeping in mind that there is a broad range of functions of these chemicals.

We must remember that behind all the "feeling" states discussed in the psychiatric literature lies a brain, one from which anxiety and depression seep out. We want to find out where this phenomenon takes place and why. What makes that happen? Should we automatically push back painful information on its way to conscious-awareness? If the person feels better with tranquilizers can we consider it a cure? Is it good enough? Or, is there a price to pay for repression?

NOTES

1. The locus ceruleus engenders norepinephrine activation (NE) modulates the cortex in response to stress or pleasure, but I shall focus on stress. See: N. Singewald and A. Philippu, "Neuroanatomy of the Pain System and of the Pathways that Modulate Pain," *Progress in Neurobiology* 56, no. 2 (October 1998): 237–67.

2. See K. H. Pribram and D. Mcguinness, "Arousal, Activation, and Effort: Separate Neural Systems," *Psychological Review* 82, no. 2 (March 1975): 116–49.

3. Joseph LeDoux, *The Emotional Brain* (New York: Simon & Schuster, 1996), p. 163.

4. C. H. Foyer and Graham Noctor, "Leaves in the Dark See the Light," *Science* 284, no. 5414 (23 April 1999): 599.

5. Ibid.

6. A. Barbazanges et al., "Maternal Glucocorticoid Secretion Mediates Long-Term Effects of Prenatal Stress," *Journal of Neuroscience* 16 (15 June 1996): 3943–49.

2

THE FRONTAL CORTEX
The Thinking Man's Brain

The orbitofrontal cortex (OBFC) is located behind the orbs of the eyes on the top layer of the brain and combines outside information with memory and personal history to produce conscious behavior. Together with the prefrontal cortex, located behind the forehead, the OBFC begins functioning at about age two and continues developing until about age twenty.

Suffice it to know that this front-top area of the brain is involved with thoughts, ideas, planning, beliefs, philosophies, logic, reason, understanding, foresight, and insight, all by integrating inside information with outside input. It also integrates lower-level feelings into conscious-awareness and gives meaning to our feelings, helping us to deal with the external world. It is the container of ambition, abstract thought, and sophisticated concepts. It involves ambition because it can set goals for the future and make plans to achieve them.

The problem is that sometimes these concepts exist solely in the frontal area without a solid connection to the subcortical structures of the brain. This explains why we can be smart but not intelligent. With disconnection from lower centers we can misperceive and misjudge.

The growth of the frontal cortex reaches preliminary maturity between eighteen months and two years. Because it has a reciprocal relationship with the reticular activating system, it must function properly to modulate the alerting-vigilance function. When severe adverse events take place before, during, and after birth, the frontal cortex is impaired; the gating system is compromised, leading to poorly controlled impulses and/or lifelong tension and anxiety. The child/adult no longer has a strong antipain, antianxiety function.

Environmental events determine the depth of the growth of the cortex; this in turn establishes how we perceive things and how we think, reason, and plan. A great deal of stress or neglect in the first two years of life doubtless has permanent consequences in brain development. It may also play into an excess "pruning" of the cortical neurons, leaving the child with less brain capacity to handle future stress. Neurons seem to go where they are needed; they atrophy or fade away where and when they are not needed. In dealing with early trauma, new brain pathways are constructed and others are eliminated. Contrarily, if there is not enough stimulation or emotional interaction between parent and child in the first year or two, there may well be a deficit in the development of synapses.

Trauma can interfere with the secretion of dopamine, an activating neurochemical often referred to as the "feel good" chemical, which is necessary in developing our fronto-cortical nerve cells. (High levels of dopamine tend to produce euphoria.) Above all, as we shall see, early lack of love, and that is always a trauma, alters the inhibitory neurohormone systems so that repression is less effective for a lifetime. It is no wonder that anxiety, which may have its roots in womblife, is so difficult for conventional psychotherapy to manage.

A properly functioning cortex works with the reticular activating system to modulate the alerting-vigilance function. Without it, one cannot slow oneself down, and the result can be a chronic hyper state or worse, an anxiety attack. Research shows that early events literally sculpt our brains. A loved child literally has a different brain than an unloved one. The work of Jean Lauder builds the case for how adversity in the womb changes the structure of the long axons which deliver information to other nerve cells. Sometimes there is excessive pruning as the brain must deal with inordinate pain, utilizing brain cells for repression instead of dealing with outside reality. Love produces an abundance of serotonin and other repressive brain hormones to help put down future pain. It also builds a strong prefrontal cortex to better integrate internal and external input. It is why a loved child is a smart one.

Suffice it to say that the mother or caregiver of an infant constitutes the rest of his nervous system. She fills in the blanks. He can cry or scream but he cannot comfort himself and therefore calm himself; for that he needs a parent's love. With loving nurturance he will develop the capacity for normal loving reactions later on. Without this nurturing he will become a disturbed adult forever unable to feel at ease with himself. How could it be otherwise when the brain is different for those in pain?

The early pain becomes a reverberating circuit.[1] What Schore has suggested is a possible neuronal loop for this reverberation. Inordinate responses flare up in the face of the most banal of events. A woman, for instance, who was never asked for her opinions or feelings as a child, will overreact at the slightest hint of lack of respect, such as a salesperson addressing her by her first name or her child sassing back. "Neurosis" was the label once given to these inappropriate reactions. It's a term we can use, but "pain" will do as well.

An imprint has a long life span that travels from subcortical brainstem centers to cortical sites and back interminably. It is the background on which current behavior is formed. In the case above, the lack of respect by parents is lodged in the limbic system, which then adds force to any situation where there was a lack of respect.

The more catastrophic the early trauma is, the more enduring the early emotional deprivation, the more catastrophic the later disease, whether mental or physical. These imprints have a deleterious effect on cortical development; that means the possibility of lifelong anxiety. With enough stress hormone in constant interplay with the rest of the hormone system, eventually there can be serious disease. Stamped-in memory constantly drives such behavior as aggression, depression, paranoia, jealousy, nightmares, drinking, and drug taking. We may "know" about the time our father left our mother, but we also need to "know" about this event by connecting with the feelings that lie in our unconscious, below the cortex. We then become consciously aware; therein lies the agony. To be aware doesn't necessarily mean agony. To be consciously aware does (if there was early pain). It is not a mystery as to why early pain trauma leads to catastrophic disease later in life. Those early traumas result in very high readings of vital functions. That force stays in the system creating havoc, eventually leading to serious afflictions. That force requires an equal and opposite force of repression as the system calls into work many of the inhibitory biochemicals. That deep repression (and it is almost impossible to convey the strength of this pressure in words) puts great pressure on the cells, which eventually disintegrate or deviate from normal.

The frontal cortex can either mobilize us or slow us down (up or down regulation). Early trauma and lack of love impair the ability to slow down, causing the child to be hyperactive and hard to control. Awash in impulses from all of the early pain he has suffered, he hasn't the cortical wherewithal to suppress the pain. He is then disciplined for his *lack* of discipline. He requires outside discipline precisely because he has lost his internal one. Furthermore, his heart speeds up due to the imprint and to his lack of control, and eventually, decades later, he may suffer from a heart attack.

At age two, this child is already on his way to cardiac problems at age fifty. He becomes the kind of adult who has to keep moving, who cannot take a vacation or relax. He lacks the cortical ability to slow down his metabolism—the "uncoupling of arousal" of which Schore speaks, resulting in ulcers or ulcerative colitis. Bowel functions also may be affected, as they are under stress as well. This kind of person may be irritable and easily set off. He sometimes may feel that, "I want to jump out of my skin." He needs things done *now*! The frontal cortex is a powerhouse of self-produced analgesics, which are inhibitory, painkilling chemicals. Stimulation of this area increases the level of endorphins secreted. That is how perceptions and ideas shut down pain. The secret is not to overstimulate the cortex too early.

The orbitofrontal cortex (whenever I mention any structure in a global way, it is important to remember that only parts of these areas are involved) sends direct messages to the hypothalamus, which can then activate brainstem structures such as the medulla as well as limbic sites. It sends excitatory catecholamines (adrenaline, noradrenaline, and dopamine) to the amygdala of the limbic system while sending inhibitory (cholinergic) secretions to the brainstem.

It sends inhibitory messages along chemical routes to the amygdala and brainstem because the input of pain demands it. Pain automatically and dialectically brings into being its oppressor to form a new state—a repressed or a partially feeling organism. The brain in all of its wisdom says, "I'll only let you feel a little at a time." The feeling may be, "Without my mother's love I can't survive."

HOW AN ANGRY LOOK BECOMES A CHEMICAL IN OUR BRAIN

How does a cross word by a father become a chemical in the child's brain? The angry words portend possible danger and rejection. There are clues in the tone of voice, the look, and the words themselves. What is going on inside the child is that the hypothalamic-frontal cortex axis is engaged to send messages to all other systems to be on the alert. This message is sent by chemical courier. It is the meaning implicit in the message that begins the chemical transformation in the child's brain. The hypothalamus then triggers the endocrine system to release catecholamines, making the heart speed up and the blood flow. Generally the process goes from the perceiving frontal cortex and other aspects of the cortex (hearing, sight, etc.) to the hypothalamus to the pituitary and then to sympathetic nervous system neurons which organize the flight or fight response to danger.

It also may be responsible for the increased serotonin output to hold back the tide of feelings. When the traumas are severe and early enough these changes may become permanent as the setpoints become altered. Terror of the father may become permanent increases in stress hormone levels. The frontal area interacts with the medulla in the brainstem to affect heart and lung function. In turn, the brainstem maintains the tone and vigor of the frontal cortex, constantly adjusting it to react to stimuli. When the brainstem is in a hyper state due to early trauma, particularly birth trauma, the frontal-limbic-brainstem areas may overreact. "Hysteria" is the label we attach to the resulting behavior. "What are you getting so excited about?" "Dunno." Now we know why the overreaction.

The frontal cortex is the most changeable area of the brain throughout our lives. If our access to our internal, feeling self is cut off, chances are we will be more suggestible to outside ideas, even about ourself. Instead of being connected to lower brain centers and paying attention to them, the cortex listens to the brain centers of others and follows suit. Others' ideas are allowed to dominate.

When warmth is expressed in the actions of a parent toward a baby, the baby's brain is suffused with opiates, resulting in a feeling of well-being in her. I have heard many of my patients cry out, "Show me that you want me, Mama!" In animal research, the loving handling of specimens just after birth increases the antianxiety chemicals such as serotonin. This level endures so that later in life there is still an adequate mechanism to handle adversity or stress.

When a father never touches his infant, is impatient and angry, and demands obedience from a two-year-old, the frontal cortical neurons are going to be deficient . . . for a very long time. Hugs and kisses during these critical periods make those neurons grow and connect properly with other neurons. You can kiss that brain into maturity.

A father who never shows happiness to see the baby, never responds with kindness to her cries is forming a new brain in the offspring. Every action of the parent may exude unhappiness with the child who did nothing more than get born and interfere in his life. The stage is already set for later unhappiness and depression. She is now on a lifelong struggle to make the father happy to be with her—a fruitless effort. It is a sense of being unwanted that the baby can feel long before it understands the concept of unwanted and unliked. And what can the baby do about it? Nothing. Her brain goes on the alert. Later on, if her mother is cold and unloving as well, she can turn to women for love. Or, more likely, the woman can turn to men who are not impassioned with her so that she can struggle to make them like her. Who can live with such a feeling when you are totally dependent on people who don't like you? And due to early trauma and its effects on the frontal area, the person cannot control herself and her needs. She will immediately act-out.

Everything changes in adult life, however, because now the child can do for the parent; can take care of her, pay attention to her, take her places, and in short, not be a needy child. And why does the child do it? Because the need has never changed and the child still needs to feel wanted. Now she is not only wanted but actually needed by the elderly parent; a complete switch and what the deprived parent needed all the time. How could the mother take care of the child when she was the child in need?

The frontal cortex accounts for 30 percent of all cortical mass. When a deficit occurs in the cortex, impulses are allowed to rule. If a husband leaves his pregnant wife because he doesn't want children, she is likely to be depressed or anxious. Faced with rearing a child alone, the mother secretes more stress hormones. This altered chemical, hormonal balance ultimately impacts the fetus's system, and may lead to premature birth or miscarriage. Of course, a mother who is chronically anxious due to her own miserable childhood is also going to have high stress levels without any current triggering event.

A hyperactive mother, who cannot relax and comfort her child because of what may have happened to her in the first months or years of her own life, is going to impair the frontal cortex of her child, not by deliberate acts but by who she is. Can you tell her to hold the baby gently? Yes, but you can't tell her to hold the baby with love; that is what is communicated naturally. If the mother never told the baby "I love you" but adored, hugged, and kissed her infant constantly, that child would grow up feeling loved.

The number of synaptic connections in the cortex continues to proliferate until age two, when it peaks. Then, in a Darwinian survival process called pruning, those connections no longer needed fade away, leaving us with the amount we use and need. Severe trauma interferes with the synaptic growth process, ultimately reflected in diminished thinking abilities—a gap in the intellect. We may then find clumsiness, lack of coordination, poor spatial sense, and a whole host of problems that rely on a well-functioning cortex.

All the latest research indicates that parental care early in life makes a lasting impression. Children reared without being hugged and touched early on have abnormally high stress levels. A study of Romanian orphans found this result. These hormones can impair growth and development of the brain. At the Society for Neuroscience meeting in New Orleans (1997), it was noted by Michael Meaney of the Douglas Hospital Research Center in Montreal that the presence of mothers ensures that stress hormones in their offspring remain at low levels. Any kind of touch to animals, including whisking with a brush, could reverse the stress levels occasioned by early maternal deprivation. It doesn't take much touch to comfort a child. My touch-deprived patients relive the time their father put a kind hand on their shoulder. What a wonderful moment that was for them.

"Have you hugged your child (or dog) today," goes the bumper-sticker. Hugging is not only like 25 milligrams of Prozac (serotonin) but hugging literally equates physiologically to a certain level of milligrams of Prozac in the body of the baby. We encourage our isolated, withdrawn patients to get an animal. It is a first step in giving and getting affection. They need to hug something or somebody. A dog will lick them back. He may not say, "I love you," but he will show it.

Touch and caress are crucial very early on. Touch produces precursors or building blocks of our built-in tranquilizers such as serotonin.[2] In this way it makes us strong in the face of later adversity. One thing that the lack of very early touch does is make us more prone to anxiety by weakening the repressive system that holds back fear stored low in the central nervous system where brainstem terror is organized, the locus ceruleus. A study by Smythe and others found long-term effects of animals handled early in their lives on the development and enhancement of serotonin precursors. This was not the case with adult animals who were handled outside the critical period.[3]

The long-lasting effects of early stress to later development has been well documented by pharmacologist David Peters.[4] In animal experiments with fetuses in the last week or two before birth a stressed mother adversely affected the serotonin output of the offspring. Peters found that stress impaired the later development of key inhibitory neurons and interfered with synaptic connections. This is important evidence for how the mother's condition while carrying can affect the child for the rest of his life.[5] The work of M. J. Meaney is instructive about how the very early environment affects brain development, specifically of the forebrain. Rat pups in his study were handled for the first twenty-one days after birth. Later in life they showed lower levels of stress hormones in response to external stressors. They also normalized, returning to baseline measurements after a stress situation quicker. The author points out that the changes in rats' systems remained *for a lifetime*.[6]

TRANSCRIPT OF A SESSION

The following is a transcript of a session with Mary.* Where it reads (cries) it is often very deep infantile crying of a baby. Then she comes out of the feeling and discusses her insights. There is a question in the reader's mind: How come the therapist says so little? I practiced insight therapy for seventeen years and was verbose. Primal Therapy requires very little intervention. In the space of a two-hour session I usually don't say much more than two or three paragraphs. But those words have to be precise and they have to count. We therapists do talk a lot at the end of the session, know as the *postsession*. Then we go over the insights and try to connect today's session with yesterday's. We also try to see how feelings experienced in the session relate to the patient's current life. It is a time for integration.

Therapist: Tell me how you feel?

Mary: Well I'm tired, I didn't sleep many hours.

Why?

I think I had taken a nap in the afternoon because I was so tired yesterday afternoon. And because my mind was racing with possibilities. I was just excited and so had a hard time turning it off. One feeling I was noticing this morning is that my breathing feels very, very shallow. That's when I noticed what's going on with my body. Just not breathing much.

Your body just feels tired?

I feel like I would like to go into a very deep sleep. I feel like I don't want to think about very much. I don't want to think about very much. I want to turn off all stimulation. And I don't really know how to get into my feelings because there isn't any one focus.

---

*Patients' names have been changed to ensure their privacy.

Is this your usual state where you are physically tired or do you think that there is something wrong?

I think that I use sleep to turn everything off. That when I get overwhelmed it's my way of . . . shutting everything down. And so yeah, how I feel this morning is normal input. It's like my body's wanting to get into that blissful state and touch it. I have touched or I attempt to touch it through sleep.

Do you feel overwhelmed?

Yeah I feel like there's a lot going on in my waking life. A lot of things need attention.

You want to talk about that?

The biggest, I think the biggest one is dealing with the children's father. He is hassling me. How to make decisions on how to go forward with our separation, and the feelings that it brings up.

Can you be more specific, like what feelings does it bring up?

It brings up the feeling that I have to be mean and I don't like to be mean. That I'm going to really rock the boat, upset his life. I don't really like doing that. It's having to do things I really don't want to do. I'd rather things just flow and there'd be an understanding. When I was going through this divorce I was so scared of getting him upset, and getting him mad because I felt it would bring harm to me. I realize that that was very much tied in to the situation with my mother. I didn't want to get her mad because that had very threatening consequences. Certainly while I was going through this with Ted, I didn't realize that that was where this big feeling was connected to, so there's residue of that. I feel like it just fogs my mind. Can I be hurt by pushing and pressing this issue? It just doesn't feel safe, it just doesn't feel comfortable. I feel like I have to walk through territory that I just don't like and would prefer not to.

So I think that's it . . . going through a situation that I don't want to.

Doesn't feel good. That's associated with having to fight. I tried to push out that kind of pressure. And yet I know what I have to do. Then I wish it was different, I always wished it was different. It's just amazing to me. I mean, here I am talking about how I've always wished my situation with Ted, this whole process of splitting apart was different. That's exactly how I feel my about my childhood. I wish it was different from being a child, I wish it was different. (Cries)

I wish there was an understanding. I wish there was a respect. Respect for my life. I wish there was no threat. I wish there was support. I wish there was caring about my life, wanting to make things easier. (Cries) I hear everything that I'm saying and I hear how applicable it is to my whole early life. I just know that my experience with Ted is distorted by this. I'm feeling like he's controlling and he's making things hard, just like. . . She just didn't care. (Cries) She didn't care how I feel. (Heavy cries) It wasn't important. The effects it had on me. There was just no thought, no sensitivity in my direction, as a person, as another human being. It didn't matter. I didn't matter. (Cries)

Do you remember times like that?

Yeah, there's a few that stick out, made very big impressions on me. One of them. . . I was about six years old, and what I did was, um. . . . It was Christmas Eve, it was Christmas Eve, yeah. And she had made liver for dinner and when we sat down to eat and I tasted it and I didn't like it. I didn't like it at all. And it didn't matter to her that I didn't like it. I had to eat it. And it made me gag, that's how much I didn't like it. And it's like it didn't matter that I had that kind of reaction, it didn't matter. (Cries)

What happened?

Well, she made me sit there and eat it. You know I was gagging on it, even though I didn't want it, she made it and I was going to eat it. And then she just started threatening me that if I didn't finish it up, then I would have to go straight to bed and I wouldn't be able to open any presents. She started taking all that away from. And I just hated it, I just hated it! I didn't like it! I didn't wanna eat it! It didn't taste good! And I couldn't finish it. And so I went to bed crying. There was just no compassion, no sensitivity. I never do that to my daughter. Never! There were a lot of times like that. When I would just go to bed crying. It just didn't matter how I felt. And there was nobody that really cared, who would think my feelings really mattered. It didn't matter.

(Cries) I wasn't doing anything bad, I wasn't doing anything wrong, I just didn't like the taste of that. I wasn't trying to disobey you. (Deeper sobs) I wasn't trying to do anything bad or wrong, it just tasted so horrible to me. I want your understanding. I wanted to hear you say. . . I wanted to hear you say, "Does it really taste that bad?" I wanted you to hear how I felt, how it tasted to me, how I didn't like it, how it made me gag and that it was okay with you that I didn't eat it. That I was more important to you than eating a piece of liver. I wanted you just to understand that it didn't taste good to me. I would have wanted you to see if there was something else that I could eat. But you were mean. You are making me eat something that tastes so terrible. (Back to adult crying) I wanted you to listen, I wanted you to listen. I wanted you to care enough about how I felt. I wanted to know that I was more important than that piece of meat. (Now as the little child) Please care about how I feel. Please don't make me do something that I don't wanna do, that doesn't feel good to me. Oh, please care enough about me and how I feel (deep child cries fifteen minutes).

(Patient is lying on the mat in the soundproof room. Here talk is directed to therapist.) Because that's how I felt when I was being molested. Please don't make me do something I don't wanna do. And when somebody does do things that I didn't wanna do it makes me crazy. My mother played right into the process. Please don't make me do things I don't wanna do. It doesn't feel good.

There were a lot, there were a lot of things I had to do I didn't wanna do. I didn't want to do it. I had to do it because I had to survive. So all that stuff of doing things I didn't want to do left me feeling alone. There was nobody to hear. (Again, back to childhood, crying) Don't make me do it, I don't wanna do it. You can't hear! Nobody is there to protect me. (To therapist) That's why I wanna go to sleep; that's why I wanna go unconscious, cause in those moments I'm unaware, I'm not feeling, I don't have to deal with what's going on round me. I get a break from it.

My brother would boss me around, if I didn't do what he wanted me to do, he'd beat me up. So many times when I was growing up he'd call me his slave. If I didn't do what he wanted me to do he'd threaten to hurt me. That would leave me with just nobody to turn to. There's nobody that cares. There's nobody to protect me. There's nobody's arms that I can turn to and say protect me, they are hurting me. No one to reassure me, "I won't let anything hurt you." That wasn't there. So I had to take it.

Who did you want to protect you?

I wanted those in my environment to protect me. I wanted my mother to care enough to protect me. I wanted to have a father who was there, who wouldn't let anything happen to me. I wanted my brother to care enough and protect me. I wanted the world to protect me. And care enough. And not let any harm come to me. I wanted the world to care.

(Cries deeply) Oh, please. Please care about me. Please love me, please protect me. Please be kind to me. Please! Please! I need to know you care. Please care. Please! I didn't do anything wrong. I just wanna be important to you. Please. I just want my feelings to matter. Please, please, please be gentle, please. Please don't hurt me. Please care how I feel. (Cries deeply for twenty minutes) And I thought when my son Rob was like six or seven, and he'd hit his sister, a rage would come up in me. It was like, you are not going to hurt her! I'm going to protect her! And this is a beautiful child! You will not hurt her! The way that I wish somebody would have protected me! What I wanted was for someone to stand up like I did for Betty and say no! no! You will not do that! I will not let you. You have to get through me first! But there was nobody! Nobody there to do that for me. And there was no way I was going to let Rob hurt Betty. I was gonna protect her. I wasn't going to let her experience what I experienced.

And I really made it a point after those situations occurred with Rob to explain why, to let him know how I was hurt, how there was no one there to protect me. How it felt and how I couldn't let that happen in my house with me there. Because I think feelings count, they count a lot. My feelings never counted for nothing. I wish someone would have felt they counted for something. Feelings are very important. I wanted somebody to care about how I felt. I wanted somebody whose arms I could run to and feel safe, somebody who would protect me. I had nowhere to go.

There was a time when my mother went away for a weekend and when she came back, she was married to someone I'd never met before. Never saw the person before. And I wish she'd taken the time to say, "Honey, how do you feel about it?" because I didn't like it! I didn't like it. I didn't like this new person. It didn't matter how I felt. She never took the time to ask me anything. Do you want this person here? How does it make you feel? I just had to accept it. And she immediately wanted me to call him Daddy. I didn't want to call him Daddy. He isn't my Daddy. And I didn't want him kissing me and I didn't want him touching me. And I just had to accept it. I wasn't asked how I felt. I wasn't important. I wanted you to tell me what you were doing. I wanted you to ask me how I felt! I wanted you to ask me: do I want a daddy? I wanted you to give me time to get to know this person and tell you how I felt. And have my feelings matter. You just threw him on me! I didn't like it. It wasn't right, it wasn't right to do that. It's not right. And I didn't like the fact that he took attention from me, the little attention I could get from you. I didn't like the fact that he mattered more than me. (Crying)

And I see how all that is true, even about being in the womb. It didn't matter. I didn't count, I wasn't considered! (Cries deeply) I want you to know I do count! I do count! How I feel does matter. I do count! And I wanted to count! You make it so hard for me!

Just the idea of life being easy. I can imagine what it would be like in an environment where I had a mother and father and family that cared. I would have loved life. I would have thought that life was magical, safe, supportive. I wouldn't have grown up scared. Instead, I get a lot of pain, that's what I get. My mother never supported my life. Not from the beginning, not as a child, not growing up. She just caused a lot of pain. It was so cruel. (Back to childhood crying) You don't care! You're so bad. It hurts me so much. I need you to be loving. I need you to be supportive. It would make such a big difference. You would be so proud of me. I could love you so much. All you think about is yourself. Nobody else matters, just you, you matter. That's it.

(Back to present) I wanted it to be different with what I'm going through with Fred. I wanted it to be different. It's the same feelings. I want him to care about how I feel. I want him to understand. I want him to care about how I feel. So it makes me fight because I gotta fight for how I feel. I gotta fight to be heard. I gotta fight to say I matter. I count. I have to fight to be heard. And I want it to be different!

It should be a child's right. I'm always so amazed at how fragile and yet resilient a human being really is. A word, a sentence can have so much impact, and it can make you hurt over and over. I've always won-dered "How can that be?" And I think, if I look at a human being like a piece of clay, and if every harsh thing you've ever said makes a mark on that clay, you can take that clay and stamp on it and make it flat, it is still going to have some kind of form. I think human beings are like clay and depending on what they are exposed to and what experiences they have, it's the sculpture they become.

(Addressing the therapist) So the truth is, feelings aren't really understood are they? It's like language that isn't spoken. We understand the language, you understand the language. You are the interpreters of the language. You'll be a new field called feelologists.

If you had a child and you can see the welts on her body, you know you've done harm. But words and criticism without any thoughts do the same thing. You can't see it. And I am so tired of all of that. It's a little hard for me to understand why this is so difficult to understand. It's a little hard for me. But I just see it clearly. Don't we have our eyes to see this or the minds to understand this? Naturally, that ties in with my feel-ings about being primitive, not evolved enough yet.

I mean feeling feelings would just change the disposition of humanity. To know there's a beginning point. To know when you're car-rying a child how you feel is so important. You know, I kid with you about the talking fetus but the truth is, more literally speaking, it's the feeling fetus. It really is. What a difference knowing you are loved. It just makes for greatness, I just really believe that. I think it contributes to a feeling that you can do anything, which opens the mind up even more. If you believe you can do anything to some degree, you believe that anything is possible.

What else did you go through?

Well, I came in today thinking I did not have one feeling. And then noticing how shallow I was breathing. And that I was tired. Which made me really just want to go to sleep. To block out the stimulation; to find that peace.

Can you identify what it is?

Well, I'll tell you what that felt like to me; I was just in the resting mode.

What does that do?

It conserves energy.

And feelingwise?

It stops me from feeling. I don't want to feel, I don't want any input.

What's the difference?

It's a protection measure. It's withdrawal. One of the connections I can make to it is it's basically a protection measure to conserve my life. And I think it deserves respect.

You know it's a mechanism you have to beware of when you want to feel, so as not to fall into that because it is so comfortable. But it's good for you to know that when you go into that state, it's a repair state. It's also a defense state in the sense that when you go there you shut off everything. You repair but you also don't feel.

But I need, really need that.

It's too much. It's a defense. That's what you need to know so when it happens you know what's happening to you. You said, "This is where I have to move to when I'm overwhelmed." And you're overwhelmed now.

"Overwhelmed" is a very familiar word I use in my life. A part of, yes, a part of my vocabulary, "overwhelmed" would be one. Too much.

You know when there is too much pain you actually live in a state of overload. We walk around every day of our lives in a state of overwhelm because we already have this tremendous amount of pain. Our system is dealing with so much. Anything in the present adds to that, then it's really way too much for anybody to cope with. This is what was happening. You might use another word called "suffering."

But I'm kinda used to it because I've spent so long in it. But I see there are other options. I feel that's the direction I'm moving in. That's why, I mean I have confidence that I will get through it all. One because I have this old pattern to fall back on, that I know will get me through it. I may be overwhelmed, I may be suffering, but I'll survive. But I also see this other direction that as I keep moving into it and feeling it, and bringing the feelings back up, it just opens the door to the experience that I want to dive into.

Now could you tell me why it feels so uncomfortable to go through this process?

I'm going through it but I don't want to do it. I feel I have to do it. And it invokes this fight for my right. I mean it ties into so much. I mean this is the hard part for me. I'm constantly fighting, from the moment they put this marital settlement agreement and they gave themselves ten years to pay me out, it was totally not okay with me. I don't think it's fair and my whole system is just set up to change it. I'm going to do whatever it takes to clear this up because I don't want to be tied to it, because we're not married anymore.

My first reaction in therapy is, I'm not going to beg for what should have been natural. I won't beg her. Yet when you made me do it, it opened the floodgates. So much suffering. That takes me to the rage, that takes me to the frantic making me lose my breath. You know, that's the right pathway. I am aware where certain things take me to. But it did feel good to be living in my childhood and connecting to all those feelings.

AT THE CROSSROADS: THE LIMBIC SYSTEM: THE THALAMUS, AMYGDALA, AND HIPPOCAMPUS

The limbic system, a ring of structures lying just under the cerebral cortex, processes and organizes feeling. Some of the key limbic structures are the thalamus, amygdala, hippocampus, and hypothalamus. The hippocampus, which contains the factual knowledge of an event, connects with the amygdala, which deals with the feeling content of that event. When our mother glared at us in anger, we connect to the limbic system to feel "she hates me." It is the first step in feeling what we know and knowing what we feel. The result is we hurt.

The limbic system combines emotions with lower brainstem sensations to form the guts and agony of experience—the "feeling" brain. The *feeling level* is what I call it. It encapsulates sensations from the first-line brainstem area. This level defends conscious-awareness against the terror of a first-line trauma and converts the terror into images and scenes. It accounts for nightmares of being strangled or a fear of enclosed places. It helps produce artistic images.

Daniel Goleman, science writer for the *New York Times*, sheds light on the split between thinking and feeling in his book *Emotional Intelligence*.[7] He writes that we have two kinds of intelligence, one rational and the other emotional, which have as their counterparts two kinds of memory, one for facts and one for emotional content. These functions are mediated in different parts of the brain. He points out, something that we all know, that many highly intelligent people make a mess of their personal lives because their impulses and feelings get the better of their rationality. Goleman cites findings on how the brain inscribes and processes potent early memories and how these memories play a powerful role in later life.

Many people cannot make decisions because they are so cut off from their feelings that they have nothing to guide them. "I don't know what to order. What did you order?" is an example of what I mean. It doesn't matter what I feel like eating because I don't know what I feel. I need to know what decision you made so I can follow suit. Put another way, the limbic system amygdala (and other limbic structures) secretes so many repressive neurojuices to deal with imprinted pain that there is a functional disconnect between feeling centers and their cortical counterparts. We are then forced to be guided by cortical centers alone.

We try to explain the reason for our rage: "If you hadn't said that, I wouldn't get angry"; "If you stopped pressuring me, I wouldn't get so upset." Such ideas are never irrational; they are responding first and foremost to past history. That is why there are so many insights after a reliving experience: Under blocked feelings lie the true source of the rage. Instead of saying, "I got mad because *you* didn't respect me," we learn, "I got mad because *my father* used to put me down all the time, and then threatened to beat me if I protested." It is now therapeutic to pound the padded walls against his behavior and let the rage out. It is never enough to *discuss* the anger.

One can be driven to drain the energy of early lack of love and never know why. Worse, one might not even realize that there was this lack. One just feels uncomfortable, not at ease in one's skin. One thing is certain: if the person doesn't keep on the move she doesn't feel comfortable. One patient kept going, traveling here and there, only to find out that she had no place to go; more precisely, to keep from finding out she never had any place to go—to escape. She was running from the core of her agonizing infancy pains compounded by a cold, hard, emotionless household from which she needed to escape.

Without a conscious-awareness the person will just be anxious.

THE THALAMUS:
SWITCHBOARD AND RELAY STATION OF THE BRAIN

The thalamus is a key structure in the limbic system and a major player in early trauma. It is fully functional after the fourteenth week of gestation.[8] Part of this structure's function is to integrate feelings and help relay them to the frontal cortex, where they take on specific context and meaning. It is after the fourteenth week that we see critical connections being made between thalamic and cortical centers. There is some evidence that the sense of touch, in part organized by the thalamus, is already registering in the womb after the third or fourth month.

W. J. H. Nauta, a pioneer in neurology, and coauthor Michael

Feirtag, describe the thalamus as "a final checkpoint before messages from all the sensoria are allowed entrance to higher stations of the brain . . . at each synaptic connection in sensory pathways the input is transformed: the code in which the message arrived is fundamentally changed. Presumably, the data could not be understood at higher levels: translation is needed."[9]

The thalamus, with help from the hippocampus, translates the message into the language of the cortex. This translation enables the cortex to provide meaning for an emotional stimulus. It enables a person to access and articulate a vague uncomfortable feeling into, "Father hates me and makes me feel bad about myself." The thalamus also relays our need for satisfaction, as in "Please be nice to me, Mom!"

If the feeling of deprivation is too overwhelming, however, the message is rerouted, and the imprint ends up reverberating around the subcortical unconscious, trying to force open the gates and connect with the frontal cortex. The reverberation is what makes us tense, nervous, sad, antsy, or driven. Many of the biochemicals unleashed against overwhelming feelings produce the same effect as if one had a virus—for example, they cause changes in the natural killer cells of the immune system. These cells stand guard for newly formed cancer cells, destroying them before they become full blown. After one year of Primal Therapy, we see a normalization of these cells.*

When the thalamus is impaired, the cortical gates fail to work properly. The gates don't have enough juice to do their job. The person cannot think straight; everything is a jumble, and confusion reigns. Her system is trying to deal with feelings or sensations that do not make sense because when the original trauma unfolded, the prefrontal cortex was not developed enough to *make* sense of it.

In rerouting the information away from the frontal cortex, the thalamus "believes" it is trying to save our lives and our sanity. Establishing a cortical connection would bring about an exact replay of the person's original reactions to the past trauma—rapid heart rate, elevated blood pressure, high fever, and prolonged secretion of stress hormones—which threaten the survival of the organism. I put quotes around "believes"

*This was our research in 1984 with St. Bartholomew's Hospital, London, England.

above, yet it is clear that the thalamus at some point participates in our thought processes.

When an early painful sensation is blocked it still sends up shoots, partial aspects of it that ultimately become delusions or hallucinations, hypertension, or palpitations. The closer an old traumatic sensation is to conscious awareness the more intense and importuning the obsession, delusion or hallucination, or physical symptom. Evolution forces it upward for connection, just as in ancient times there was a migration upward and outward when the cortex was forming. Alas, the thalamus and other related structures turn it away. Each traumatic imprint always tends to go with the flow to the higher centers that were developing in our history. The frontal cortex is the final way station for feeling.

It has been found that psychotics who hear voices really do hear voices—their own. Their own speech centers are activated during these episodes. They don't know it is from their feelings and speech centers but they are really hearing something. Their feelings, "My parents are trying to hurt me," become ideas that speak to them: e.g., "The man on the corner wants to hurt me." They sense danger, not from inside where it resides, but from outside where it is projected. Because they do not have internal access they must focus externally. That is why when they get further along and do have inner access they can resolve the feelings, and the hallucinations and delusions disappear. Sometimes when a patient is approaching a heavy feeling in a session they may have a transient hallucination. This is nearly always accompanied by radical shifts in vital signs.

Many of my patients enter therapy with an absence of any optimism. Their whole system has gone into (the original) fail mode—pessimism. One patient started a session feeling depressed, helpless, and cynical: "What's the use? Nothing will do any good. This therapy can't work on me." Her attitude was given impetus by her birth experience, during which her mother received heavy anesthesia. In making her way through the birth canal she had been hampered by drugs which imprinted her with a feeling that nothing she could do would make any difference. Then, in a childhood where nothing she did could make her mother love her, the pessimism and defeated feeling became reinforced.

Here we find first a physiologic-brainstem memory. With the advent of words it becomes "hopelessness." Not a different memory; a more elaborated one. Hopelessness later rises to the cortex for a label. Sometimes it is so well masked that one has to go to a therapist even to find out that one is drowning in hopelessness. It goes by many names in psychotherapy—"masked depression" is a favorite. So first we have a physiology of hopelessness; then the suffering component on the limbic level; and finally the idea of it. All three contribute to the overwhelming feeling. The system can feel hopeless; and this feeling can already be doing damage to organ systems long before we suffer from it consciously.

As a child one female patient felt she had nothing to hang on to. In adulthood she adopted one mystical, New Age idea after another in search of an anchor. She was a sucker for pushy salespeople because she didn't know how to resist, how to say no. Her overpowering and demanding father had taken that ability away. Against any real obstacles she wanted to give up, felt resigned and beaten, pretty much the feeling she had at birth. It was imprinted and enduring. She relived where all those key feelings began and put them back into the past where they belonged. On those rare occasions when the feeling arose again it was bereft of its previous power and she could decide not to give in. She had the power to change her life.

One of my patients whose blood pressure is normal experienced a rise in blood pressure to 220/110 as she approached the deep hopelessness she experienced as a child. Then as she dropped into the feeling the pressure dropped radically. These readings indicate the connection between feelings and blood pressure. The rises in vital signs gives us an index of the magnitude of the feeling. Feeling hopeless in therapy finally allows one to be shed of it. Because the struggle to get love in the present is driven by that shattering feeling. It is the basis of all manner of act-outs. Too often, there isn't even a struggle for love as the person just gives up on ever getting it. She withdraws, has no friends to help her with her feelings, and becomes more depressed. She can be encouraged to make friends, go out and meet people, but it is fighting against a powerful imprint which says, "Give up, don't try. It is of no use."

Patients who are mired in hopelessness usually enter a session with very low vital signs, the very same vital signs as happened in the original trauma, because that trauma has been triggered off. One of the ways the memory is carried around is in the low vital body temperature, and in the lower lymphocyte production of the immune system. In short, psychosomatic means not that something psychological affects the soma or body. Rather, it means that events are impressed into the physical system as part of the memory. It is not one or the other. It is both at once. There are painkilling receptors on immune cells that are the same as what the brain manufactures. Pain goes directly to these cells, changing their immune function.

After a feeling, body temperature drops considerably, as does blood pressure. The body switches to the conservation, energy mode. Why? Because originally (in anoxia due to anesthesia at birth, for example) that is what was required. When these patients leave the session it is often with a higher vital sign reading. Reliving normalizes because imprinting the trauma destabilizes. I don't know of any way a therapy can alter the body temperature radically as we do. It is evidence that humans are one unified entity; feelings are reflected in temperature and other vital functions and it all moves together toward normalization. The temperature militates toward normal readings while the patient reports that she feels much better. However, if the patient reports that she is feeling much better but physiologic measurements do not reflect it, we shall have to take another look. It often happens in abreaction where the patient discharges tension-energy but has not connected, leading to a self-delusional state. The vital signs meanwhile drop in sporadic fashion and not all together. It is one index that the system is not in harmony.

ORGANIZING MEMORY: THE AMYGDALA

After the thalamus helps code information of the memory, the amygdala (right and left sides) and hippocampus consolidate it. The amygdalae lie adjacent to the hippocampus on the inner surface of the temporal lobes, forming a kind of crossroads in the brain. The need-feeling "I need my daddy!" may be coded and stored by the thalamus and concretized by the amygdalae and hippocampus. If the need is not fulfilled it signals "danger" and is sent via the hypothalamus to bodily systems, where it alters our physical functioning, eventually making us sick.

The amygdala's connection to the frontal cortex and hippocampus allows us to feel a feeling, name it, and get a handle on it. It can transform a hollow sensation in the pit of the stomach into a feeling of emptiness, loneliness, and abandonment. It has been found recently that the amygdala regulates "stop" versus "go" mechanisms in the frontal cortex so that the two work together to inhibit pain impulses. When the amygdalae are calm, there is less energy surging forth to make one feel bad. In that case, the frontal cortex can block upsurging feelings. It does this by thinking thoughts that are the obverse of inner reality: "I feel wonderful. I have found God and he is protecting me." Reality equals I feel lost, unprotected, and unsafe. Or the person can begin ruminating so that certain thoughts become obsessive: e.g., "Doom is imminent."

The thoughts are actually expressing a deeply hidden sensation-feeling. Somewhere, the system feels that doom (the actual feeling on the rise) is imminent. It is now projecting this feeling into the world. The person sees doom everywhere. Not that there isn't a possibility of serious trouble. One can never predict the future. But in these people it is exaggerated. It becomes the end of the world. And indeed, the end of the world and life for the person may have been these imprinted life-and-death experiences early on. Death and catastrophe always lurk because death did lurk and was indeed just around the corner. The person will find one thing or another to focus on but the content is always the same—the end of everything—the apocalypse.

THE DOPAMINE CONNECTION

Recent research has found a correlation between lowered dopamine and depression.[10] Often, the investigators allude to genetic factors involved. It is my belief that most of us are not born with genetic deficits in dopamine. So much happens in utero, at birth, and just after to account for alterations in dopamine setpoints. New research shows that stress before birth results in an alteration of dopamine levels in the right brain hemisphere. This eventually results in heightened emotionality and the inability to regulate emotions properly.[11]

It is no accident that a hug or a kiss raises dopamine levels. There must be some intrauterine equivalent to a hug that produces a feeling of comfort. That equivalent I believe is a mother comfortable in her skin, happy to have the baby, who eats properly and has a well-balanced internal system. I don't think depression is "caused" by genetically lowered dopamine. More likely it is a bad uterine environment and then a stifling, repressive home environment that alters dopamine levels and sets the stage for depression.

Low levels of dopamine are implicated in attention deficit disorder. Many of the drugs treating it tend to enhance dopamine supplies. I am convinced that plenty of early love and a decent womblife would avoid such deficits, particularly since lower dopamine is more evident in the left brain, where ideas and ideation help suppress upsurging impulses. It is this hemisphere that needs a boost from dopamine in order to repress brainstem impulses. And it may be this hemisphere that has its resources depleted by lack of love early on.

There is recent evidence, as well, of the role of dopamine in drug and alcohol addiction. It seems that the more the dopamine system is enhanced by drugs the more likely the addiction. Chemically it takes the place of love; the better I feel inside, the less dead and numb I feel, the more I want the drug that helps me feel that way. Cocaine keeps dopamine levels high, and is addictive. Dopamine plays a role in how well we sleep.[12]

In a study in Paris by Merle Ruberg of the Salpetriere Hospital, it was found that when electrodes were placed in a brain region known as the substantia nigra, where Parkinson's disease begins to kill off brain cells, the patient would often cry and become depressed.[13] They said such things as, "I no longer wish to live." The depression lifted as soon as the electrode was taken away. Here we are beginning to see the relationship of depression, hopelessness, and brain-cell death. This is the area of dopamine production which seems to falter with Parkinson's disease. Hence the need for L-dopa to enhance dopamine levels in these individuals. It may well be that imprinted pain depletes dopamine supplies through the need for constant vigilance against the imprint. After sixty years of vigilance the system cannot put out the supplies anymore. It needs outside help. This vigilance may have started in the womb against a trauma, such as the mother's smoking or drinking. It starts so early that we can easily be led to believe that it is genetic in origin.

When someone has been up-regulated during gestation (anxious mother drinking many cups of coffee) then as an adult, taking a downer can be an important moment as the person thinks to herself, So that's what I've been needing all my life. Of course she will go back for more. Someone who is up- or down-regulated will always feel out of sorts, and will feel better with some outside help that normalizes.

THE AMYGDALAE: MOTHER NATURE AT WORK

When a connection is made in the nerve fibers leading from the amygdalae to the frontal cortex, the feelings churning below begin to make sense. But when gating systems are active, the feelings are disguised. You know the old saying, "You can't fool Mother Nature"? The amygdalae and their little helpers in the brainstem are as close to Mother Nature as we can get. The frontal area, however, is a sucker. In disconnect mode it can believe anything. All we have to do to manipulate someone's ideas is to lock on to their need. Then the person becomes absolutely dumb because he sees only fulfillment of need and nothing else.

Opiate-containing fibers run from the amygdalae to the sensory systems, where they serve a gatekeeping function. They release painkillers in response to emotional states generated in the hypothalamus and limbic structures. When a young girl suffers incest, painkillers are released and the message is blocked en route to the frontal cortex. The terrible suffering, however, does get through. The person is miserable and does not know why. Even if she acknowledges the incest within her frontal cortex, nothing will change. The misery will remain. Sometimes repression or inhibition is so effective that even the suffering component is blocked, and the person feels nothing. There may only be a vague sentiment that one is not getting anything out of life.

The amygdalae contain raw feeling. They provide the hurt, and the hippocampus attaches the name "humiliated" and sends it to the frontal cortex. During a reliving, the amygdalae also fire off information to the thalamus, which translates it for the frontal cortex: e.g., "They are putting me down!" When the message arrives at the cortex, it deactivates the left prefrontal area, giving sway to the right brain, the "feeling" side. Now we have a connected feeling.

The amygdalae contain the feeling part of an event; the "tone" and "guts" of feeling; the *feeling of feeling*. It is the feeling of feeling that I believe is missing in so many individuals, and so many psychotherapies, for that matter. Moreover, the limbic area, specifically the hippocampus, contains the history of the feeling. Thus, the feeling is first felt as, "My friends are pretty insulting." Then once locked into the feeling, it translates into, "My parents always denigrated me." This then, with proper therapeutic techniques, becomes, "Daddy, say I'm good. Say I'm good, please!"

Not surprisingly, during dream sleep the amygdalae are very active, while the frontal cortex is far less inactive. Dreams symbolize feelings. We say, "I had the scariest dream last night." Actually, it was not the dream that was scary but the "scary" imprint that produced the dream. Those feelings are with us all the time, which accounts for why we have the same dreams over and over. The only time I take dreams into account in therapy is when we address the underlying feeling in it. That is what is real and historical. The story is the cover-up. Like Watergate, we not only want to catch the criminals, we want to know who is orchestrating the whole thing. The dream story is what the limbic system and aspects of the right cortex do to disguise real feelings. We don't want to address the disguises because they keep on changing. Feelings and needs do not.

Limbic structures such as the amygdalae undergo a critical period of maturation from before birth until age two. Long before the cortex is myelinated and ready for action, the amygdala has been dominant in processing emotional information. It is one reason why the unconscious is the unconscious—because the upper-level thinking cortex isn't "aware" as yet. Nearly every vertebrate has an amygdala and a serotonin inhibitory system. These date back some several hundred million years. Dogs and cats can't articulate feelings, but they can feel and act on them. Pain pathways and the serotonin system seem to be similar in all vertebrates. Moreover, they seem to occupy the same places in the nervous system. Limbic structures are also similar in most mammals, so it is not a stretch to compare animal reactivity with our own. Where the two diverge is in the area of ideas about those feelings.

The provocation of feelings imprinted from past events may take place when an outside trigger, say the sound of menace in a parent's voice (or anyone's voice, for that matter), sets the amygdalae in motion, which signals the hypothalamus-pituitary to produce stress hormone, putting the overall brain system on alert. The anger is internalized in a child's limbic and cortical areas. When the amount of stress hormone becomes excessive it threatens to damage brain cells. Usually, the threat is far more subtle. If there are no words, no emotional contact, no parental warmth in the first weeks of life, the infant's system is driven into the stress response; here the imprinted danger is lack of love. It is an absence that puts the baby in stress. That is what is truly subtle. When someone tries to remember bad scenes from her childhood there may not be any terrible scenes at all; just nothingness, no warmth, no love, no touch, and no caring . . . nothing to hang onto. Here the feeling alone *is* the memory, and it is sufficient to be engulfed by it; to connect and integrate it. Our brains can transform nothing (a lack of eye contact) into physical damage. It is not "nothing" to the brain. It is deprivation of need. No hormone works alone; that is why it is called the endocrine "system," a cascade of hormones that work together, and a cascade of deviations when pain intrudes.

If we overlook the amygdalae of the patient during psychotherapy by ignoring deep feelings (and by that I don't mean that the patient sobs or cries *about* her childhood) we will end up with a bright, passionless human being. Worse, she cannot even feel that she doesn't feel, and never knows the feeling of feeling. Someone who has wonderful insights into her behavior can be totally self-absorbed, uncaring of and insensitive to those around her.

Sometimes, early in life parents perform an amygdalectomy on their children by simply not being there for them. Thus, the child's feelings aren't directly suppressed; they are simply ignored, which amounts to the same thing. The result is that the feelings stay inside unconnected, unexpressed, and unresolved. Therapy should produce amygdaloids, those in touch with their deep, feeling self.

ARE WE CONSCIOUS FIRST AND THEN UNCONSCIOUS?

The amygdala (together with other limbic and brainstem structures) can react in a delirium of rage, fear, or sex before the cortex knows what is going on because such *raw emotion is triggered independent of, and prior to, thought*. That is the way feelings overcome us. Was something painful in our conscious and then put into the unconscious? No, it never made it to conscious-awareness. The amygdala has already been very busy when finally the prefrontal cortex becomes aware and tries to stop those rising feelings; before it can put a stop to our eating binges, for example. Deep-lying imprints are in control. It is clear that needs that involve survival are going to be more potent than ideas about those needs. When someone is out of control the person is usually in the control of low-level imprints and out of control of the frontal cortex. So many "how-to" books concentrate on controlling ourselves, our impulses, rages, etc., and yet the imprints will never cease to dominate our lives ... until they connect with top-level cortical processes. Feelings are not businesses to be "managed." They are meant to be felt.

A person out of touch with his feeling self may enter therapy for what he believes is a sexual problem. With little access to lower structures such as the amygdalae, a man may be asexual, with a low libido and subdued passion. The amygdalae provide an erection. A man may not realize that this is the problem, however, because it is like hunger; if you have lost your appetite, you don't see that your problem is that you are not eating. The key in psychotherapy for sexual problems is to have access to the amygdalae as well as other limbic sites.[14]

Antonio Demasio, in his recent book, *The Feeling of What Happens*,[15] notes how we can act on unconscious feelings. He cites the case of David, who had massive damage to the hippocampus, leaving him with no ability to lay down new memories. There was damage to the amygdala as well. Damasio conducted an experiment with him, known as the "good guy, bad guy" setup. David had encounters with someone who was very nice and kind to him, and other encounters with someone abrupt and unpleasant. David could not recognize these people once out of his sight.

He had no ability to use history to guide him in his behavior because he had lost that ability. He could not say to himself, "This person is mean and to be avoided." He could not integrate his experiences or articulate them; yet, he always gravitated to the nice people and away from the unpleasant ones. He was guided by an unseen and unrecognized force— by history, by feelings due to forgotten experiences. David was literally and physically disconnected from his history yet motivated by it, exactly the point I am making for those who are not necessarily damaged but who are disconnected from lower centers through repression. His was an organismic response rather than a consciously aware one. Here we have a neurological paradigm for understanding depression; for example, being driven into moods for no apparent reason. Suppose David had regained his connections to lower centers. He would no longer be driven by his unconscious. This is exactly the point I am making about regaining functional connections to lower centers by the lifting of repression. With prefrontal-limbic conscious-awareness (consciously integrating unconscious feelings) there would be no more depression. The unconscious would be made conscious so that it would no longer be possible for us to be pushed around by unconscious feelings, which is what depression is about. We apply a sophisticated term to it, "mood swings," but our whole organism revolves around deep-lying feelings that we have no idea exist. These experiences often occur years before we have a fully functional frontal cortex to make sense out of them. Consciousness, as I have observed in my patients, is THE antidote for depression.

I received a letter in the mail today from one of my patients, Regina, which exemplifies the point I am making: "I want to share with you my experience of waking up on the first day of this new year (the millennium) totally in tears. Why? After watching all the celebrations last night across the world without one glitch, no terrorists, electricity failures, or plane crashes, I realized that for the past year all the bad things I thought were going to happen to me, all the disasters I have been obsessing about was not my intuition at all but rather was coming from the past reality that lives inside me. It was like a big mirror in front of me showing me that it was my past that was the problem; I felt I had to protect myself, buying a quarter ton of grain. I had to be prepared for what was coming my way. It had already come by, like I had been lied to by myself; that I was going to get hurt if I didn't prepare enough. So I obsessed about Y2K. Tormented myself with 'what ifs.' I cry now because of all of those feelings of not being safe, and I know where they belong. Displacing those feelings onto Y2K made me realize how I refocused what was inside to the outside."[16]

Some of my male patients who are constantly sexually excited find that when their emotional pain from early trauma is diminished, so are their sexual urges. Events during womblife have such a profound effect on later life. It has been found, for example, that exposing pregnant rats to morphine feminizes their male offspring.[17] The whole sexual balance can be thrown off by events in the womb. Morphine is a repressor/inhibitor. We produce the same chemical ourselves, with possibly the same effect on later sexuality. If we repress enough we repress our sexuality.

Hypersexuality in adult life can originate in the brainstem from an imprint that actually has nothing to do with sex. To then treat satyriacis as a sex problem is to miss the point. Sex is but one way primal energy is released. And the energizing portion, though affecting sex, can be of anoxia at birth. So we treat sex when we should be treating anoxia. It is never harmful to treat the symptom so long as we understand that *is* a symptom—of something else. Old need can stir up sexual interest in a man or woman—for example, a childhood without a father might divert the sex impulse toward other males. Pain is converted into the sex drive. The desperation of the sexual need is commensurate with the early deprivation of love, given impetus by the body's reticular activating system, which puts the system on alert. Then childhood events, a tyrannical or absent father, channel the drive. Homosexuality may be the result. (More on this later.)

For women who suffered incest and thus are afraid of men, the sex drive, as soon as it appears, can be diverted toward women. Sexual interaction with men would reactivate the pain of incest and overwhelm the woman. Hence, she turns to women to fulfill her need for love and, more importantly, to keep the pain at bay. Many of my lesbian patients suffered incest in childhood.

We are not going to fool the amygdala ever, but we can fool the cortical derivatives of it. Example: a girl has been sexually abused by a father very early in life, but somehow she learns in therapy to forgive him. The father and daughter are now reconciled but the problem is that she cannot forgive an imprint. And the amygdala cannot forgive; that is not its job. It's like forgiving her physiology. The old feelings are still in place, now layered over by cortical "forgiveness." Layer over enough and we lose access to the real feelings. Oddly, this layering may make one feel wonderful. So what's the problem, one might ask? What's wrong with feeling good? If we could *feel* good it would be wonderful. If you think you feel good that is another matter. It means being unreal; living in a state of unreality only to be struck down prematurely later on by a hidden reality.

A young woman I treated relived being sexually attacked by her stepfather. Her hands automatically crossed behind her back (her stepfather pinned her hands behind her back), her back arched way back, and her heart rate climbed to 180 beats per minute. This woman was afraid of men and sex in the present, but the imprint itself was decades old, yet most of her relationships were dominated by it.

One patient found that whenever she was under the slightest pressure, such as preparing a paper for class, she got a migraine headache. In her sessions she relived her birth, during which she did not receive enough oxygen (her mother was given heavy anesthetics). The pressure, which constricted her blood vessels, then dilated them, was her imprint. Any pressure she felt later in life gave her a migraine, left her upset and unable to function.

The amygdala is formed long before the neocortex (new cortex) is developed, both in personal development (ontogenetic) and in our long history from animals to human beings (phylogenetic). At one point in personal and phylogenetic history the amygdala had to do all the work. It didn't have a hippocampus and neocortex to help specify matters and guide feelings. It just channeled instincts. It added its measure of fear to the equation.

As the pain impulses accumulate they tend to overwhelm the receptor system. The result may be free-floating anxiety. It is free-floating because the imprint occurred long before words came along to circumscribe and contain it. When the amygdala is calm there is less energy surging forth to make one feel bad. In that case, the frontal cortex can block anxiety attacks and/or obsessions and compulsions. One might be tempted to say that the new drugs "cure" obsessive-compulsive symptoms, but in reality, they don't cure anything; they defer! The same imprints are still there, simply held in better check by drugs that suppress them and keep the message from overwhelming the frontal cortex. The belief is a self-administered drug. The cortex knows what it is doing when it concocts beliefs. Those beliefs go to where they must to help us survive. It is not always a good idea to dissuade someone from "irrational" beliefs. They serve an important function in the psychic economy. And if we tie the belief to history it is not as irrational as it may seem.

THE REPOSITORY OF TRUTH

The amygdalae are the repository of truth. A young man suffered an anxiety attack when he was asked to make a presentation in front of his co-workers. The true reaction here may be to the loss of oxygen, not stage fright. Getting up in front of people took on a life-and-death importance. This man suffered from anoxia during birth. His current fear resonates with his past terror, and as a result he feels he is dying again. "There's nothing to be afraid of. They're your friends," he may be told by a counselor. Yet the amygdalae have found a great deal to be afraid of; together with the brainstem, the old anoxia and fear of death intrude into the presentation and it again becomes life-and-death. The current fear kicked off the chain of pain, evoking the primordial terror at the start of life. Yes, there were later fears in his childhood that counted as well. But the visceral anxiety had its roots before he saw his first person. If the original terror was not compounded later on, there would be far less fear in making the presentation.

When someone is in a state of craving drugs or alcohol, it is the amygdala that is very active. When an addict is in the throes of needing a fix, it is the amygdala that is the driving force, according to Dr. Hans Beiter of Massachusetts General Hospital. It is sending out its message of pain and the need for something soothing for that pain. It is not surprising that antidepressive drugs work on the amygdala. It should be noted that most depressions are high activation states, despite the phlegmatic, energyless look to the person.

Finally, because the amygdala and other structures that process feelings also secrete repressive, inhibitory hormones, they control access to those emotions, influencing what we are aware of and what we are not. Damage to the amygdala prevents someone from recognizing fearful expressions in others (and presumably in themselves), another indication of this structure's role in emotional perception. Impaired amygdalae due to a load of pain can make us less sensitive to how others feel. The amygdala plays a key role in emotional speech and crying, so when my patients cry "Mama, please hold me!" in a five-year-old voice, we can be sure the amygdala is involved. It is my assumption that the more remote the memory the more ancient the brain structure mediating it. Ancient brain structures seem to be more involved in the more arcane and remote memories of infancy and before.

Another reason why insight therapy involving the late-developing prefrontal cortex is not as effective as it could be is that the frontal area is trying to do the work of a very old brain dealing with feelings. It is trying to gain access to feeling and deep sensation. The old brain, the amygdala and hippocampus, won't tolerate this attempted intrusion and forbids access. It is a dialogue of the deaf. The old brain simply can't hear or understand what the frontal cortex is rambling on about. Michaela Gallagher, a neuroscientist at Johns Hopkins University, has found that a fully functioning cortex can keep the amygdala and its feelings in check. Another way of putting it is that a person would be hyperreactive and overly reactive to stimuli if the frontal cortex were not intact. But the overactive cortex is exactly what we don't need in order to feel. Its hyperactivity becomes a defense against regressing to the feeling level. It is why our patients are in a darkened, quiet room.

THE HIPPOCAMPUS: ACCESSING CHILDHOOD MEMORIES

Situated behind the amygdalae, the hippocampus forms the tip of the ram's-horn shape of the limbic system (see chapter 1). The hippocampus handles the context and circumstances of an event; the amygdalae, the emotional content. If, at five years of age, your mother says to you for the hundredth time: "You are useless and stupid. Get out of my sight!" the circumstances and feeling of the event are imprinted by the hippocampus and amygdalae, respectively.

A more precise meaning is added by the thinking cortex so that the full connection may be: "Mother hates me!" The subconscious logic of the young child is likely to be: "She's angry because I'm bad." Because this is so devastating for a child to grasp, endorphins are secreted to inhibit the full connection. The feelings are now gated and kept unconscious. The struggle then begins, as the child, and later the adult, strives to get others to like her. The feeling is unconscious and acted out unconsciously.

The hippocampus lays down new memory, working with the frontal area to consolidate feelings. Once the load of memory is shifted to the cortex it can be brought to awareness. The hippocampus now has space to continue naming new feelings and needs and can lay down new memory based on current stimuli. In consolidating feelings, the hippocampus, with the help of the amygdalae, scans personal experience, looking to history for clues. If that history is loaded with pain, the clues are difficult to reach. The person either overreacts or underreacts—talks too much, eats too much, has no sex or not enough sex, and so forth.

The hippocampus is one of the few brain structures that continue developing with age. Researchers at the Salk Institute in La Jolla, California, have found an increased number of hippocampal cells as a result of either mental or physical exercise.[18] I believe that love received very early in life also helps the brain to continue to develop.

Consider the hippocampus to be the handmaiden of the amygdalae. Both have direct connections to the thalamus. Fear can travel from the thalamus to the amygdalae, or, to the thalamus via the cortex, then to the amygdalae to be engraved in many ways. For some, just getting up in the morning, relatively undefended, can produce a flash of fear. Fear can travel from the thalamus to the amygdalae, without the frontal cortex, for an immediate, emergency reaction. This is called *emotional learning*. One area of the amygdalae has brainstem connections that increase heart rate and other automatic functions. A traumatic birth skews the brain so that thalamic pathways to the amygdalae take precedence over cortical ones. The frontal area is then used after a feeling as a "mop up" procedure.

The hippocampus also attenuates emotional response. When heavy pain is imprinted, it puts a great burden on this structure. Eventually the hippocampus begins to break down, or atrophies, and memory becomes faulty and truncated. As degeneration continues, there may be permanent memory loss. It has been found through autopsy that hippocampal cells in psychotics are in total disarray.[19] A number of studies of severe mental illness have revealed that as frontal cortex function diminishes, the hippocampal area becomes overactive. Emotions roil while the integrative centers are disintegrating.

A massive discharge of feeling from the amygdalae shuts down the hippocampus. This is another way that the pain message is prevented from reaching the frontal cortex. The hippocampus says, "I've had enough. I'm not delivering the message. It's too much trouble." It keeps the frontal cortex in the dark. No one can tell the person what feelings lie deep down because no one but that person can feel them.

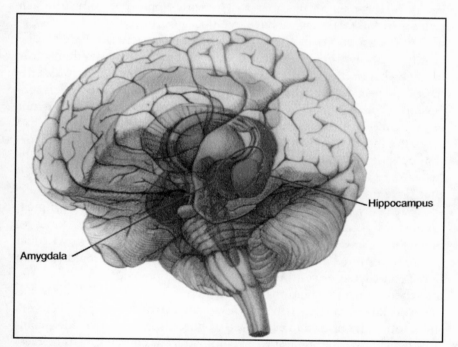

Fig. 2. Hippocampus: Laying down new memory; retaining memory as a fact. Amygdala: The feeling of feeling; memory as an emotion.

Any trigger, say a parent's look of disgust or a boss's tone of contempt, can cause the hippocampus to retrieve the memory. This is accomplished by its scanning mechanism: The trigger resonates with a past coded feeling, dredging it up from the limbic storehouse and launching it toward conscious-awareness. The information activates physical systems, producing anxiety and signaling the danger that the original event is approaching consciousness. It is the early womb trauma plus the birth trauma that produces the visceral reaction we call anxiety. It happens because some current event (an angry tone by someone else) sets off the prototype. The danger in the tone sets off primordial imprinted fears. There is an oversecretion of cortisol-stress hormone because that was the original lifesaving physiologic reaction. The problem is that this reaction occurs without connection because it is practically impossible to gain access to the memory without a systematic approach, going through lesser pains first. So now we have free-floating anxiety.

We need access to our feelings to lead an intelligent life. One may be able to logically work out mathematical problems while simultaneously living a chaotic life filled with drugs and dangerous acting out. A brilliant businessman, for instance, knows the art of making the deal, is successful, social, yet his life is empty. His life looks good but he is not enjoying it. As one of my patients said, "I have a fascinating job. Too bad it doesn't interest me." A man can spend a lifetime trying to feel important because he was never important to the people who counted, namely, his parents. We can make a mess of our relationships because we lack that "love imprint" early in life.

When my patients fully relive a feeling they emerge with a great number of associations and insights covering very different kinds of behaviors. "Now I see why I have been late all my life, and why I could never be confined at school in a classroom," they say. "I couldn't stand being constricted or confined, first in the birth canal, then in the crib, and then at home where my parents were so very strict." Feeling has given meaning to their behavior. One patient had to appear before a judge. She was opposed in court by a psychopath who lied. She felt completely helpless. She came into a session afterward and felt first, helpless in general, then helpless with her parents who controlled her every move, and then finally the helplessness at birth when her mother had been given a massive anesthetic. This helplessness was the prototype upon which all later experiences elaborated. Helplessness became a compounded feeling, reinforced time and again.

The prototype of helplessness directs many later-life characteristics such as fear of change, rigidity, and lack of spontaneity. The unconscious

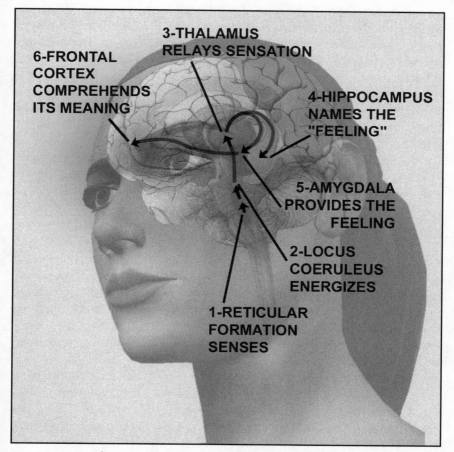

Fig. 3. Frontal Cortex: meaning and comprehension; integration of feeling; scans history and recalls similar events; enriches the stream of consciousness. Amygdala: Helps galvanize the system when it detects danger.

is warning, "There is nothing you can do about your situation." If you couldn't do anything to save your life originally, you are indeed helpless.

THE PAIN OF ANOREXIA

One anorexic young girl I treated was forced to perform oral sex on her mother's boyfriend from age six to age nine. When she later developed anorexia and bulimia and would binge and purge, she was unconsciously throwing up what her mother's boyfriend had ejaculated into her. Rejecting the sperm fluid was a survival mechanism; her body was rejecting an alien and threatening force. This all happened after age five. I could never have made the connection she did in her feelings because it would be my cortex trying to figure out a low-level imprint in someone else's brain.

Anorexia is often brainstem originated, whereas the conscious decision to fight it is located far away from the brainstem. Engaging in such a dialogue between the cortex and the brainstem is a conversation that transcends millions of years of development, asking the frontal cortex to do the work of the brainstem. It is no different than trying to use willpower alone to battle anorexia.

It is known that "speed" can reduce appetite. The person who is speedy through internal overstimulation may through this fact alone lose his appetite. Anorexia may be treated in a soothing and encouraging group home environment, a halfway house for example, and sometimes the symptoms may be eradicated, but the dynamic behind it is never eradicated. Yet it is very important to treat the symptom because it can be fatal. Not treating the cause, however, can also be fatal.

The lower brain knows more about its own internal reality than any outside expert. My patient's anorexia continued because her survival mechanism was stronger than any therapeutic approach. In these cases conventional psychotherapy can be of no help except on a superficial level. Often both patient and doctor believe progress is being made, when actually the doctor is dealing with one reality while the patient's brain and body are dealing with another.

A patient of mine, Sandra, recounted her struggle with anorexia and her road to recovery. The following case history of Sandra again points out some of the origins, not only of anorexia but also of suicidal tendencies. In her case, she almost died at birth. She was engulfed in death feelings at the start of her life which became imprinted so that she was obsessed with it. It is not often that the person wants to die. It is rather that the imprint is that death can end agony. It is that equation from birth that drives the person both toward and away from death. When hopelessness is added to the mix there is a feeling of impending death together with the feeling that there is no use in trying to change anything. Most of my death-obsessed patients tell me that their feeling is that death is immediate, not some far-off event. What is immediate is that the death sensation from birth is rising toward awareness and produces obsessions.

SANDRA'S STORY

My mother didn't want me; she tried to abort me. When that didn't work, she starved herself so she wouldn't look pregnant. She finally started eating during her (my) seventh month because she had started to show. When I was born I was anorexic and couldn't keep anything down. I feel now that I keep myself on the brink of starvation because I've had that feeling from the very beginning.

Before I was born my mother lost a baby during the fifth month. The same thing happened to me, only I was somehow strong enough to survive.

Today I feel that same toxicity, and with it the death feelings that have plagued me all of my life. I have always had a slight sensation of nausea, especially just after eating. My impulse has been to regurgitate anything that came into my body. I see now that I have been reenacting that poisoning experience in the womb. I must have had the impulse to regurgitate to survive in the womb—and maybe it was even that impulse, or a primitive version of it, that kept me alive. Yet that impulse almost killed me later on when I began to lose so much weight.

Whenever I am in a situation of stress or vulnerability, those same early death feelings come up, and my body is obliged to push them down.

In sleep I sink down to what feels like a baby level of consciousness; as a result, I get terrified and have trouble getting to sleep at all. In sex I'm vulnerable, so I just shut off when I get too excited. I have been suicidal for years, and now I see why. Even before I was born I was surrounded by death and had to fight it off!

I followed the same pattern of blocking my feelings in therapy. As feelings would come up I would get overwhelmed, push down the feeling I was dealing with in the present, and just abreact or release helter-skelter all of the energy trapped inside me. I was always regarded as a "hysteric." I couldn't focus on any one feeling because I had a volcano inside of me to be dealt with. None of my body processes functioned right because my body always held the death feeling captive. Those feelings had to be taken care of in Primal Therapy before my body would work again.

THE BRAINSTEM: INSTINCT AND SURVIVAL

The lowest part of the brain, which leads to the spinal column, is called the brainstem. Composed of many structures, the brainstem includes the reticular activating system, the medulla, and the locus ceruleus. It is the first organized central system to handle and register events, particularly before birth and for several months thereafter.

When a threat arises the brainstem sounds the alarm and energizes the body. It is involved in the regulation of vital functions such as breathing, blood pressure, and heart rate. All of these are instinctual, automatic functions. The brainstem rallies the troops by activating the rest of the brain and body with nerve fibers that go directly to the frontal cortex and also to the limbic system.

Signals of fear engraved in brainstem structures such as the locus ceruleus are sent to the upper-level cortex, which then assembles it into a phobia, an obsession, or anxiety, the origins of which for the person are deeply sequestered. "Why anxiety?" one might question. Because anxiety takes cortical processing, otherwise it is low-level terror. You need to be "aware" of the visceral rumblings. Anxiety is only amorphous terror. Anxiety is an "aware" state. We feel terrible, know something is wrong, but don't know what or why. When I took an MRI for my back, enclosed in a tight metal sheath for one-half hour, in order to avoid anxiety I instructed the technician to tap hard on my feet (they stick out) at irregular intervals so that I could not process the fear cortically. It worked. No anxiety; no ability to produce and assemble the fear cortically.

Think of the brainstem as the reptilian brain.[20] It is what we have in common with our animal ancestors. Traumas occurring during gestation connect directly to this system. This is why, during a feeling, a patient "recalls" in the language of brute physiology and anatomy, with crossed legs, shortness of breath, grunts, gagging, and coughing. Using the proper techniques, we can access this primitive level.* If the patient cries during a session, it is the wail of the newborn, not the scream of a three-year-old. When a patient relives something that happened at age six, the cry is distinctively that of a six-year-old. As she descends down the chain of pain, however, the cries automatically become more infantile. By the time she arrives at the brainstem, it is no longer a cry; it is a grunt or a moan. Even a baby cry during a birth Primal tells us it is not a true event.

Anoxia can never be explained. It is a physiologic state, not an idea. That is why anxiety is so amorphous. It is pure physical, visceral sensation— a choking, a tightness in the chest, churning stomach and a constricting band around the head, dizziness, vertigo, shortness of breath, skipped heartbeat, etc. This anoxia occurred long before the development of the logical cortex which could have made sense of it. The more confined the current visceral reaction (grinding stomach, colitis, diarrhea, for example), the more likely the origin lies in the preverbal past. The prototypic reactivity that got its start at birth is now the first line of response to any new threat. In the face of current threat the hippocampus scans history to find the prototype in order to dictate reaction. It is based on the instinct for survival.

The brainstem has its own memory system. The way we breathe, for example, and the force and cadence of our speech or our general energy level have their origins in this first-line area of the brain. Those whose style of speaking tends to be piercing are often driven by the force of imprinted sensations, the domain of the first-line. Though speech itself is a higher brain function, the energy of forceful speech can be driven by

---

*The publication of our techniques is for another book. It takes six years to learn them. Making them public runs the risk of abuse.

the reptilian brain. When we are sick, however, we often lose that force of speech. Why do sick people look sick? Because a viral attack, like an attack of feelings, puts us under stress, which uses up energy. The voice, for example, is no longer booming and stentorian.

THE WORK OF THE FRONTAL CORTEX: ON DEVELOPING STRANGE IDEAS

The brainstem maintains the tone and rigor of the frontal cortex. It needs a certain amount of input to maintain itself in good working order. The frontal cortex has direct access to the medulla and thus affects heart and breathing functions. The frontal cortex, in reciprocal fashion, regulates the output of the brainstem.

Too much input from the brainstem leaves us easily distracted and unable to concentrate. Picture a fist thrusting upward into a jigsaw puzzle and scattering the pieces here and there. That is roughly what happens when input from below rises unattenuated toward the frontal cortex, which is desperately trying to put all the pieces together. The frontal cortex becomes fragmented and loses cohesion. Paranoia, for example, is a last attempt to ward off fragmentation. It is an attempt by the cortex to gather up all one's fears and put a rationale to them. When paranoia fails we have a mentally ill person. So here we have an example of being psychotic (paranoia) to keep from going completely crazy. At least the paranoid usually functions: can hold down a job, take care of himself, support a family, etc.

One patient, who suffered from paranoia, believed the newspaper vendor down the street wanted to kill him. In our sessions he finally arrived at the brainstem imprint of anoxia (loss of oxygen) at birth. The imprint climbed upward to the frontal cortex where, four decades later, the feeling was transformed from "I'm going to die," to "They want to kill me." The imprint knew death was lurking but because it failed to connect, the cortex did not know the reason for this feeling. His paranoia grew until he became delusional, focusing all his fears in the present. The bizarre newspaper-vendor scenario developed because of the great force of his life-and-death pain at birth and because his defense system had been weakened by so many hurts in his childhood. His parents also hurt him almost every day of his life. They did not want children. He was an accident, and they were going to make sure that he paid for it because he robbed them of their freedom and their lives. If the imprint had originated not at birth but much later in life, we would rarely see such a delusion as this patient had.

Nightmares are a sign of the cortex and parts of the limbic system pushed to the extreme. The *feeling* in the nightmare is the exact replica of the original trauma; the feeling, not the images. The images are a disguise for the sensation-feeling. We do not waste time analyzing the images and the content; we can go straight to the bottom of it. We use the symbols and images in the dream. The patient lets himself be engulfed by the feeling, then rides the vehicle of feeling down the glidepath to its roots. If the feeling is too strong, however, we will not let the patient go there, particularly a new patient. Generally, the brain won't let that happen as the gates slam shut. But if the gates are weakened by compounded pain through one's life, then we help out. It could be that at this point tranquilizers are needed. They do exactly what a mother's kiss would have done. Nightmares mean faulty defenses, a breakthrough of heavy valence pain. Usually, dreams can manage all by themselves to wrap up the feeling in images. It is only when that fails that we have nightmares. Dreams are the disguises for primal feelings; otherwise we would awake and be in reality. They help keep us asleep. Some of us remember our dreams because they have partial access to that level.

Trying to reason with the patient above and convince him that no one wanted to kill him was useless since his body and brain knew that death was around the corner. This was not a "thought disorder," as reported in the psychiatric literature. In fact, it is not a disorder at all. It is an attempt by the body's last cerebral defense to make sense out of a hidden feeling. It is a compensatory mechanism to help us stay sane, at least somewhat sane. Its function is to keep connection from happening, as that means vital signs in the danger area.

Drugs that calm or suppress the upsurging brainstem message only ameliorate the syndrome. Not surprisingly, those drugs also dampen obsessive-compulsive symptoms such as constant hand-washing or checking the locks dozens of times a day. It diminishes the work that the cortex has to do by slowing down brainstem and limbic impulses that terminate in the neocortex. It doesn't matter whether it is obsessions, attention-distraction, or paranoia; it all involves the frontal thinking cortex and its limbic connections. It is obvious why the same pill suppresses all of them to one degree or another.

Obsessions, ruminations at night while trying to fall asleep, and mystical ideas are the cortex's way to handle and hold back feelings. It certainly feels more comfortable to believe you are protected by a mighty force than to feel totally naked and unprotected. When our feelings match our ideation the system can finally rest.

FEELING OUR HUMANITY

Whenever brainstem imprints are involved, I can hear it during a feeling in the pattern of crying; the sporadic, truncated sobs; and the loss of breath. When I see a normalization of function—lower body temperature, for example—I feel secure in the knowledge that disconnection was the culprit and reconnection to the original event the savior. I am able to state with assurance that reconnection restabilizes the system, because I have seen it time and again in my patients. There is nothing quite as soothing as getting rid of nagging tension and anxiety, of shaking that feeling of being unloved.

Feeling is what makes us human. In Primal Therapy we help the patient feel uncomfortable, but only for a short time. If we were not meant to connect brainstem instinctive forces with higher brain levels we would not have such a direct linkage of nerve networks.

There is a biologic need to be whole and to reconnect; a memory of wellness, of what we once were lies in each of us. If the body normalizes with the *reexperience* of early feelings, then we can assume that it *deviated* with the original experience of that pain. When the patient relives a trauma that doubled his blood pressure and brings it back to normal later we don't have to figure anything out. History ties the symptom to the past.

NOTES

1. Allan Schore describes the reverberation process: "This posterior cortical-prefrontal-subcortical limbic-prefrontal-posterior cortical loop would activate a reverberating (self-reexcitational) circuit that mediates a long-term memory function." Allan Schore, *Affect Regulation and the Origin of the Self: The Neurobiology of Emotional Development* (Hillsdale, N.J.: Lawrence Erlbaum and Associates, 1994), p. 297.

2. J. W. Smyth et al., "The Interaction between Prenatal Stress and Neonatal Handling on Nociceptive Response Latencies in Male and Female Rats," *Physiology and Behavior* 55, no. 5 (May 1994): 973.

3. J. W. Smyth, W. B. Rowe, and M. J. Meaney, "Neonatal Handling Alters Serotonin (5HT) Turnover and 5HT Receptor Binding in Selected Brain Regions," *Developmental Brain Research* 80 (15 February 1994): 183–89.

4. D. Peters et al., "Effects of Maternal Stress During Different Gestational Periods on the Serotonergic System in the Adult Rat Offspring," *Pharmacology, Biochemistry and Behavior* 31 (1989): 839–43.

5. Ibid.

6. M. J. Meaney et al., "Early Environmental Regulation of Forebrain Gluto-corticoid Receptor Gene Expression: Implications for Adreno-cortical Responses to Stress," *Developmental Neuroscience* (Montreal, Canada) 18 (1996): 49–72.

7. Daniel Goleman, *Emotional Intelligence* (New York: Bantam, 1995).

8. B. Dalens, "La Douleur Aigue de l'enfant et son Traitement," *Annals Franciases D'Anesthesie et De Reanimation* (Paris) 10 (1981): 40–41.

9. W. J. H. Nauta and Michael Feirtag, "The Organization of the Brain," *Scientific American* 241, no. 3 (September 1979): 88–98.

10. See *Time*, 5 May 1997, p. 78 for a summary of the research.

11. M. Weinstock, "Prenatal Stress Increases Anxiety-Related Behavior and Alters Cerebral Lateralization of Dopamine Activity," *Life Sciences* 42 (1988): 1059–65.

12. It should be added, however, that different neurotransmitters work differently in different parts of the brain. Thus, dopamine can be inhibitory in some lower areas and inhibitory in the cortex by stimulating the frontal area to be more effective.

13. "A Shocking Case of Depression," *Science News* 154, no. 22 (28 November 1998): 344.

14. See our own research, *The New Primal Scream*, obtainable at The Primal Center, Venice, Calif.

15. Antonio Damasio, *The Feeling of What Happens* (New York: Harcourt Brace, 1999), p. 46.

16. Personal correspondence, 1 January 2000.

17. R. Gagin, E. Cohen, and Y. Shavit, "Prenatal Exposure to Morphine Feminizes Male Sexual Behavior in the Adult Rat," *Pharmacology, Biochemistry and Behavior* 38 (1997): 345.

18. H. Van Praag et al., "Running Enhances Neurogenesis, Learning, and Long-Term Potentiation in Mice," *Proceedings of the National Academy of Science USA* 96, no. 23 (9 November 1999): 13427–31; G. Kempermann, H. G. Kuh, and F. H. Cage, "More Hippocampal Neurons in Adult Mice Living in an Enriched Environment," *Nature* 386, no. 6624 (3 April 1997): 493–95.

19. Stephen Plotkin, University of California at Irvine, in "Study Links Schizophrenia, Cells," *Outlook*, 16 May 1996.

20. Paul MacLean, *The Triune Brain in Evolution: Role in Paleocerebral Functions* (New York: Plenum Press, 1990).

3

SOUNDING THE ALARM
The Reticular Activating System

Rather than relaying global information to higher centers, the reticular activating system "measures" the amount of information passing through and activates the brain sufficiently to deal with that level. The system matures early, before birth, activating the highest level of neurological functioning available at a given stage of development.

Pain mobilizes the system, keeping it alert, signaling danger and possible damage. Organizing this information is the reticular activating system. This netlike structure is one of the key areas of norepinephrine concentration, which helps keep us vigilant. One specialist explains: "Both norepinephrine and dopamine [the activating neurochemicals] send their axons (the long connecting arms) into the cerebral cortex . . . highly complex and intricate patterns of intellectual activity in the cortex are influenced by evolutionary primitive catecholamine systems."[1] This means that brainstem sites send long connecting axons, nerve networks, to the frontal cortical area for meaning. It is the way that the brainstem imprints activate the ideational mind and keeps it churning and obsessing. This, then, keeps us from relaxing and sleeping. We are overactivated, not by thoughts, but by nonverbal imprints that drive us to think and ruminate. Why can't we sleep? Because we are letting go of our cerebral defense system as we approach lower-level structures, the very ones that signal pain.

When pain is imprinted, the system may overstimulate the frontal cortex. This is when we see obsessive-compulsive behavior or phobias as the frontal area hurries to discharge the imprinted overload. Or, depending on the nature of the early trauma, such as massive anesthesia at birth, the reticular activating system shuts down and may not provide sufficient stimulation to keep the frontal cortex active and effective. The result is a phlegmatic personality with passivity and unfocused, scattered, thought patterns. This is also the pattern of a "loser" who can't seem to get anything done. Sometimes ideas, traveling on descending reticular pathways, shut off sensations and feelings and keep the impulses from flooding the frontal area.

The frontal lobe has direct connections to this system and can control physiologic states. Animal studies indicate that caressing or holding these animals can attenuate or modulate the reticular activating system, making them less excitable. You can tranquilize the reticular activating system through either touch or drugs. Touch is far more effective. I have watched patients writhe in agony as they beg for touch from their parents. During critical periods, caress and touch are essential to human brain development. After that period, all the touch in the world will not completely erase the damage; a quantity of touch deprivation will remain. And that is what often drives compulsive sexual activity in women—and men, for that matter. When the system is activated, as in sexual excitement, the whole panoply of buried feelings threatens to emerge as well. If the imprint of high levels of excitement resulted in "shut down" originally then high levels of sexual excitement will result in a shut down of the sexual experience. When something is very exciting, as in sex, the brain scans its history for an equal level of excitement and searches for the correct response. If the original response to massive stimulation was shut-down (as in the birth trauma), then there will be shut-down again. Here is one possible origin of frigidity.

Let me be clear about this. When a high-valence (force) event takes place in adulthood, such as sexual excitement, it forces the limbic structures to scan for other equally high-valence events such as the birth trauma, and triggers it all off. It also dredges up other traumas during childhood, so that now there is a high-level pain on the rise plus the deviations that took place—for example, wearing Mother's panties. The sex drive is now compromised by one's life history. Perhaps there will be an incessant homosexual fantasy as sexual excitement mounts—the need for a father's love in a man. This need, normally well repressed, has become unhinged and intrudes into the sex act. If the current event, a joyful basketball game, is not of such a high valence, it might not trigger off the sexual fantasies or deviations.

THE LOCUS CERULEUS: AT TERROR'S CENTER

The locus ceruleus is an important center of fear and pain reaction in the brainstem. Located high up in the brainstem (see chapter 1), it secretes noradrenaline, an arousal chemical, in response to preverbal trauma, birth accidents, or early lack of touch and warmth. When noradrenaline connects with its receptors we experience pain. The locus ceruleus is a primitive structure that knows only sensations and has little to do with feelings. In evolutionary terms it predates the development of feelings by millions of years.

The locus ceruleus is made up of only a few hundred to a few thousand neurons, yet its branches, or axons, extend throughout the brain. This enables the locus ceruleus to activate the nervous system in a global manner. But although the locus ceruleus responds to pain, it also has a dense concentration of opiate receptors that squelch pain. In other words, the home of pain is also the home of pain suppression. Early imprints galvanize the system to accommodate pain, then provoke the system to suppress that pain when it reaches inordinate levels. A number of animal studies involving pain (delivered by electrical stimulation or by pinching the tail) have been found to affect the locus ceruleus in terms of both stimulation and inhibition.[2]

Because the locus ceruleus is a key center of terror, this sensation will ultimately disrupt the work of the thinking cortex as terror is sent upward by the reticular activating system for cortical connection.

The drug clonidine is a brainstem blocker that inhibits the firing of noradrenaline neurons in the locus ceruleus. Bruce Perry of the Baylor University Medical Center found that "rats exposed to perinatal stress (around birth) show major alterations in their stress response later in life."[3] Abused children have been found to experience in later life "frustration, anger, pain, helplessness, startle response, sleep abnormalities, impulsivity, and altered cardiovascular regulation.[4]

Perry also found that stressed and abused children responded well to clonidine because it regulated the activity of the locus ceruleus. It helped improve sleep, stabilized heart function, slowed restlessness, and decreased hypervigilance. Also helped, Perry learned, were many of the impulse-ridden traits such as aggression, stealing, and uncontrolled outbursts.

I treated a woman who as a newborn was left for days without her mother who was hospitalized with tuberculosis. That experience of being in a new world with no support or warmth has been imprinted as both terror and loneliness. Most of her brainstem structures contributed in their own way to the valence of pain, secreting dopamine and/or norepinephrine to mobilize the brain and body, making her hyperactive.

Her pain of being left alone was blocked by neurotransmitters, then rerouted to other centers. The energy of it, however, was enough to shatter her concentration and elevate her hyperactivity. In high school, she received Fs and Ds. Many of her teachers thought she was "dumb," and her parents reinforced this idea. She finally felt her terror, her fear of life, and fear of trying. Her whole life was dominated by fear. This woman is now a successful doctor. She was suffering, however.

When stimulation reaches inordinate levels over time, locus ceruleus activation *decreases*, assuring that the pain message will not reach conscious-awareness. The locus ceruleus usually responds to incoming stimulation with large bursts of neural activity followed by a quiescent period. These bursts may account for panic attacks. These panic attacks are responding to imprints. The locus ceruleus just doesn't go off on its own without reason.

The locus ceruleus isn't subject to logic; in the presence of early painful imprints, it simply reacts and mobilizes us. One can say, "There's nothing to be alarmed about," but the alarm is internal. A person in an enclosed room feels suffocated. Another person panics when riding in an elevator. The locus ceruleus and other lower structures contain the nonverbal postbirth message, "I am suffocating in the incubator," resulting in panic, the same physiologic reaction as experienced in the incubator.

Clonidine has been used for high blood pressure for thirty years. It can tell us about the relationship of pain and blood pressure.

Stored terror can leak out in myriad ways throughout one's life: through phobias, talking fast, hyperactivity, anxiety, and panic attacks. Bad dreams and nightmares are good examples of leakage.

In morphine withdrawal, as might be expected, there is more firing in the locus ceruleus. The system is again in danger, and the locus ceruleus, through stimulating the upper cortical brain, is making us aware of it. We can slow the firing rate of locus ceruleus neurons and also of the neurons in the medulla with medication. The sudden stoppage of drugs acting on the brainstem increases the output of noradrenaline(speeds heart rate, dilates blood vessels)with therefore more arousal. This means more pain and therefore more need to quell it; i.e., withdrawal syndrome. As discussed earlier, the sudden withdrawal of effective brainstem drugs can be dangerous and may lead in some cases to seizures—massive discharge of brain neurons. It is the excess firing of the locus ceruleus that makes the withdrawal subject so uncomfortable. She is agitated to the extreme without knowing why, which makes it all the more devilish. Taking medication that slows down the firing restores comfort.

All the reticular activation system and locus ceruleus know is to get ready for action. They mobilize our defenses: A poor night's sleep permits deep-lying imprints to emerge from storage. The closer that imprinted event is to conscious-awareness, the more the cortex is compelled to produce ideation. You cannot talk the person out of the ideation because it is anchored in an unconscious feeling. Tranquilizers may continue to block the pain, but once they are discontinued, the resulting output of noradrenaline increases heart rate and dilates blood vessels, getting ready again for an anxiety attack. We always pay a price for artificial manipulation.

NOTES

1. M. Huttunen and P. Niskanen, "Prenatal Loss of Father and Psychiatric Disorders," *Archives of General Psychiatry* 35 (1978): 429–31.

2. See: S. L. Foote et al., "Nucleus Locus Ceruleus: New Evidence of Anatomical and Physiological Specificity," *Physiological Reviews* 63 (July 1983): 868.

3. Bruce Perry, "Clonidine Decreases Symptoms of Physiological Hyper-arousal in Traumatized Children," Submission to *American Academy of Child and Adolescent Psychiatry* (17 February 1996): 313.

4. Ibid., p. 314.

4

THE HYPOTHALAMUS
Carrying the Message of Feeling

In addition to the thalamus, amygdalae, and hippocampus, the limbic structures are connected to the hypothalamus and its adjunct, the pituitary. The hypothalamus regulates hormone production and directs the immune system via the pituitary gland, which lies just beneath it. The hypothalamus also helps regulate heart rate and blood pressure. If the hypothalamus is overloaded with pain, the body will either over-secrete or undersecrete hormone, causing changes in heart rate and body temperature.

Along with the brainstem, the hypothalamus is involved in the body's "homeostatic regulation," controlling breathing, heart function, blood pressure, digestion, electrolyte balance, visceral tone, and other vital functions. The hypothalamus is a final common pathway through which the limbic system sends feelings into the bodily system. It is what makes the feeling of being criticized churn the stomach, diminish the natural killer cells and the lymphocytes of the immune system. Contrarily, stimulation of the hypothalamus can increase the antibodies to combat foreign substances and/or infection.

The hypothalamus needs love, too. Its connection to the frontal cortex affects the growth of brainstem neurons. The way it shows its need is that it keeps us constantly vigilant and then makes us sick if it doesn't get what it wants. I am reminded of a patient who had dermatitis. We found that constant caressing during sessions greatly ameliorated her condition. What eventually eradicated the symptom was when she relived the feeling of her body crying out for touch from a mother who was unable to show physical affection. She lifted her arms and screamed and pleaded for weeks about this.

Feelings travel to the hypothalamus and manifest into such symptoms as stomach cramps, heaviness in the chest, rapid heartbeat, and high blood pressure. The symptoms indicate that the system is in disharmony. The person may be aware of malaise, but she can't shut it off because she cannot shut off the early feeling.

Birth trauma skews the hypothalamus to favor sympathetic output, revving us up. If a baby is "born" with allergies, the hypothalamus and other structures that help process allergies may have been affected in the womb. If an infant is not loved in the first year or two of her life, the hypothalamus can be impaired, resulting in a chronically sick child, one continually plagued by allergies, infections, and fever.

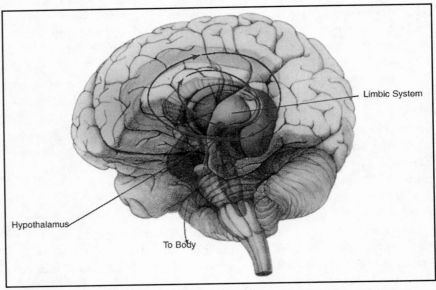

Fig. 4. Feelings in the limbic system regulate hormone production.

Stimulation of the hypothalamus can increase antibody levels that combat foreign elements (such as pollen or cat dander), antigens, viruses, and so forth. Autoimmune diseases such as arthritis are another possible outcome. A specialist in immune function, Hugo Besedovsky of Davos, Switzerland, has written about the mechanisms involved in the relay of electrochemical messages from the cortex to the hypothalamus, which then tells the immune cells to increase or decrease their activity.[1]

Messages from the hypothalamus also tell the sympathetic neurons to get moving. One of my patients was constantly on the go, as if he were trying to stay out of harm's way—which he was. As a child, his parents fought constantly. He felt helpless, believing there was no way out. When he stopped rushing around, utter helplessness and hopelessness set in. Constant activity was his defense against feeling that there was nothing he could do to change his family life. In our sessions we discovered that at birth, he had been squeezed and stuck in the canal, blocked by a tumor. This was confirmed by his parent later on. We could never have guessed about this last experience of being squeezed. The sensation and the body contractions with the pain all delivered up its truth. *His act-out was being driven by the feeling to keep him from feeling the feeling. Let me hasten to add that we do not look for birth trauma, and we do not expect it. The patient's body offers it up when it is ready and not before. There are times when that trauma does not exist. This is frequently the case in home births where no anesthetics are used.*

The hypothalamus is in part responsible for palpitations, tachycardia, and other heart disrhythms brought on by arousal through the secretions of norepinephrine. If the hypothalamus activates the sympathetic nervous system, the parasympathetic system largely shuts down. The resulting imbalance is why it is often so difficult to fall asleep, or why we cannot concentrate. Activation from early pain doesn't cease because we want to sleep. On the contrary, as we start to fall asleep and let go of some cortical defenses we are even more activated. With lifelong oversecretion of stress hormones to combat the imprint, supplies are eventually going to be exhausted. Sleep means the suppression in progression of the higher levels of conscious-awareness, starting with the cortex, moving to the limbic system, active in dream sleep, and then descending to the brainstem and deep sleep. It also means liberating lower-level imprints.

At the back of the hypothalamus is a major center for agony. Whether the pain originates from a fall down the stairs or from the memory that "Mommy doesn't like me," the agony is the same. The heart speeds up, more stress hormones are secreted, blood pressure climbs, and brainwave amplitude may climb. The system has gone into combat mode because a need is struggling to be fulfilled. That need may be "Love me a little! Please don't hate me!" When a patient lying motionless in a quiet room suddenly experiences a radical increase in heart rate, we know that she is beginning to relive the feeling. The feeling involves year after year of not being able to articulate, "Love me just a little!" "Be kind to me." It may not seem like much now but in childhood no child can stand being disliked. Parents are everything to him, and as we have seen, love means proper development of the brain.

The message "Love me!" is never complicated because it is organized in structures that cannot construct complicated syntax. Indeed, if someone is reliving infancy trauma and exclaims in complicated sentences we know it is not real. Even if the person uses adult words like "recognize" we know again that it is not a true experience.

When the feeling rises to the top, first there is agony as it comes close to conscious-awareness, and then the alerting system (sympathetic), which has mobilized the entire organism to fight the connection, relaxes as the parasympathetic system takes over. There is then rest and repair. After such a connection I've seen systolic blood pressure drop one hundred points in minutes. Here again we note the dialectic: the structures that organize feeling are also the ones that repress it through the secretion of neuroinhibitors. While the message from the limbic feeling centers is relatively simple, the message when it emanates from the brainstem is simplicity itself—"I'm strangling. It's hopeless. I can't breathe! I'm dying! I'm suffocating. Don't crowd me!" Most often there are no words at all, just sensations—feeling crushed.

As I pointed out earlier, manic and depressive states are not different diseases but differing levels of effectiveness in blocking feelings. When a manic finally becomes depressive, much of the feeling energy has been drained by the manic behavior, allowing repression to prevail. Those same feelings of hopelessness have not vanished but are more effectively repressed because less force is making its way to the cortex and limbic areas.

I have been discussing love at length. Now let us turn our attention to what love is made of. It is not some ethereal concept existing in the air; it is something concrete and can be accounted for by the levels of certain hormones in one's body and by specific structures of the brain. As the reader might imagine, pain has something to do with changing the levels of the hormones of love. We can try to be loving and warm to our mates but there are biological limits to overcome.

THE CINGULATE CORTEX

The last brain structure to be discussed is by far not the least—the cingulate cortex. This is somewhat like an arc overarching the limbic system and enveloping limbic structures. Remember again, that the limbic system has to do with feelings and their expression. NIMH scientist Paul MacLean believes that the cingulate cortex acts like a receptive organ for the experiencing of emotion. It has three basic functions: (1) The cry of separation, (2) play, and (3) nursing and other family-oriented behavior. It distinguishes us from lower animal forms, representing the evolutionary transition from reptiles to mammals. It is heavily involved in love—maternal care and, eventually, altruism.

Let us take the separation cry. This cry is characteristic of most mammals and is crucial to survival. The newborn/infant needs love to survive. The cry is a shout for love to come running. It is responsible for the primal scream; to end the agony of isolation by the infant. There is no greater pain for the infant than that of being separated from the mother. We need contact to survive. MacLean believes that the earliest mammals were tiny, nocturnal animals who lived in semidarkness. The cry was the healing tentacle to end separation. When we damage or extirpate the cingulate cortex we effectively stop maternal behavior. There are aspects of this structure related to the perception of pain. So here again we see the relationship of need and pain; deprived need becomes pain. The key feeling is a need for closeness and physical contact.

Not surprisingly, this area is heavily endowed with internally manufactured opiate/painkillers. When infant animals are given small doses of morphine their separation cries diminish. When they are given opiate-antagonists, they cry again. Here again we note how painkillers ease the agony of separation; and conversely, separation for an infant is agony. It is a pain that endures, which is why adults need painkillers—to stifle the cries of being unloved early in life. The cingulate cortex is also implicated in empathy, the ability to feel what someone else is experiencing inside. When the president says, "I feel your pain," he means, "My cingulate cortex understands your feelings." When we relate on a feeling level it is this structure that is involved. It often eludes the grasp of those who rely on numbers, words, and figures to explain psychological behavior. It is another universe of discourse that was the central, highest form of "thought and communication" in lower animals.

If we are to go on surviving and caring about our fellow beings we need to make sure that the cingulate cortex is not neglected.

NOTE

1. H. O. Besedovsky, "Immune-Neuro-Endocrine Interactions: Facts and Hypotheses," *Endocrinology Review* 17, no. 1 (February 1996): 64–102.

5

THE SYMPATH
AND PARASYMPATH
Shaping Personality in the Womb

I mentioned early that the hypothalamus controls the two divisions of the autonomic nervous system, the parasympathetic (the parasympath) and the sympathetic (the sympath). The sympathetic system directs energy-using processes such as the fight-or-flight response. It mobilizes us, raises body temperature, and reduces peripheral circulation to conserve blood for the muscles—which may explain a pale face or cold hands and feet. Frequent urination, increased sweat, dry mouth, and higher-pitched voice are other effects.

By contrast, the parasympathetic branch controls energy-conserving processes, those of rest, sleep, and repair. It dilates blood vessels, making the skin warm, and promotes healing. When we are in the parasympathetic mode, our musculature relaxes to save energy, and our voice lowers to a slow, mellifluous timbre.

A healthy person has a good balance between the two systems. Ideally, the two work together in harmony so that we are more "sympathetic" during the day and more "parasympathetic" during sleep. But birth trauma or a harsh childhood can push us in one direction or the other. For example, during a difficult birth when the mother is heavily anesthetized, the neonate cannot help himself to be born because he has been shut down. This event imprints despair and resignation—a parasympathetic mode that directs future responses: a person might give up easily or feel overwhelmed by the smallest of things (struggle-fail). On the other hand, if the neonate has struggled successfully to be born, the imprinted mode may be sympathetic (struggle-win). The person does not give up easily and is optimistic and tenacious.

I have found specific personality types based on the two kinds of very early experience we have. The prototype that is imprinted is, by and large, life-saving. After that the brain will scan history to see how to react in the present, and it always will fall on the prototype. There is an entire configuration in the parasympath: lower body temperature, slower pulse, and low blood pressure. One key feature is the slightly lower thyroid output. In some cases during a birth reliving the body temperature can drop two to three degrees. Since the patient has no idea what is going on it is largely an unfaked reaction. The reason for the drop may be due to massive anesthesia given to the mother which effectively shut down the neonate's system. Further, there are specific ideas that accompany these drops, usually forerunners of the feeling that is coming up. Feelings are preceded by ideas as the lower-level force moves to frontal awareness. Ideas pave the way, so to speak; they speak of what lies below. That is why, with the right techniques, we can focus on ideas and regress down to origins. Patients come in bereft of optimism; resignation reigns as the whole system goes into (the original) fail mode. The person feels hopeless as death approaches and finds there is nothing she can do about it. She may start a therapy session depressed, helpless, and cynical: "Nothing will do any good." "What's the use of trying? This therapy can't work on me." The reason for this attitude is that she is close to birth-death feelings. She could not try during the birth sequence being up against massive anesthetic odds. The vital signs accommodate to this fact; thus it is all of a piece—low vital signs with despair and resignation. In short, "hopeless." She also could not try after birth when she was left alone day after day, when her cries went unheeded because the parents thought it correct to "let her cry it out."

Parasympathetic men have a low, leisure, deep voice. An air of lassitude is projected; the metabolism is slow. Other attributes include introspection, dreaminess, and emotional detachment. Parasympaths are often night people, meeting the dawn of each day as they met birth—sluggishly (anesthetized). Each morning is a sort of flashback to the birth event.

The sympath, however, fought mightily and successfully during birth. This configuration also has a marked gestalt about it: higher pulse rate, elevated body temperature, a more cheery and optimistic demeanor. Male sympaths have a higher, squeakier voice. The sympathetic proto-type changes the setpoints of many biologic systems. The sympath has trouble applying the brakes in the face of reality. Push, push was the early lifesaving mode. He maneuvers his outer life to conform with his inner feelings. He is the salesman who won't take "no" for an answer.

When the sympathetic system is activated by life-and-death danger stemming from birth, it deactivates the parasympathetic system. Anxiety and heart palpitations then prevail because the parasympathetic system, which normally orders the sympathetic system to rest and relax, is ren-dered temporarily underfunctional.

The parasympathetic system plays a major role in depression. Early skewing of the parasympathetic and sympathetic nervous systems alters personality in a definitive way: passive to active, reflective to impulsive, internally directed to externally directed, artistic to practical, dreamy to pragmatic, or vice versa. Birth trauma can warp personality for a lifetime. It is, of course, not just the birth trauma, but the nine previous months that will dictate in some respects how the birth trauma is reacted to. A chronically smoking mother has already seen to it that even with slight anoxia at birth, the predominant mode will be parasympathetic.

Even after early events have been relived, the basic personality cannot be completely changed, for it has been reinforced by repetitive behavior. The parameters can be changed, however, so that the individual is neither exceptionally energyless nor exceptionally overactive. In cases where the child's behavior or actions were not rewarded by the parents, chances are the parasympathetic system will predominate because the memory of despair endures. I treated a woman whose mother died during childbirth. The father blamed the child for her death, and nothing she could ever do was good enough for him. There was no love to strive for, only the avoidance of his anger. She became lethargic and introverted. She gave up by the age of three. It is the sullen child syndrome.

As long as an overburdened hypothalamus has not been skewed to the sympathetic side, the parasympathetic side can help put an end to anxiety and panic attacks. However, the system cannot be at its best if there was prebirth neglect, poor diet, or alcohol and drug use on behalf of the car-rying mother. An October 1998 report by the National Organization on Fetal Alcohol Syndrome found that children whose mothers consumed alcohol excessively while pregnant exhibited mental defects and mental retardation, growth deficiencies, behavioral maladjustments, and central nervous system dysfunction.[1] Clearly, not all of this is simply due to skewing of the autonomic nervous system. There are many other con-tributing factors. I offer skewing because I see it so much of the time in my patients. At least two-thirds of my patients are skewed to the parasympa-thetic mode. If they are not, generally, they do not come to us for help.

There is no doubt a question in the mind of the reader about the occa-sional cigarette or drink by a pregnant woman. I doubt that one cigarette will do much damage, but when the drink or smoke is continuous it will disrupt the integrating capacity of the fetus and deviations will take place. In the adult one drink will not do much damage. Five drinks can produce a drunk. In the fetus five drinks may produce more than a drunk; it may change vital biologic functions as the little system scrambles desperately to handle the input. Much better to abstain. A life is at stake.

If a patient begins a Primal Therapy session with low body tempera-ture, he is likely to be in parasympathetic excess. This happens with our depressive clients because they are often on the verge of feeling a trauma with original parasympathetic reactions—the prototype. They are in a par-ticular mood but don't know why. To reiterate: reactions of depression/sui-cide in the present are the exact reactions from the original imprinted trauma. The hippocampus has scanned history and come up with what was lifesaving originally. It will again and again. Giving up originally was life-saving; struggle was a threat. We put the patient back into historical con-text so that the mood and feelings match the scenes in which they origi-nated. The scene may not be an actual image, simply an anatomic-physio-logic configuration. Reactions are dictated by the nature of the trauma. If a baby is not given to the mother right after birth but instead is put into a layette, the prototype may become resignation. The baby is imprinted as listless and apathetic. Institutionalized children who receive very little love develop this behavior pattern of lethargy and passivity. It is when all three brain levels line up with the same feeling that suicide is a possibility. When someone feels hopeless in the brainstem, limbic system, and in the present life, there is palpable danger. A little bit of hope in the present can lower depression enough to avoid suicidal impulses.

Being a victim of parental cruelty may well rest on this prototype of giving in. In adult life, one may take the role of victim as an unconscious demonstration of this cruelty. Through her attitudes toward others, the person is saying, "I am being abused. Help me!" This is also known as the loser syndrome: "I won't succeed until you see that I'm hurting."

I treated a patient who could not express himself in any confrontation. Two hours into our session, he was reliving a childhood in which his mother constantly reprimanded him. He felt helpless to fight back, particularly because of her violent temper. That reactivated a deeper, related memory in which he was strangling on the umbilical cord. His face went beet-red for a half hour. He came out of the session with the insight that his inability to fight back was from the primal imprint of being choked at birth, compounded by his mother's treatment of him. The patient remarked that whenever anyone told him off or criticized him, he would go mute, just as he did with his mother. It would take an hour for him to think about what he should have said.

For some babies the birth process is a near-death experience imprinted on a naive brain. It is no wonder that certain traits and ways of reacting are stamped in; these traits were nothing less than survival tactics. The proper processing of feeling requires the harmonious efforts of both the sympathetic and parasympathetic systems.

In sympathetic excess one feels "wired." Sympathetic neurons hold and process imprints in the brainstem and limbic system. But some fear-energy manages to seep upward, making the sympath toss and turn in bed, thinking about this project or that, what she will do tomorrow, what she should have done today. This is called *obsessive rumination*. After enough fear-energy is expended through worry, she finally falls asleep. But the terror catches up, and she has a nightmare. She wakes up; her frontal cortex has become "aware" to keep the limbic-brainstem terror in the unconscious. One brain is being used to escape from the other. She takes a sleeping pill to calm the fear. The pill puts the brainstem to sleep. She wakes up the next morning still wired, jumps out of bed, and starts another busy day. It is an interminable cycle.

Some individuals are so totally shut down that they don't even feel the sympathetic energy. These individuals are far removed from their feelings and usually do not come to therapy. If the pain is so steeped in the unconscious, it can be absorbed by the unreal systems of belief. In this case, the person does not suffer. Instead, she may adopt "crazy" ideas, such as a belief in the occult. One sees this in past-lives therapy. Past-lives therapy is now the rage in the New Age field; anything but reality. It is never enough to deal with life and its problems in this world, they have to harken back to ancient Egypt to find their previous lives. Too often, the person has found she was a princess in some ancient kingdom. All of this is predicated on the notion that our ancient history is imprinted in our nervous systems and we have only to tap into it. In this way there is no reality to deal with. I have never seen such a phenomenon in the thousands of relivings I have seen. My patients do report that when they took LSD before therapy such things did happen as they skipped over their whole lives to plunge into mystical notions. Past-lives is a key sign of overload and symbolization, to be taken only as a pathologic sign.

The sympath has learned that effort and struggle is lifesaving; the parasympath has learned that too much effort can be life-endangering (it uses up too much oxygen). The parasympath is more reflective, more brooding, and more likely to be depressed. The sympath is the picture of optimism, less reflective, and rarely depressed.

Think of it in evolutionary terms: sensations came first; feelings came second; thoughts came last. Feelings were in place long before the capacity to be paranoid.

A thought disorder cannot be considered without reference to its limbic-brainstem underpinnings. Ungated feelings and sensations, not compulsive thoughts, are what drive us crazy. The thoughts arise because of pressure from feelings that cannot connect to the frontal cortex.

There are no "thought disorders" as proposed in the psychiatric literature and by literally every drug company flogging tranquilizers for such disorders. Paranoia is believed to be a thought disorder. But it is actually a disorder of *feelings*, of underlying brain processes brought on by changes in the system of the carrying mother. Schizophrenic mothers are five times more likely to have a schizophrenic child, not necessarily because of heredity but because a deeply disturbed mother produces a deeply disturbed physiology that surrounds the fetus, eventually disorganizing limbic centers.[2]

The body automatically directs a person's sex drive based on need. If a man puts on panties and a dress, his behavior may be directed toward fulfilling an old need—that of an absent mother early in life. If the need was not fulfilled in early life, it goes underground. In my clinical practice, so many of our "dress up" males developed because a working mother left only her garments as a reminder. The need is to have a mother nearby; failing that the man takes the next best thing, symbolic reminders—panties. For a woman deprived of a mother, the repressed need may emerge during adolescence and turn its focus toward women. The result may be lesbianism. It may be hard to remember that our parents were everything to to us as children.[3] A girl, deprived of physical comfort by her mother, may at the age of fifteen find herself touched by a girlfriend. It feels so good that it can begin to determine sexual direction. She wants more of what she needs. She is past the age of getting warmth from her mother so she does the next best thing. She finds it in girlfriends.

This woman may come to me not because of her lesbianism but because she suffers from anxiety attacks or other problems from early lack of love. The lesbianism may feel so right that the person is convinced it is normal and maybe even genetic. She has a female lover and would not want it any other way, because her need for a loving woman could not be anything but what it is.

One patient felt as though he was coming out of a lifelong trance. He was the second of twins to be delivered but was in a breech position (feet first) in the womb. He had to be turned around in the womb, which was extremely painful, and finally was born after several hours. He believed he lost consciousness at that point due to pain and the suffocation. His lungs filled with fluid, leaving him with the feeling of drowning. After he was born, his mother was ill from the procedure and unavailable to comfort and reassure him.

The terror was magnified and remained so throughout his life. He had an absent father. His mother had to work to support them both. He was awash in pain all of his life. One could see it in photos taken during his childhood. Born in Slovakia, he was sent away during the war without his mother. He clung to his sister, who later died in an explosion, leaving him totally alone. He was prepsychotic, with occasional delusions and hallucinations; he was sure that the man at the parking kiosk was mad at him because he saw him smiling. Despite this delusion he functioned very well.

His repression of the horrendous pain rendered him almost unconscious at all times; indeed, he was in a trance. As he began to integrate his needs and pain he started to come out of the trance, less immersed in lower-level feelings. That is really what a trance is: being locked into lower levels of consciousness without the frontal cortex to make things clear.

A THERAPY OF EMOTIONAL EMERGENCY

When patients come in contact with old feelings in Primal Therapy, large portions of the frontal cortex shut down while lower centers take over. This is what happens in emergency situations when instinct takes over to save our lives. At that point we don't have time to think about our options; we need to react. In therapy the alienated, dangerous feelings on the rise signal an emergency, compelling the lower centers to take over. There is an attack by feelings. Parts of the immune system go into action just as if a virus were attacking.

The brain treats feeling as if it were an alien that must be repelled at all costs. The lower feeling brain treats it as a current threat. One reason is that the lower centers do not have a time code; it is the cortex that measures time. That is why we need the cortex to properly place a feeling in the past so that it no longer intrudes on current life. As we note elsewhere, the limbic-brainstem processes are mature long before the frontal cortex is activated. That is why Freud called his unconscious the Id, "timeless."

Feeling therapy is nearly always an emergency because if they weren't a threat they already would have been felt. We need to let the patient give in to that emergency and descend the evolutionary chain. We take great care not to ask questions of the patient who is close to feeling. We don't want explanations, and we do not want the patient to be using words for a wordless early trauma. In short, we don't want the frontal cortex involved until we reach the insight phase of feeling. Thoughts are too often the enemy of feelings.

In a session in the darkened room, the therapist sits behind the patient. The patient usually begins by discussing something in the present, a fight with a friend, for example. She may rage about it or cry. She will go on and on about the current situation. Some thirty minutes later she may drop into something similar from her childhood. Her mother always had to be right and would tolerate no dissent. "Let me have my feelings, Momma!" she might scream. She goes on automatically about other similar scenes in her childhood, as the limbic system seems to offer all relevant scenes up to conscious-awareness as though all coded under one overarching feeling. And indeed, the scenes are coded by feeling. Once the patient is locked into the feeling she may grow quiet for a time, gagging a bit or choking, and then silently and slowly gain deeper access. This is dangerous for new patients: too heavy pains too soon for conscious integration. After one and a half or two hours she will open her eyes, blink, and seem to come back into the present. Then the insights begin, and it is then that the therapist takes a much more active role, discussing her current life and how these feelings have played into her previous behavior. Everyone else became her mother, setting off her rage. After the feeling, she sits up, feeling refreshed and not at all wiped out as one would imagine, and bids us goodbye. She decides when to come again. The power is hers.

As soon as a feeling or early event reaches conscious-awareness in the frontal area, it locks in. A solid connection is forged, and the body system returns to normal. That is the connection that should have taken place originally had not gating interceded to save the frontal cortex and the bodily system from being overwhelmed. Enough earlier feelings have been connected so that the system is ready to tackle deeper pains.

This will happen as long as no outsider—i.e., therapist—dictates what the patient should feel and when he should feel it. The patient's brain system and body will take care of all of that. We must learn to trust biology and the individual and abjure ourselves of the need for power. When a person conquers her claustrophobia after feeling the terrible fear and anguish of being punished and left alone in a small room as a child, the connections and insights are made automatically. There are even more widespread insights as the patient slips down into a birth sequence of being left alone for perhaps hours or days in an incubator.

After reexperiencing and connecting their feelings the vital signs of my patients return to below starting values. Repressing feelings generates

heat in the body, but once those feelings are allowed to surface there is a
drop in body temperature, often a permanent decrease from one half to
one degree. (We measure the vital signs of every patient in every session,
before and after.) When a patient abreacts—when the energy of a feeling
is released in sporadic fashion and does not hook into the past solidly—
vital signs fall sporadically or do not fall at all. It is one key check we
have on connection.

So many self-help books focus on how to control ourselves, our impulses, our rages, ignoring the imprints that will never cease to dominate
our lives. Now we understand why most violent prisoners still remain a
threat to society after they are released. No amount of rage-control
therapy will help because the cause of the rage has not been touched.
Counseling only provides us with reasons *not* to act-out. In the end,
though, it is the feelings that win, especially when those feelings are
driven by brainstem energy.

In the 1950s, Kaiser Permanente Hospital invented a "convenient"
way for mothers to deal with newborns. They provided a drawer that slid
in and out. When the mother was done feeding the baby, the infant was
locked away in a drawer. The terror of this trauma is an effective way to
dysregulate the cortex and other brain cells. If a study were to be conducted of those children, now adults, the effects of this rather monstrous
concept would be evident, all despite the best of intentions.

If you have seen someone reliving birth, as I have, you come to
believe that the energy used to keep these sensations and emotions suppressed for all those years must eventually affect the body's cellular structure. In our therapy sessions we see what massive, awesome pain most of
us hide inside. It takes an equally massive inhibition to hold down these
terrible pains. The sudden release of this early pain can be explosive.
Now add a measure of parental indifference and lack of warmth right
after birth and throughout infancy and you have compounded pain with
a damaged frontal cortex and limbic structures. That means chronic suffering. High anxiety in the carrying mother not only is accompanied by
cortisol secretion but lingering secretion will eventually damage limbic
cells of the baby. This is a straight-ahead demonstration of how lack of
love early on can damage the brain.

Bruce Bower in *Science News* notes that, "For twenty years studies of rats and other nonhuman animals have suggested that sustained exposure to high concentrations of stress hormones provokes cell loss in the hippocampus."[4] He implies that chronic high levels of cortisol can result in damage to the hippocampus and result in the cognitive diseases we often associated with later age. It can mean that the loss of memory after the age of sixty may be the result of an imprint at birth which provoked chronically high cortisol levels throughout life. And that is why it is so devilish to try to find exact causes of memory loss when we focus only on physiologic and neurologic events in old age.

An analogy at this point might help our understanding. When a doctor gives a patient painkillers over weeks or months, the patient is warned not to stop abruptly. The reason . . . seizures. To put down internal, deep forces either with our own manufactured suppressants or with pills causes the suppressed material to build up. To have it released all at once means a widespread, explosive eruption of feeling all over the brain—a seizure—as defenses weaken against the tidal force. We see something close to this in our therapy—a random, massive, unfocused eruption when feelings build up and come close to conscious-awareness. It is the focus, a scene or memory that funnels the feeling into proper channels and avoids a seizure. But if too much comes up too soon the focus is lost and the brain is overwhelmed.

In sleep we become unconscious in stages ranging from the present awareness to deep sleep. Sleep involves repression of higher layers of consciousness. At some point approaching deep sleep the person is literally in the same brain and physiologic state as a six-month-old: no conceptual-intellectual defenses against terror. That is what is so terrifying for those reliving preverbal trauma. There is nothing in their heads that can conceptualize or figure out what is happening. It is stark fright, often organized by first-line imprints in the locus ceruleus.

Speaking of physiologic memory, in recent months we had two patients reliving childhood meningitis and scarlet fever respectively. In both cases the patients ran a fever during the reliving.

Let's take as an example an infant given little attention in the first months of life. As an adult, terrible loneliness is activated in the limbic system and drives the cortex into hope ("Maybe someone will come and keep me company. I'll call up my friends. Maybe they will come and drive my loneliness away"). That action takes place before reflection and is one way we defend against the feeling. And if our parents said, "Wipe that frown off your face" enough times, even happiness can be a defense; the pretense is that all is well when it isn't.

If the person could experience the sadness and its causes, perhaps she wouldn't be depressed. After all, it is that sadness and so many other feelings that play into depression. Sadness engulfs so many disparate experiences in which the child could not communicate her unhappiness to her parents. So many of my patients come in with high blood pressure or migraines and tell me that they had very good childhoods. Months later they are writhing on the padded mat, bewailing their early misery, even as the migraine is disappearing. Nobody suggests this pain to a patient. It evolves from revisiting one's childhood. If we learn to rummage around in our personal brain files there is no telling what we can find. No patient is ever told what to feel or cry or scream.

One of our current patients was just dumped by her boyfriend of two years. She was devastated and begged and called him repeatedly. He warned her not to call anymore. She couldn't stop herself; she became a stalker. Then, finally, she fell into a depressive funk for weeks, couldn't go out of her apartment, never called her friends, and gave up on life. The feeling she finally got to was a heavily anesthetized birth where she was overwhelmed, and she developed the "struggle-fail" syndrome, giving up quickly in the face of any adversity, and then moving up the brain levels to the relationship she had with her shut-off parents, emotionally distant, so distant that she gave up trying for love, kept to herself, and was known as a loner. When she saw a chance for love as an adult she became tenacious and obsessive. She was clinging to hope. And that is what made her situation hopeless—she was so deprived and needy that she drove men away. The more she needed the less she got.

The aim of Primal Therapy is to hook up the frontal cortical memory with the unconscious suffering (limbic-brainstem) component to achieve conscious-awareness—a frontal cortex fully connected to limbic-brainstem structures. That is access. Consciousness is the ultimate goal of therapy: making the unconscious conscious. We seek to take the pressure out of the system even while necessary palliative measures are taking place. We do insist that the symptoms be treated, no matter what their cause. We need to quell a migraine or high blood pressure with medication so that we can function.

NOTES

1. See the *New York Times*, 19 January 1994. The subtitle of the article notes, "When the Mother Drinks So Does Her Baby."

2. E. Cantor-Grace, "Link between Pregnancy Complications and Minor Physical Anomalies in Monozygotic Twins Discordant for Schizophrenia," *American Journal of Psychiatry* 151, no. 8 (August 1994): 1188–93.

3. R. Gagin, E. Cohen, and Y. Shavit, "Prenatal Exposure to Morphine Feminizes Male Sexual Behavior in the Adult Rat," *Pharmacology, Biochemistry and Behavior* 38 (1997): 345.

4. Bruce Bower, *Science News* 153 (25 April 1998): 263.

6

THE THREE LEVELS
OF CONSCIOUSNESS

The three levels of consciousness are based on the three key brain systems discussed earlier: the brainstem, the limbic (or "feeling") brain, and the neocortex. In my nomenclature I refer to them as lines. The first-line involves the primitive nervous system, mostly the brainstem. Although the nervous system's structures are competent at birth, they actually begin working during gestation to coordinate physiological development.

FIRST-LINE INSTINCTUAL CONSCIOUSNESS

The first-line is the visceral mind, the caretaker of sensations. Vital functions are largely under its control: breathing, cardiovascular activity, hormone output, digestion and urinary processes, among others. Traumas that occur before birth and for several months after are likely to affect these functions. Hence, if an adult patient presents with chronic colitis or palpitations, we may anticipate a first-line trauma is involved—something that happened before the infant was six months old, and possibly at birth or before. This may help to explain why some people have far lower pulse, blood pressure, and body temperature than others. The setpoints for these

106

have been established by events in the womb. They may also have been partially set by heredity. Because these setpoints can change in therapy it seems that genetics is not the predominant cause. Our consulting physician has remarked for the last twenty years that advanced primal patients coming to him invariably have lower vital signs.

Compulsive sex is an example of brainstem driving. The way one expresses one's sexuality depends on life circumstance, but the energy of that drive is established very early on. We look to the brainstem for this symptom. I have never seen anyone shed tears while reliving birth. And speech is impossible since language is a higher-level function which comes later. During birth reliving there is a characteristic foot and arm position. (I omit it to avoid future problems with patients trying to simulate the experience.) This sign cannot be faked because the patient has no idea what she is doing during the primal. The moment the patient comes out of the sequence and begins speaking, the foot position changes—clear evidence of the integrity and unity of each level of consciousness.

The use of words automatically places the individual on a higher level of consciousness accessing different brain structures. It is in the reliving that we observe the distinct three lines corresponding to the key three brain functions. The first-line can, however, store the cataclysmic sensations of approaching death, the frenzied breathing and writhing body movements such as those that arise when traumatic birth memories break through the repressive barriers. These same memories tax the body for years and decades and can play a role in the development of cardiovascular disease, stroke, and even cancer. There is mounting research evidence that traumas in the earliest months of life change the neurobiology.[1] These traumas can change the course of limbic system maturation.

As Martin Teicher of McClean Hospital, Massachusetts, points out, these traumas "may provide the biological substrate for a panoply of later psychiatric consequences, including affective instability, inability to modulate anger, poor impulse control, limited stress tolerance, episodic aggression, memory impairment and hallucinatory phenomena."[2] These authors found that of twenty-two patients who were involved in incestuous relationships as a child, 77 percent had brainwave abnormalities.[3] The implication is inescapable: serious early trauma results in brainwave deviations, and these deviations portend possible psychiatric problems since brain deviations are the substrate for later thought disorders.

STEVE

I was born cesarean, removed because the doctors were afraid I would die due to the drugs during delivery. All my life, I've had a pattern of intense activity followed by intense inactivity. I have always done things as if I had very little time left and I needed to complete them while I still have energy. I could only keep this up for awhile, however, and at that point I'd get very tired and would have to "crash" or do nothing for awhile. This manifested itself in many ways, most notably in drinking or drugs, followed by a hangover where I could do nothing but rest and not function. Then the cycle would repeat. The sad part of this is that I've spent my entire life not experiencing what I've done. I've always been removed when with friends, doing things such as sports, playing music, and with lovers. I always want to go back to these memories for a second chance, or I reexperience them with sadness at how complete each experience really was, at how great my friends really are, how good my life really has been in many ways, I just wasn't really "present" to experience it. And it's very simple, I was too busy shutting down pain—the physical pain. To have experienced what I've done in my life would have meant also feeling these hurts in my body. And they're real physical pains. They hurt. They're unpleasant. But I think I'm beginning to put them in their proper context. I've been "counterphobic," meaning that I will force myself to work out, for instance, when I begin to feel tired. I usually seek out challenges and sometimes danger. This has been the only way I can feel alive. As above, I usually have to reason my way through things, such as buying a car, closing a business deal, etc., because I can't sense what's happening. My pain gauges are overloaded, so they malfunction. I have to depend upon other facilities to ensure my successful survival. I can't say that this has changed yet, but I do know that feeling the pain in my body somehow helps me make sense of my life and is a relief. I do have a sense that as I continue to feel this pain the overload will lessen and I will have access to the senses I so badly want and need. To me, it's no different than any other handicap, such as a missing limb, deafness, blindness. It may be less extreme, but the effect is almost as limiting.

While the situation with Steve is self-explanatory, Myra's case is different; a most atypical event that we rarely see. Here is a dramatic example of how events in the last trimester of pregnancy can have a lifelong effect. She was overloaded and became unconscious—the prototype for later being overloaded and going blank, not understanding or listening. To have witnessed this event (filmed) is to see the awesome power of early events and how they remain pristine for all of our lives so that in her forties she was reliving an event forty years ago as though nothing happened in between. For the imprint, nothing has. It is unaffected by experience because experience doesn't touch it. Only *the* experience counts; the reexperience of the original event. Now we understand Marilyn Monroe. Not all the adoration in the world altered the fact that she was in an institution with little love early on. That adoration never entered her system. It was blocked by pain and repression. Only if she felt profoundly unloved early on, in context, would she finally be able to feel loved.

Myra

One day in a therapy session we saw something strange, a patient in convulsions, seizurelike activity not indicative of birth; no typical arm and leg positions. It went on for days and even the patient was confused. We checked with her mother and found that in her eighth month of carrying she put a plug into a 220 outlet and received a massive shock. It also shocked the baby. The child was born in a coma that lasted for three days, no sign of life or movement as before. Then she revived. But all previous memory was blasted out and later her prototype was to go blank when in overload. The shock was obviously overwhelming. When stimulation was too much—e.g., when she received instructions from her boss that were slightly complicated—she could not see or understand what was right before her. She blanked out as the old unconscious event and original reactions came to the fore, arriving at the cerebral cortex, rendering her helpless. She became, in effect, unconscious. Most of her life was spent, according to her, "in a daze." The shock to the mother in her eighth month was the same as shock therapy. Her reaction to an overload at the age of two and three was to immediately shut down, it became the prototype. She grew up unconscious. She couldn't understand the simplest courses in school. The minute in life when she was overwhelmed she was "as if in a coma or a daze" knowing nothing and seeing nothing. Later overload—too many things to do at once, even reading a lengthy book— was enough to shut her down completely. She bought only thin books. Everything was too much because her unconscious stress level was very high already.

As she began to relive the shock and connected it with the cortical processing centers for integration she found herself less and less in a daze and more able to understand things. The brainstem imprint which controlled her life and her later thinking was no longer reverberating solely around lower brain centers but had access to higher frontal integrating centers. It happens to many of my patients who were heavily drugged at birth. The physiologic equation, originally and currently, is: stress leads to unconsciousness. Or, a variation: stress leads to drinking alcohol, which leads to unconsciousness. Why is this so? Because the original stress is a *current* imprinted memory. New events resonate with this memory and produce the same prototypic reaction. The prototype controls behavior because it is the first memory of trauma and survival, occurring in an early life-and-death situation.

Regarding being drugged at birth. A new study reported in October of 1999 by the American Society of Anesthesiologists shows that between 1981 and 1997 the incidence of drugging mothers with painkillers during birth tripled. The news articles heralding this "improvement" said that finally women were opting for what made them feel better, while doctors stated that women should not suffer needlessly during childbirth. I agree, women should not suffer needlessly—but, not at the expense of the baby who will incur suffering for the rest of his life! Drugging is not an improvement; it is an expedient, and one that can be dangerous. The full contractions of birth are necessary for many reasons including stimulation of the respiratory and urinary systems of the baby. Contractions are not a trauma if they help the birth process along.

With early trauma the system stays either in the excitatory mode or in the depressed, down-regulated mode for a lifetime depending on the type of reaction to the early event. It depends not only on the reaction of the baby but also on the circumstances, particularly, the kind of drugs, if any, given to the birth mother. Heavy anesthesia often sets the stage for depression later on given repressive circumstances in the family home where the child is unable to express herself. Later depressive reactions are, as I have explained, exactly what the original reactions were to the drugged birth: "I can't try anymore. It is all hopeless. What's the use? Nothing does any good." In other words, the basic feeling becomes compounded over the years. It is the same feeling based on three different levels.

A depressive who comes in with a body temp of 96.0 degrees, blood pressure of 85/65, and a heart rate of fifty-five, will generally leave the session if she has felt and connected with the underlying feeling, with normalized signs of a nondepressive. That is, a blood pressure of 120/80 and a body temp of 97.5 (the average for my advanced patients).[4] Then when the patient states that she feels better we can believe her. The anxiety case comes in with exactly the opposite readings. After the session all vital signs normalize.

What seems to happen under conditions of threat, for example, the fetus being strangled by the umbilical cord, is that catecholamine production is radically increased. This engraves the imprint—as a memory of survival—more deeply into the system. It becomes a prototype. The down-regulated prototype directs many later-life characteristics such as fear of change, rigidity, and lack of spontaneity. Don't make a move! Danger lurks! The prototype is the first major response to a life-and-death experience. It becomes a template for all future reactions to threat.

THE SECOND-LINE: EMOTIONAL CONSCIOUSNESS

The second line—the emotional level of the limbic system—begins to develop before birth and continues until full bloom at between two and three years of age. Over time, the infant relates to an ever larger world than the mother's breast and cheek, establishing emotional attachments to friends, parents, siblings, and other relatives. This is the level of feeling states, tears, and sobs. There are many individuals who are first-line, brainstem driven: impulsive, rageful, driven without cease, impatient and inattentive, unable to focus and concentrate. Very often these individuals do not develop an adequate limbic/feeling band. There is some kind of emotional empathy missing. Their first-line dominates and prevents them from properly developing the emotional level. Great athletes are sometimes completely in touch with their first-line and very little else. A postgame interview with some of these athletes is not a marvel of intellectual discussion. But on the field the football player knows where to run by instinct. If he had to think about it, he wouldn't be a good player.

A patient may start a session crying on the second-line at the age of ten when his parents gave away his favorite dog. Soon, though, he will have a radically different infant cry as he moves into a mode with infant memories of having his teddy bear taken away as punishment when he was age two.

When there is gagging and coughing in the middle of a childhood reliving scene (second-line), it is called first-line intrusion. We see this quite often. We are then faced with the decision to drain off first-line energy or suppress it with tranquilizers. If it continues to intrude then the patient cannot have an integrated feeling and will leave the session worse off. If we use techniques to allow the intrusion more complete access, the patient can drain some of the brainstem (first-line) energy and then return to her feeling.

A traumatic event such as the parents' divorce, which occurs at the age of five or six, largely involves the second-line, although it has first-line components because of its catastrophic meaning—there is no more family. The suffering component of pain is stored on the limbic level. It is on this level that the child can become tense. Anxiety is a much more primitive reaction, involving the viscera or guts. These visceral responses were the highest level of brain operation when the trauma occurred. Once imprinted it dictates visceral reactions to adversity later on: e.g., the example earlier of anxiety when making a presentation, stomach cramps, a tightness in the chest, butterflies in the stomach, palpitations, having to urinate frequently. One way we know about the origins of a trauma is by the kind of reactions there are. A churning stomach may be a reaction to mother's anger when the child is six, but the bodily response itself is first-line prototypic. It is preverbal in origin, which can mean an imprinted intrauterine trauma.

It is why ideas are of no use against anxiety. Ideas are trying to use the new cortex to suppress a 300-million-year-old instinctual response. One can never get one level of the brain to do another level's work. Anxiety, to be resolved, needs to be experienced as a fully visceral reaction without words. It can have words when the reaction is attached to scenes in childhood but there comes a time when the prototype is reached in its naked state, a time when the cortex was still not adequately developed.

When individuals remember with the limbic structures, they remember pictures of childhood, of scenes, images, and smells of the kitchen. Particularly smells since it is the ancient reptilian smell brain that elaborated into the feeling brain of humans. It is how we often get patients back to their childhoods. And when they remember a room at the age of three they can describe the color of the linoleum and the arrangement of the furniture; something verified by parents later on, and something the patient could never do before the reliving episode. They can smell Mother's baking as if they were again in the kitchen as kids.

The goal in any profound therapy should be to retrieve feelings from limbic and brainstem structures, taking care not to stop with limbic imprints. When full retrieval happens the person will normalize. This does not obviate counseling, child guidance, marital advice, or help with everyday problems. Too often, however, problems in a marriage stem from rather deep imprints in one or both of the partners.

When a patient is in a past feeling there is a flow of words and ideas that is unequaled by cortically originated ideas. There is an effortless spouting of insights that goes on for a long time without the patient seeming to dig for ideas or consciously scan for thoughts. I have remarked over and over that this kind of thought pattern is qualitatively different from purely left-cortical processes, which are purely intellectual.

THE THIRD-LINE: INTELLECTUAL CONSCIOUSNESS

The third-line prefrontal and orbitofrontal cortices begin to play an active role at about age two, and continue developing until around age twenty. Mediated by the brain's frontal lobe, it organizes all things intellectual. Third-line consciousness integrates the lower levels, helps inhibit impulses, deals with the external world, and puts meaning to feelings. It is the site of sophisticated concepts. It does the preplanning and can see the consequences of one's acts.

The problem is that concepts can exist solely on the third-line without solid connection to the lines below. When that happens, we are smart but not intelligent. Our feelings cannot guide us. Those who never feel hungry, who can go for days without thinking about food, are an example. Some individuals can go for months without sex, feeling no lack and no need. You need first-line access for good sex. Too much access, however, due to poor gating produces hyperreactivity with poor impulse control. These individuals often cannot control their sexual desires or impulses. Poor gating can lead to premature ejaculation or nymphomania, not to mention rape.

A long time ago, when our ancestors had to hide from adversity, the migration of brain cells upward and outward gave them an evolutionary edge. Thanks to this evolutionary development, we inherited the ability to understand and speak language. The neocortex third-line deals in logic, rationality, concepts, calculation, and reality testing. It can be "reasonable" and develop complex philosophies.

Third-line consciousness finds "reasons" to explain other people's behavior and our own, enabling us to project motives onto others, have faulty perceptions, and bend logic in accord with our internal truths. It is one way to deflect criticism. It is the third-line that organizes obsessions. The feeling centers are working overtime due to early lack of love, while the frontal cortex is attempting to stem the tide. It uses obsessions to absorb and control the feeling. Obsessions arise out of the clash between deep-lying first- and second-line feelings with the frontal cortex. The result is an overload of this cortex and the manufacture of obsessions. Tranquilizers work because they dampen the amount of input arising out of the two lower levels.

Nonrooted insights occur on the third-line. When there is no sub-conscious anchor, insights remain on this level without touching the instinctual-feeling base. When first-, second-, and third-lines are co-herent and connected the person can finally trust herself and know what her motives are and the motives of others as well. She is conscious.

The left hemisphere digs into our past for the facts of feeling, while the right brain dredges up the raw feeling itself. It is both sides working together that convert amorphous suffering into specific feeling. It means an end to obsessions; finally the left side knows what the right side is feeling. That is connection.

Thus we have three levels of consciousness, each separated in evolu-tionary time, involving different brain structures and serving specific functions. Damage to one level will not necessarily affect another. One can have one's motor functions impaired but retain crystal-clear percep-tion. Those in a coma are operating on the first-line, with the two higher levels inactive. They behave on a rudimentary level, but they are "func-tioning." If you touch them with a pin, they may make an effort to pull away. Holding the hand of someone who is under anesthesia can help attenuate pain. The person still senses this contact even though he is residing on another level of consciousness. Physical contact is important. In Primal Therapy we hold the hand of a patient to attenuate the pain and put her into the feeling zone. We take care not to hold on too much or too long so as to bring the patient from the past back into the present. Too much comfort blocks feelings. It is a tricky affair.

Each level of consciousness contributes to conscious-awareness. To be aware is third-line. To be consciously aware, or fully conscious, en-compasses all three lines working together in a fluid way—the right and left hemisphere and the brainstem with the limbic-frontal cortex func-tioning in harmony. In a normal, healthy person, these three distinct minds correspond to specific brain structures and function as an inte-grated, balanced mental apparatus. They allow the person to be a feeling, thinking being. Thoughts can readily reach lower levels of consciousness. It is consciousness that helps us avoid unhealthy activity such as smoking or overeating. One is no longer a victim of one's impulses.

Health means optimum coherence or connectedness among levels, harmonious functioning that serves survival. When the levels become disjointed in some way, there is apt to be illness later on. The instinctual first-line is charged with saving our lives in an emergency. Trauma interferes with this harmony, causing one to do what one knows one shouldn't do, such as consuming alcohol or taking drugs. Without these aids we would have to deal with too much pain.

When my patients are in a feeling and travel from the present to the remote past, then back to the present, it is called a 3-2-1-2-3 sequence. It is a completed feeling: accessing the deepest levels of the brain and then returning to the integrating frontal cortex, where the memory is laid to rest. The levels form a chain of feeling, or a chain of pain. It is why someone reliving a childhood memory can delve into something deeper as the session continues. No one has to point the patient there; it is automatic because early trauma has its representations on each succeeding brain level. If a mother and father were loving and kind, warm and happy, a baby will eventually have this access without any therapy. If they were not, it will take deep, probing therapy to offer this kind of access.

One of my patients was upset because she had not been invited to a dinner party. She came into the session on the third-line, feeling "left behind." As the session progressed, she took the feeling down to the second-line, where she was left out by her parents, who related to each other emotionally to the exclusion of their children. (The children were not allowed to eat with the parents.) Finally, she felt her birth. She was the second of twins. The doctors weren't aware of her at first, and she remained inside the womb for what she now considers an inordinate amount of time. She suffered physiologically, which later was elaborated by the limbic-frontal connections as being left behind or being left out (actually left in, but feeling left out).

The first memory is strictly physiologic, but as the brain develops the nerve networks on higher levels interpret the memory in their own way; the feeling brain in terms of images, poetry, paintings, and dreams, while the thinking cortex provides the label or meaning for it. Luckily, these representations are what we follow until the patient's brain leads us back to origins. We don't start with the original pain. We always try to start with the key representations on the higher levels. The brain will do the rest if we don't interfere and try to "treat" the patient. Now we understand why a patient who feels hopeless and depressed in the present can travel down the levels of consciousness to a birth trauma where there was heavy anesthetic preventing any kind of reaction. This prototype leads to resignation and feelings of failure. There were no alternatives to choose from. When my patient with this kind of imprint found that his girlfriend had left him, he was again stuck in the same feeling, not seeing any way out, feeling overwhelmed and defeated. He was totally immobilized, all the way from the beginning. When we see a certain behavior, immobilized, and we treat it as a separate entity, we are leaving out all of the accompanying aspects of the memory.

If there is a first-line origin to a trauma and the therapist does not know how to get the patient there safely, the patient will not normalize. You can, in short, be third-line "well"; be well-adapted, do fine in school, have a good marriage, and still be loaded with pain. If the person is satisfied with that goal, then that is fine. But she should at least be informed that there is much that lies below.

The patient above who was left behind at the dinner party understood her anxiety. The unconscious had been made conscious. No more anxiety. It is not in one session that this is resolved because our repressive system allows only so much feeling to be felt at one time. When too much pain is allowed access we have overload and either total shutdown or mystical symbolization as the cortex does gyrations to handle the pain. The original life-and-death trauma is of such a magnitude that it takes many, many primals for resolution. We wouldn't want to try for resolution in a single session.

The frontal cortex is an integral part of feeling. It isn't just yelling or crying in itself. It is having access to the limbic feeling in order to have a proper understanding of it; dealing with the limbic cortical circuits that make the feeling complete. Until you include the frontal cortex, you can scream and yell, cry and sob, pound the walls and never make any progress. But if you use only the frontal cortex without accessing lower levels, you still will not have a complete feeling.

Trauma stretches across all levels of consciousness and eventually lodges in the neocortex. Therapy involves retrieving memories on all three levels. Final connection is retrieving memories with all three levels involved: instinctual/survival, feeling, and cognitive.

THE HEMISPHERES OF LOVE:
THE LEFT AND RIGHT HEMISPHERES

When a baby witnesses emotion in a parent, nerve cells fire in the right hemisphere of her brain, and blood flow to this area is increased. These cells also fire when the baby reciprocates that emotion. The right side responds to love impulses from the parent. Similarly, it lights up when a patient *relives* emotional trauma from infancy.[5] It is yet another way we know that the reliving is a real event. When a patient *recounts* an old trauma it is largely the left brain that is involved. The guts of the agony meanwhile lie a few centimeters to the west and south. That is the journey we see in our patients who begin the session recounting a lack of love at age six. The cortical-limbic networks operate more from the right side of the brain. Feelings, in short, militate to the right feeling brain centers more than the left and end up in the right frontal cortex.

Verbal, analytical, problem-solving processes are carried out by the left side of the brain, whereas feelings, emotional attachment, and creativity are the domain of the right side. Hence, I would consider the right side as indeed the hemisphere of love. R. J. Davidson believes that the right side is the hemisphere of seeing the big picture, including the totality of the relationship to the parent.[6]

The left and right hemispheres each have their own specific functions. The right hemisphere is larger than the left and processes emotional imprints. It is the site of feelings, of holistic and global thinking. The left hemisphere governs thinking, planning, and conceptualizing. The frontal cortex is mature halfway through the second year of life. It is at this time that the right brain is largely mature, whereas the left brain is just beginning to mature.

It is interesting that the right side is more associated with withdrawal away from confrontation. It seems that parasympathetic skewing favors the right-side social/emotional withdrawal syndrome. Some of what I discuss is of necessity speculation. It is not completely out of the blue sky, however, since there are many decades of clinical experience to go along with it. Nevertheless, sometimes the reach can be beyond the current facts; an atavistic leap into what are only possibilities. But if we don't see possibilities, however, we shall make no great leaps. These possibilities must have some relation to current research, however. I have been writing about the birth trauma and imprinted childhood pain for thirty years. Research is now catching up. (A recent issue of *Newsweek* has a cover story on the effects of womblife.) We should not retreat from positing possibilities. This is another way of saying that science is not just statistics. Ideas count, too.

Perhaps I am the shoemaker who sees only shoes in the world; being a therapist, I see only pain in humans. All scientists have to be careful of this because when we have a hammer, everything in the world looks like a nail.

RIGHT-BRAIN EMPATHY

The right brain is empathic, able to sense what others are feeling, able to discern whether someone is sincere. It keeps us in touch with ourselves and our feelings. Because it develops earlier than the left brain, it is more sensitive to the emotions of the pregnant mother, bonding with her, organizing the limbic structures as they relate to cortical knowledge. It is one way we know that feelings precede thoughts, particularly abstract thought, and are stronger than thoughts. The right brain is dependent on feelings. It needs "love" from the mother to continue developing. It has strong interactive circuits with limbic-feeling structures, and therefore dominates when feelings are involved.

Schore comments on how the infant uses the mother's right brain "as a template for the imprinting, the hard-wiring of circuits in his own right cortex."[7] This hemisphere is largely responsible for how the child and adult relates to others. Defective relationships in the first two years of life reduces the amount of cortical synapses and changes the structure of the right side.

When a mother is overexcited and demands too much attention from the baby, the baby is overloaded and overwhelmed. When a mother is underexcited and is not responsive, the rapidly developing nerve circuits between the frontal cortex and limbic system of the baby are impaired, more so on the right hemisphere than on the left. This is known as a *lack of attunement* in the current literature. The brain must have optimum stimulation to develop.

When there is prolonged stress in infancy, a constant lack of love, parental indifference and nonresponsiveness, it is the right brain that suffers. It often won't or cannot tell the left brain what is wrong or even that something is wrong. It may be because the left brain is not fully developed as yet. As we grow older the left brain goes on its merry way, oblivious to the right brain's suffering. If one wanted to create a psychopath, someone without real emotional attachments, one has to inflict neglect, lack of touch, and indifference early in life. Cortisol levels in the baby then skyrocket, and "feeling" cells begin to die. The right hemisphere is then unable to empathize with others' pain, or even see it.

Early stress affects the right hemisphere-limbic connections, causing a switch from left to right in dominance. In our research with Drs. Erik Hoffman and Leonid Goldstein of Rutgers University, we found a normalization and a more even balance between the two hemispheres after one year of Primal Therapy.[8] Hoffman writes, "In the course of therapy bilateral amplitudes become more symmetrical."[9] The brain is more harmonious. What seems to happen with imprinted pain is that an asymmetry between halves occurs that may be due to differential pressure from lower levels. The pressure seems to be higher on the right side. Therapy helps to restore symmetry.

Those who have an impaired right-side brain may have a "wooden" face, a lack of expression, or an impassiveness. They may have lacked a spontaneous, warm, reactive relationship in infancy with their parents. As time goes on, there is a tilt to the left side as feelings are buried away. The left thinks analytically in minute detail about externals, as opposed to the right, which organizes self-awareness. The left brain listens only to the words while the right brain moves to the music.

The right hemisphere is incriminated in all sorts of psychopathologies, from autism to psychosis and depression. During anxiety states it is the right brain that is highly activated. Reactivating the painful memories stimulates the right brain and its limbic counterparts.[10] Those infants who cried when separated from their mothers showed greater right frontal activation than those infants who did not cry.[11] To be accurate, however, it is also the left brain that has been implicated in schizophrenia. I think that this has a lot of do with the left brain doing what it can, using paranoid ideas to handle feelings from the other side.

It makes sense that the right hemisphere, damaged by early trauma and lack of love, underlies so many disparate disorders. When reliving these early traumas, it is this hemisphere that is heavily involved. A vast array of illnesses, mental and physical, stem from not being touched and caressed early in life, from unhealthy habits of the carrying mother, from the chaotic first several years of life, and from births that are difficult and involve heavy use of anesthetics.

The effect continues into adulthood, where learning difficulties such as dyslexia may persist. A right-brain deficit can affect how well someone forges lasting friendships, and how easily they develop strong emotional ties. It isn't so easy to have a steady, warm relationship with a right-brain defect. The left side rationalizes and apologizes, and two months later there may be another violent outburst from the right, which forgot what the left said in its apology. In a disconnected brain, the left brain is unable to control the right.[12]

The right hemisphere generally is not involved with words, at least in the complex sense of words. This is logical, since it is called on to handle preverbal trauma. When my patients tap into vivid early scenes the emotion usually follows. Neurochemicals such as serotonin have blocked the transfer of information from the right side to the left, leaving the adult with no access to her emotions. She believes whatever she is told because she no longer has feelings to guide her. Clearly, there is a right-brain consciousness and a left-brain consciousness, *but conscious-awareness involves both.*

Emotional memory (called *implicit memory*) is right brain, while memory of facts and figures (called *explicit* or *declarative memory*) is left. When my patients regress to a lower level of consciousness it can be with predominantly right-hemisphere circuits that lead them down to limbic pathways and from there to the brainstem. Meanwhile, the left hemisphere has been only vaguely aware of what is going on in the right. As someone descends to the lowest feeling level the left brain can lock in and start explaining the person's previous behavior.

THE LEFT ANALYTIC BRAIN

The left brain dissects and deduces but is capable of recall only in an abstract way. If we try to get well in therapy uniquely through the left-brain insights we enter a labyrinth of concepts with no ultimate exit. It means getting only half well. The left will be well-adjusted while the right is a mess, as is the emotional life. But the left brain can still run a computer, get good grades and succeed at work. *It is not possible to get the left brain to do the right brain's work.* We must heal the site of the wound with the brain that was wounded.

As we grow older, we develop more sophisticated left-hemisphere rationales for our feelings. Ideas may change, but they are still confined within the parameters of feelings and imprints. "No one is to be trusted" is what a cynic acts out every day. His ideas follow his past history. If he never had a loving parent and never felt secure, a parent who never kept his word, he may not trust others. Many patients have this experience. They tread cautiously and cannot give themselves over fully to any relationship. This is the left brain carrying out right-brain dictates, carrying out orders from an unseen, unfelt source.

The right brain provides feeling—meaning—to a situation. Robots have no feeling; they don't reflect on their behavior. Neither do predominantly left-brain people. The right side is aware of inner states, of what causes one's moods, for example. The left is aware of the outside world and uses that outside focus to stay far away from feelings. It becomes involved in keeping track of football scores, basketball history, box office receipts, and economic trends. It can also send up terrific insights in psychotherapy without ever feeling anything. Right-brain memory, when retrieved, may well be without words and contains the guts of the pain as the limbic hippocampus and amygdala send secret, suffering messages forward to the cortex.

The left hemisphere stays aloof. It can make us say, "Oh, how terrible." But to feel, empathize, and "know" how terrible something truly is we need the cooperation and assistance of the right hemisphere.

The retrieval of emotional memory is done by the right-side hippocampus. It brings feelings to the frontal cortex for connection. We need that frontal cortex to be aware of our inner state. The frontal cortex can do all sorts of things with feelings, including symbolize them and rechannel them into mystical ideas. "God is watching over me and won't let anything bad happen to me," says a person who in truth was never watched over and protected early in life. The pain/need has been transformed into its opposite: symbolic fulfillment by a deity. It is fulfillment concocted by the cortex, deceiving us into believing we feel protected when we don't. The person feels safe and protected, not by the deity, but by the word "God." Cortical ideas are very good repressors.

The frontal area makes us "feel better" through the release of opiates set off by the idea, "God" in the case above. When the amount of opiates active in the system is measured, we find that the higher the level of inhibition or gating, the better we feel or don't feel. It is an oxymoron: Not feeling makes us feel better. This is what confuses so many of us. The frontal cortex is quite inventive when it comes to handling feeling. The left cortex can decide, "Love is a myth. No one needs fulfillment," while the right side is crying out for it. That silent cry eventually works its way through the physical system until there is a bleeding ulcer, a stroke, or a heart attack. It raises the blood pressure because the system is gearing up for permanent combat against an unseen enemy—catastrophic feelings.

The limbic system has more two-way nerve fiber networks on the right-side cortex than on the left. Love aids in the development of this hemisphere. A nurtured child is more empathic and sympathetic, more willing to acknowledge and understand the feelings of others, to be a good parent herself one day because she has had an expanded capacity to feel ever since she was an infant. Early love is literally forming the brain. Don't feel hopeless. There is a great deal one can to to ameliorate early pain even if it cannot be erased.

THE BATTLE IN THE BRAIN BETWEEN IDEAS AND FEELINGS

Ideas cannot change imprinted feelings. It is counter-evolutionary, a logic in reverse. The brain adheres to its evolution: the right feeling hemisphere was and is developed before the left critical one. Feelings change ideas, not the reverse. There are many more ascending tracts from limbic centers to the frontal area than descending ones from the frontal cortex. Feelings predate the development of ideas and are stronger; whereas the brainstem-imprinted sensations are far stronger than feelings and ideas combined because they are more tied to survival.

What is happening to our feelings? The emotional pain in the limbic area is moving to the cortex to make us aware of it. But it is blocked and deflected by a number of structures, not the least of which is the thalamus. It then moves toward the association cortex where feelings are scrambled and redefined. "I'm not really jealous. I'm not angry." They are made nonthreatening. In the meantime, our hand immediately reaches for a cigarette to keep the system calm and continue the repression.

In a study by child specialists R. J. Harmon and Paula D. Riggs, clonidine (a brainstem blocker) was given to five preschoolers with post-traumatic stress syndrome. The children became less aggressive and impulsive, experienced fewer emotional outbursts, and slept better.[13] Clonidine is effective in treating adults with anxiety or obsessive disorders because the roots of anxiety lie in primitive brain structures that process imprints from the remote past. All of this tends to confirm our clinical findings that very early imprints affect brainstem sites and form the basis of so many later symptoms. The symptoms may differ from person to person, but the launching pad is the same.

In obsessive worry the right-side thalamus and amygdala, together with the reticular activating system, may allow too much input to be released to higher centers and specifically to the left frontal area, causing the cortex to work overtime. The ideas are not driving the person crazy; the feelings are driving the ideas, which make the ideas seem crazy. Fear from an early trauma makes its way to the frontal cortex. Part of the suffering gets through the gate and reaches the frontal cortex, where it is translated into constant worrying: "What if I have a car wreck?" "What if there's an earthquake?" "What if I lose my job?" The bad news has already taken place. If the pain is even stronger the ideas may project themselves into the bizarre range (e.g., "I know an earthquake is going to happen any time and California will slide off into the sea").

The brain is indeed a miraculous structure in the way that it protects us from harm, and in the way one half doesn't know what the other half is up to; a bifurcation that is one more survival mechanism. The neurons, filled with a kind of jelly, know when harm is on its way and construct the forces to repel it. That jelly can conjure up colorful images and "tell" a part of the brain to produce painkillers. It is, after all, just a piece of matter. But what extraordinary powers!

Until we travel below the cortex we will constantly fall prey to drinking, stealing, migraines, ulcers, drugs, and what have you. There is a choice: either let the feelings up for connection, joining the right side of the brain with the left, or push them down by ignoring them, redirecting them, drugging them, or convincing ourselves that they don't exist. This is the dilemma every psychotherapy must confront. Whenever deep pain is ignored it is tantamount to denying our physiology.

My colleagues and I did measurements of imipramine 1984 in England, in conjunction with Open University and St. Bartholomew's Hospital, London. It was a double-blind study directed by Professor Steven Rose of Open University, with the cooperation of Professor Bernard Watson of St. Bartholomew's.

We measured imipramine binding to blood platelets. Imipramine is a serotonin reuptake inhibitor as well as a norepinephrine inhibitor,* so we assumed that what was going on in the blood system would match what was going on in the brain. When we speak of uptake inhibitors, all we need to know is that the final result is more serotonin and epinephrine in the synapse and that means better repression or inhibition. Imipramine binding is lower in depressives.

Blood platelets biochemically resemble neurons, which include possession of transmitter uptake and binding sites. The levels increased with our therapy so that imipramine binding to platelets, though lower in depressives, normalizes in our therapy. With this normalization the patient then had increased antipain and antianxiety capacity. The repressive systems worked better.

Here are Professor Rose's conclusions:

---

*When there is an "uptake inhibitor," it means that the chemical serotonin will not be taken up or taken back. The result: more serotonin in the synapse to aid repression.

1. Self-referring individuals entering psychotherapy show a level of maximal specific binding of 3H-imipramine binding to blood platelets about one-half that of a control group of self-defined normal subjects not in therapy.
2. Six months after beginning a course in Primal Therapy, their average imipramine binding level had increased until it was indistinguishable from control levels, and this increase was maintained for a further six months.
3. Eleven of twelve subjects showed some improvement in score on an arbitrary psychic assessment scale over this period, and there was a positive correlation between this improved assessment score and increased imipramine binding.

When we discuss imipramine binding, we need to be thinking, "serotonin" (or even easier, "Prozac"). We are measuring something that we think is being mimicked in the brain. The importance of this research is that beginning patients, often highly anxious, are low in binding. As Primal Therapy continues, however, they come up to normal levels. By resolving feelings their repressive system is more effective. They are therefore more comfortable and at ease, and this is what we found with our questionnaire.

The study represents, to our knowledge, the first attempt to relate a biochemical measure commonly used in biological psychiatry to a psychotherapeutic treatment. Its positive outcome should encourage more extensive experimental and theoretical study of biochemical markers in psychotherapy.

Who is to say that I don't feel good when I do feel good? The body is to say, for it may succumb to heart disease, ulcer, or stroke because of this self-deceptive state. We may want to smoke no matter what the research says. Our cortex will find reasons for doing it. We rationalize that a smoker in Russia lived to 110 years of age, convincing ourselves that it is possible to escape harm. The need to quell the pain is overpowering; no one is smarter or stronger than this need, and no one ever overcomes it. It is basic to survival. Self-deception, we must remember, is part of the defense apparatus and is necessary, just as the delusions of the paranoid are. Nothing is quite as infinite as self-deception. It is part of the human condition. Let us think before we attempt to disabuse our patients of their strange or irrational ideas because it is the cortex trying to rationalize unseen, unknown forces.

NOLAN

I came from Australia to Venice, California, for Primal Therapy because I was always miserable, alone, scared, and hiding from people. I was unable to change. I drank heavily for eighteen years, for relief and to be able to be with people. However, my behavior, feelings of guilt, and the horrible hangovers were finally too much. I went to Alcoholics Anonymous, but after nine years of sobriety in the twelve-step movement and after many different therapists I was desperate. Reading Dr. Janov's books gave me hope. I was furious with my parents. With the payoff package from my job of eleven years I came here—which was amazing for me, as I was so scared of going anywhere alone. The hope of a happy life meant everything to me. I've been here for two years now and so much of therapy has been learning about myself.

Incredibly I never realized how anxious and depressed I'd always been. I have spent years trying to solve all my problems through thinking. This was a great defense against feeling how much I was hurting. I've always been in conflict with people and been unable to deal with the feelings. I'd either go away hurt or attack them in angry rages. Now by feeling the pain of a current event and then tracing it back to similar pain in my past, I'm able to understand why I hurt so much. It's also enabling me to be closer to people. For example, one of my roommates here told me I was her friend and that she liked me—magic words for me. It means everything to me to be liked and wanted.

We became friends but I gradually realized that our relationship was all about her needs. That she had said this to me so I would look after her. I realized that my feelings didn't count. I finally exploded in the group session feeling all the frustration and anger. I wanted her to be there for me as I was there for her. Through this relationship I've been able to go back and feel how my mother said all the right words but didn't care about me—all the pain of not being wanted—and how I've struggled to get her to love me.

The worst part of this therapy is to feel how much I wanted to love my parents and needed them to know that. But they didn't care about me. This has affected all of my relationships. It feels like death to me—to be unwanted. Recently I've been feeling how I wanted my Auntie Maisie to take me with her. I cried as I remembered how much I wanted to be with her. I loved her and knew she really cared about me. I was only three years old and knew even then that my parents didn't want me. My life has been about misery and hopelessness. By going back and feeling the horror of my childhood it gives me hope of a future. My father committed suicide—I felt I was heading there, too. As I feel more of my feelings I'm getting closer to my children. Before therapy it was too painful to be with them because it triggered my own feelings. Now through connecting these feelings to my relationship with my father, I'm able to let them be themselves more and listen to them.

I want to be a loving father—my father seemed to hate me. It reached the stage where he avoided me wherever possible. I was devastated. I was in group talking about my children. I kept saying, "I'm sorry" over and over. I had a picture in my head of me holding them in my arms and yet they were still hurting. I realized I was the one who was hurting them. That set me off sobbing. Later I had a memory of being in a playpen and seeing my parents closing the door leaving me on my own. I was crying and begging them not to leave me, "I'll do anything—just don't leave me." The pain of not being wanted was too much—anything rather than that.

After resting I felt the relief of feeling the pain and had some insights: When my children need me it brings up my need for my parents and I run away exactly as my parents did. By feeling how much I hurt I find I'm much more compassionate with my children.

It's so hard for me to get going. I'm always waiting. I'm learning by being more in touch with my body, to keep going at my pace. Before I used to deny the feelings of wanting to give up. I used to feel pushed. I could never relax. I could never do enough to please my father. Now I'm getting closer to the feeling that it is all too much. I'm starting to ask for help—to accept that I need it. It was instilled into me very early on not to ask—to be strong and not show any signs of weakness. Now it's such a relief to be able to be human at last. To be able to cry and sob about all my pain.

For me Primal Therapy is about connecting what happened to me in the past with my present behavior—the lovely relief of "Oh that's why I do that!" I have started to realize why I'm so scared of people by reliving the feelings of how terrified I was of my father—total terror that left me paralyzed. I thought I was a coward because the feeling seeped through me so completely. I'm learning I can actually function while being afraid. Before, the feelings were so overwhelming I was immobilized. Now I know they are feelings and I know where they come from and how they affect me. It's not easy but little by little I am doing it.

I keep coming back to Primal Therapy because I want to be a fully feeling person. Before, I was surviving, not living. I feel like I've been frozen and I'm slowly thawing out. After years of searching I believe this is the way for me.

ROGER

Why Primal Therapy? The answer seemed so obvious, I had never properly considered it. Why go through all this pain? Wasn't it bad enough the first time? Why dig it up? What benefit is to be had? I'll try to keep these questions in mind as I write.

I'll start by telling you about my most recent session. To remind you, I've been in therapy now for about sixteen months. It has been an incredible journey.

April 20

I began talking about how dishonest I felt my boss had been in group the week before. She had been telling everyone how well she treated her employees. It hadn't bothered me at the time but this morning I'd been obsessing over the news that she was going to fire me from a job. I had done nothing wrong. It felt so unfair. She didn't trust me. She had wanted to dock my pay a few days previously, over something that was not my fault. I stood up to her but I felt guilty, as if I had done something wrong. I really wanted to tell her that she was wrong—to leave me alone. A therapist encouraged me and I was into the rage immediately. It pumped out from my belly, filling my arms and legs—incredible rage. I just wanted her to stop. I calmed down and then it flashed through my mind. I had always wanted to get this angry—to be powerful in my dealings with people.

I realized that I had always felt guilty when challenged by authority, even if I had done nothing wrong. I must have been made to feel so bad as a child. The rage and frustration was still there. I wanted to tear the place apart. I started breathing violently and uncontrollably. I went with it. The frustration was killing me. My body doubled up and then straightened. I felt as if I couldn't breath. Then wrenching coughs that reached right down to my lower abdomen.

As I came out of it, I suddenly had some space. It felt so familiar—being small and being told I was wrong and bad. Then it crossed my mind like a shadow: "It's like when my father beat me." I felt ashamed and didn't want to talk about it. I curled over. I was crying now. "Please Daddy. Please, I'm sorry, Daddy. I'm sorry, Daddy." I felt so wrong. It hit me how much my father meant to me. I would do anything for him. He was huge. He was everything. I loved him so much. I had done nothing really bad—probably made too much noise. He used to wake from an afternoon nap and come at us like a crazed animal, smacking whichever of us was nearest, first. I could see myself watching my brother being beaten and the look of agony on his face. I knew I would be next. I would plead, "Sorry, Daddy," and curl up to protect myself. I let in as much of it as I could.

I really wanted someone to take all this pain away. I thought about my mother. She didn't protect me. She was scared of my father as well. I was struck dumb by this. How could she do nothing? She's my mother. I didn't know what to do with this. I stopped crying for a while and just lay there. "I still feel sad," I said to my therapist. I asked her to hold me and I let myself go. I sank into the terrible aloneness.

After the crying, I talked calmly about what had happened with my boss. I knew I would have to stand up to her in the future. It still felt hard that I would have to do it—that I couldn't change her—but it was okay.

So how does reliving feelings like these help me? Well, immediately I stopped obsessing about the situation at work and felt quite comfortable with my boss when I saw her next. I know it will happen again. I won't change the pattern of my whole life with one session. But next time it will be a little easier. The point is that knowing about the causes does not change the behavior. As I was nervously standing up to my boss the last thing on my mind was the way my parents treated me. At that present moment I could not make the connection. What this therapy allows me to do is follow the feeling from the present to the real causes in the past. I can then make the connection and cry out all the hurt that had been preventing me from responding normally to my boss. Before therapy I knew my father beat me and my mother was weak and never there, but that did nothing to alter how powerless I felt when challenged by authority. The facts were not unconscious—but the truth was. Only connecting to feelings like these has made any difference.

I am also finding how little I knew about my own behavior. I thought I functioned well. Most of the friends who knew I was coming to Primal Therapy couldn't understand why. I seemed well-adjusted and had a close and steady relationship with my wife. It was an act and one I almost believed myself. My friends never saw the outbursts of rage I was prone to. I would be teaching a class of twelve-year-olds and suddenly lose my temper. The trigger was usually having my authority questioned by a child. As the situation became increasingly frustrating, I would suddenly snap. I had no idea at the time that this had anything to do with my own experiences as a child. I certainly did not associate it with the difficulties of my birth.

I remember as a child being fascinated with superhero comics and later becoming obsessed with being strong and building up my body. I never seemed to be strong enough, however. I could still be hurt. As a young adult I read books on how to win friends and influence people. I was on my way to developing my adult personality. I slowly pushed away the painful memories of my childhood. It is only in the last few months that I have been willing to let my parents back in to my life—to admit that I still need and love them. I see them more clearly. I know that I might have to start asking them questions like why they divorced. I was never really told. Now I might be able to risk what I never could then.

Before therapy I clung to the hope that things would miraculously change for me one day. I wanted someone to do it for me. I acted this out in my relationships. Even therapy became part of that hope. It took feeling the hopelessness—which goes all the way back to my birth—to change anything. In my birth I needed "someone to do it for me" to bring me into life. I couldn't do it on my own. The feeling of being paralyzed by the drugs in my mother's system after a tremendous struggle to be born—this has given me some freedom in the present to start doing things. Crying out the need to be helped has allowed me to start helping myself. I know no one will do it for me. It is the beginning of growing up. The beginning of freedom.

At the moment I feel a new surge of creativity. I was a painter and for years I struggled with my art. I would have days when I felt like Picasso, followed by days of feeling worthless. Reliving the ups and downs of my birth has lessened this struggle. I know I used my talents to feel special with my parents. I have cried over this need. I wanted to be worth something—to be loved without having to try. For the first time in my life I feel as if I can do something without beating myself up that it is not good enough. That I am not good enough. I can even write this article without being paralyzed that it's not the right style. It is a great feeling. The dialectic is everywhere in this therapy—the more I feel the past, the more I can do in the present.

So why Primal Therapy? Why dig up these old feelings? I suppose the simple answer is because I can feel now. I had no idea what that meant before therapy. I no longer live in my head, or in the terrible sensations of my body. I can be with people in a way I never could before.

THE CHAIN OF PAIN

Long nerve circuits extend from the brainstem and limbic system to the frontal cortex. When a current event triggers traumatic past memory, the brain knows only one thing to do: either deliver the message or shut down. When someone is criticized and feels great anxiety, his underlying feeling may be, "I'm bad and I won't be loved (by my parents)."

If you have a raw sensation imprinted in the brainstem area, in order for it to be resolved it must be acknowledged, named, and integrated—that is, experienced. Not *reexperienced*, but experienced for the first time. The memory may be held in the cortex with absolute clarity, but the suffering component, stored subcortically, has been only partially experienced. When a bruise from a beating at age six reappears on the body of an adult patient in the same place, you see how memory remains untouched by years of experience, and how aspects of memory can be hidden for a lifetime. (Photos of this have appeared in previous works of the author.) Finally, you become aware that memory is far more than intellectual recall.

Once a memory comes to the fore, it seems to bring with it all related traumas from deep in the brain, and the person becomes overwhelmed. The cortex simply can't separate out the different kinds of trauma and react to each specifically in a proper time sequence. In our work tranquilizers may be administered to quell the deeper aspects of the chain of pain so that later, less traumatic hurts can be felt and integrated. Drugs are used only as a way station en route to resolution. They are not the therapy and not an end in themselves, but we want to give the therapy every chance to succeed. The drugs are making up for the lack of early caring and touch. They are literally what would have happened to the brain chemistry had there been early love.

A patient of mine began to feel weak during one Primal Therapy session after about a year of therapy. This was a woman who was constantly on the move in her life, but now she could hardly move, could hardly breathe. She first went through a feeling of trying everything she could to get her mother's love, but nothing helped. Two hours later she slid fully into the state of weakness and helplessness she experienced at birth after being anesthetized (via the drug administered to her mother) and unable to do anything to help herself. We encouraged her to let the feeling of exhaustion overtake her completely.

Her constant activity in her present life had served to keep her from feeling this helplessness. She always had to keep on the move with this project or that to keep the helpless feeling away (there is nothing I can do about my situation).

The sensation of weakness my client felt was compounded by her relationship with her mother. Her father had left the family after she was born, and her mother had to go to work to support the family. She took out her anger on the children, blaming them for everything that went wrong. From the start, my patient felt she was in the way. That feeling endured. As an adult, she would hold back in a group and would constantly apologize for everything she did or said.

This woman was struggling so hard to be *loved* that she never really felt the depths of being *unloved*. Her behavior was a frantic dash away from her feelings. In our sessions we stopped her from trying to be the "perfect" patient, which brought her fears of being unwanted to the surface.

Because the original traumatic sensations are elaborated in the feeling-limbic centers and later represented in the frontal cortex, we have only to start with the perception of weakness in the present (the sensation), then allow the patient to fully sink into the sensation of fatigue (the feeling of weariness), and from there to the helplessness (the original trauma) and exhaustion. If the patient starts with a sensation, extreme fatigue, we can be sure that there are deep brainstem aspects to the feeling. We then help the patient work her way back out through each level. (This process may take hours over the course of many sessions; it is not as simple as it may sound.)

The system can only react to a certain amount of pain at a time. It then shuts down again. So we titrate the pain, allowing so much each session and then waiting for another session to go on with the same pain. The amount of pain in these traumas is ineffable; literally awesome, something I as a conventional therapist had never seen.

After reaching the sensation level, my patient proceeded directly to her exhaustion/helplessness at birth. When she descended to birth, she uttered no words. For over forty minutes she arched her back and butted her head against the padded wall. She seemed to be suffocating. When she finally worked her way back up to the feeling level, then to the cortex, she was able to scream, "I give up! You won't love me anyway!" The fatigue was saying, "I can't try anymore. Don't make me." She returned to that feeling dozens of times in many sessions afterward, the force of the feeling was so heavy and stressful.

When a patient comes out of a session she lies there, still for a few moments, blinks, and then opens her eyes. All report that they have been far away. They look as though they just woke up, and in a sense, they have. They are coming out of the dream brain into the prefrontal aware state just as though they were just coming into life. It takes some minutes before the insights and integration begin. She has stayed in the session for all the time she needed. It is the end of the fifty-minute hour. I couldn't imagine stopping a session when a patient is still feeling bad or is crying.

This sinking into deep and remote past events does not and should not happen in the first weeks of therapy. If a patient has that kind of access early on, it is usually a sign of deep disturbance, of faulty gating. It means the pain level is very high and the repressive system faulty. It can mean that there are heavy valence brainstem imprints. In any case, it is often a sign of brainstem memory domination. If it does happen prematurely in therapy it is then that we will use tranquilizers. Those drugs operate exactly as gates, something the brain should be able to do by itself.

The prefrontal cortex focuses in the present, blames this person or that. Those who are disconnected from their history act as though the old trauma were unfolding right now. There is no other choice. Reexperiencing it is in essence a cortical acknowledgment, integrating early sensations and feelings and placing them in historic context.

Sensations (feeling crushed, smothered, suffocated) make their way from deep in the brain to the right frontal cortex, where they are expressed in "pure," simple words or short phrases. The patient may scream, "I give up! I'm drowning! I can't go on!" In that scream is a whole history of trying, failing, and then giving up entirely . . . the "struggle-fail" syndrome. The brainstem-cortex connection is largely right brain where the phrases are short, specific, and uncomplicated, and are direct outflows of deep imprints. It is the left brain that complicates things, twists reality, and produces convoluted notions and complex syntax.

Let us sum up thus far: when a newborn is handled, touched, and caressed right after birth and thereafter it sets in motion what is for all intents and purposes a new brain. It builds the internal serotonin/inhibitory system to keep the individual at ease and relaxed. It increases and enhances the frontal cortex, which is chiefly responsible for shutting out extraneous input in life, for organizing feelings, for thinking, reflecting, and above all, inhibiting sensations and feelings from deeper brain layers. If we cannot shut out extraneous input we have attention deficit disorder, cannot focus or concentrate, and are easily distractible.

When there is early love, the mobilizing forces in the brainstem are modulated by the frontal cortex. When there is a lack of love and a weak frontal area there is runaway activation and lack of control. The neurons do not mature properly. A strong frontal cortex moderates feelings in the limbic system. A weak one leads to hyperactivity. The same early trauma that makes impaired frontal cortex control also produces the hyperactivity. The impulses bubbling up force the child and then the adult to keep active.

THE TRANSLATION OF FEELINGS INTO SYMPTOMS

There are direct connections to the hypothalamus from the frontal cortex that cause stress to be translated into physical symptoms. It "instructs" the hypothalamus to instruct the pituitary to secrete certain hormones, including those of stress. The frontal area cannot manufacture the catecholamines but can order it done by other brain structures. It is the frontal cortex that absorbs activation from below through the use of ideas and beliefs. There are direct fiber networks from the brainstem to the frontal area that work in a two-way fashion, holding back impulses and stimulating the cortex when necessary. It even stimulates the frontal area when it is not necessary—e.g., a racing mind when one is trying to fall asleep.

The frontal cortex sends activating chemicals to the amygdala so that we can feel what we think and vice versa. Each limbic/feeling structure has both ascending and descending networks. When they are blocked the pressure builds up in our systems. Whatever influences feeling and emotional well-being early on will help build the frontal integrating cortex. Most conventional therapies work on enhancing the frontal cortex against deep-lying impulses. That is the one way to go about it if all one wants is control. If we want integration it is another matter. We must soften those impulses so that the frontal cortex doesn't have so much to do. Even though there are counterparts of feelings in the frontal cortex, the deeper feeling structures develop earlier. This is why we need to get down into the baby brain to relive experiences that impacted us long before we had the capacity for thoughts. After a reexperience, thoughts are important. They help us understand what we went through and how it changed us originally.

The lack of love puts the system in danger. The brain sends out stress hormones to accompany the alarm, and this prolonged secretion damages the growth of the feeling centers and the frontal cortex. This in turn decreases the immune system function, decreasing lymphocytes to surveil and kill invading bacteria. There is a reason that the majority of prison inmates are on drugs before they enter prison: emotional deprivation right after birth and in the first two years. Most of these people were ruled by pain and needed drugs to control it. They were also victims of such early pain, compounded with deprived childhoods, that the cortical control centers were compromised. Impulses make their anger outbursts become out of control, make many of them unable to wait or think through and see the consequences of their acts. One needs a strong frontal cortex to inhibit oneself against overriding impulses.

One of my female patients constantly provoked her mate's anger even knowing he would beat her. Her only physical contact with her father was when he put her over his knee and spanked her with his bare hand. She still needed it, knew it was "crazy," and still did it. She needed physical and emotional contact.

SUZANNE

The following is a transcript of part of two sessions. Suzanne is describing her reliving of an attempted abortion by her mother with caustic materials. It was verified later. At the third month of her pregnancy her mother did try unsuccessfully to abort her. During her primal session she curled up into the tiniest ball possible and wedged herself into the corner. Because she did not have the characteristic arm and foot position, the therapist, who first thought it was a birth primal, was suspicious and inquired more into what had happened. Here, after the primal, she discusses and then cries about what it all meant to her. Most of the techniques by the therapist have been left out. Suzanne's act-out had been to try to create and live in an unpolluted atmosphere: first, because her family situation was "toxic," and also because of the attempted abortion with chemicals that the mother ingested. She was on a quest for a protective environment. She finally discovered what the source of that toxicity was, and how she projected this toxic feeling onto her environment. The prototype here was established long before birth, that of withdrawal from danger. All of us withdraw from danger, except in her case it became an exaggerated and often inappropriate reaction. It is no different than the photographs taken recently of fetuses that withdraw and scrunch up their faces in pain in the presence of a needle puncture.

Session I

I tell you I had to start smoking cigarettes again because I noticed that for the week that I stopped, stuff was shooting up so fast I couldn't deal with it. I had doubled my Zyban [an antismoking drug]. But what I noticed was that by the fifth day of not smoking, the sixth day and the seventh day it was coming up so strong, that all day long I was an emotional basket case. So I went to the nicotine.

What's been going on the past two weeks since I was here and stopped smoking is, every single morning I wake up and I am sick to my stomach. Very nauseous. Feelings of I don't wanna live. Every morning. It really starts to wear me down because what I wanna do is just have the experience once of waking up in the morning and be glad to be awake . . . to be alive . . . like, what a beautiful day. Added to this is the feeling of being scared. What I want to have die is that feeling of wanting to die. But it won't leave me alone; it has such a grip on me. It's got my will (her mother tried to abort her with a very strong saline solution plus something else caustic).

There was this chemical all over my body making me sick. A lot of my problems seem to stem from that. Being scared. Being toxic. Not wanting to move. A sick feeling. I lie in bed at 5 o'clock in the morning and I want to crawl up into a ball and make that feeling stop. I just hate starting my day like that. It constantly puts me in tears. I just couldn't take it anymore, so I reach for the cigarettes, because they help calm me down. I needed to function and yet I am swamped with the feeling of wanting to die. I don't want to live if that is how I have to feel. This comes up with Janis (daughter) because she is living in my condition and because it is extremely toxic. How much can she take? I am not present for her and she's gotta deal with a mom who cries all of the time.

It distorts everything in my whole world. Every morning when I wake up, my hands are hot, my feet are hot, my whole body is hot. It won't let me go. Yet, I can't let myself start feeling it because I'm not sure where it will take me. I'm so relieved when that feeling isn't there.

Therapist: What is it exactly?

The feeling of being sick to my stomach. I can't see any beauty in life. There is something inside me that keeps coming up. (Cries and sobs)

I hate it . . .

I hate it . . .

I want to stop. I don't want to feel that way. It won't let me go. It's just shaking my insides. It feels so terrible. That's what it's doing. I wanna throw up, I feel nauseous. It's so strong (wretches, crawls into a ball).

I guess I was twenty-one and I was leaving New York to come to California. It's so interesting because there was that feeling of being afraid of life, afraid of myself. When that feeling would come up all through my life I never understood what it was. Why was I afraid? It was the f——— memory!

I am just crying because I hate it. It makes me so sick. And it sticks to me like glue. It just sucks me in. It's a whole-body sensation. And it pulls me out of the present. I don't want to live like a vegetable. That feeling is tied into so many other feelings, it's tying into my brain.

There is so much to cry about. Janis said to me today, she's been monitoring my smoking. She's made a little calender. She asks me how many cigarettes I smoked today and she writes it down; she says, "Mom, you've started smoking again." And I said it's because too much pain was coming up too fast and the cigarettes help calm me down. She says, "I really want you to stop smoking, Mom," and I said, "Well, you mean to tell me you'd rather have me crying a lot more than smoking cigarettes?" She said, "Yeah." I said, "Are you sure you can deal with that?" She goes, "I'd rather have you crying than smoke cigarettes." I'm thinking, I'm totally thinking, I'm gonna have a toxic effect on her. She's got a mom who's going through this and we're not 100 percent together. I feel so guilty, because this week I was thinking about when I was growing up, my mother had asthma and I hated it when she got sick. So I guess that's how Janis must feel. And then I think that it's not fair.

That's what the feeling makes me feel when it comes up, that I'm this sick person. I'm not gonna make it, it's gonna swallow me up. And it's gonna stick to me all day long. I feel so messed up. I don't wanna move, I don't wanna go outside. I don't wanna talk. The imprint is so big! It's like being tortured.

There is a whole feeling on the inside of my body. It's frantic. I don't want to lose my breath. It does make a difference knowing where the feeling is coming from (she had the primal of womblife the day before). A couple of times these two weeks when the feeling would come up in the morning, it helped to know where it was coming from.

I always knew there's a very naive and innocent side to me. And I can see how it came in handy because if I had really realized everything I had been through I would never have made it. I think being naive, not realizing, helped me not think it through. Janis sees me go through this, sees my ups and downs. I hate it, I feel so guilty. I let her know that she'll never have to experience this because she was wanted, she was loved right from the beginning, and she'll never experience this. (Still crying) Every night there's this fever that goes on at about 4 or 5 in the morning and my feet are so hot and my hands are so hot. It's like my mind is trying to burn this right out of my soul.

Session 2

I found it very interesting yesterday when I left here. There was this joy because I had plunged into the memory of the abortion. I just felt happy, more alive. I just felt that somehow I was happy in going through that whole process and the intensity of the effect that it had. Maybe it has to do with knowing that it's a specific memory, and the relief that I'm not crazy. You know when you don't know where catastrophic feelings are coming from you have to think you're crazy. That somehow in going through the process my body's reaction was pleased to finally have the opportunity to express it.

I slept well but I was up at 4:30, 5 o'clock, only the sick feeling wasn't as intense, it still came up and the longer I stayed in bed without moving it was coming up stronger. By 6 o'clock I thought, oh, there's that familiar feeling of nausea coming up. But I still feel that sick feeling. I was lying down in bed, trying to sleep. At 6:30 it is stronger; I want to contract, go into that little ball. It is still there now. It is very much right there. I go into not wanting to move. So I got up and sat on the couch in the hotel room. And I don't wanna move. I could spend the whole day like that if I feel like that. And the only thing that gets me going is movement, action. The feeling has a paralyzing effect on me. I don't have free will. It's like somebody's always picking on me, won't leave me alone.

(Screams continuously, "Leave me alone!!!!")

And I wanted my stepfather to leave me alone when he molested me. Sometimes I feel so traumatized it feels like I just want to go into a corner. It's like I needed some kind of touch. Just a kind hand on my shoulder. I'm not asking for much. I would have been able to feel some-thing. And my body just feels like it's pins and needles. It's like I'm looking for some kind of touch. (Hold me, Momma, please, please hold me . . . Cries deeply for a long time. Reaches out pleadingly.)

[Back to the present]

In those moments, it's like I'm dancing. It's like it's okay. There's a time when it stops hurting and it's like a breath of fresh air and I feel okay. I feel I'm not hurting. I have a feeling that's where my optimism and my joy comes from. Those little windows when everything just stops hurting and the feeling is so fantastic.

I keep thinking about when I was fourteen and I had what I call "The Main LSD trip." And now I see so clearly the parallels, what was coming up was the birth experience, not the birth experience but what happened to me was, I sat in one place for over ten hours and I was afraid to move. And my whole body, it was just so sensitive. It was like I could hear through walls, I could feel everything and I just couldn't move. I had to stay there. Now I see I was reliving that whole thing. "Don't move. It will be okay if you don't move." My body was so sensitive, it was like one big nerve. And then after that whole experience that's when I started doing barbiturates and downers because it was the only thing that could take the edge off my body feeling like one giant nerve and it was the only thing that could calm my body down. I started with the barbiturates, with Tuanols and Quaaludes. I was just feeling too much. The only reason I stopped doing those is because I got hooked on them and took too many. I went to a doctor and told him what I did, figuring that he'd understand and be able to help me understand. He didn't.

It makes perfect sense about my reactions in life when I'm feeling too much or there's too much input. I withdraw. That's the imprint, to withdraw from what is trying to kill me. What's true about me to this day is that I could never hide how I was feeling. I was one of those people who you see wearing their feelings on their sleeve. I had no myth. How I was feeling was there, like an open book. You could just read it. And the way I navigated through life was on my feelings. It's like if I felt safe, I would move forward. If it didn't feel safe, I moved away.

It seems to me that part of this experience, the effect that it had was to affect my nervous system; to be more sensitive. I'm very sensitive to how others around me feel. My nervous system was just overloaded and as a result it magnified everything so I've had the feeling of thinking it is all too much. So in the womb my reaction was to shut it off by withdrawing and becoming as small as possible, contracting. And I still do it. I guess that's what Dr. Janov calls the prototype. It seems to be that I'm prehardwired. I have to be strong no matter how bad things are. I mean obviously that's how I have survived my whole life in the worst situations was being able to find something good, something that I learn, something that made me wise and stronger.

Therapist: It saved your life for one thing.

I've always had this optimism. The optimism is the possibility in life. You know I don't think I would have survived otherwise. That's what I cling to. Those little windows. And I'm always striving to get back to that. But it makes sense because that's when the pain stops. As intense as the pain is, if I were to swing over to the other end of the spectrum, that's how great not feeling the pain is, it's like dancing on the rooftops, the joy, that's the magic.

There is nothing like wanting nothing; except to enjoy the beauty of the day, the magic of looking at a flower, of seeing the sun shining. It's just all very simple. There's no ambition, there's nothing in there except wanting to breathe. I have to tell you it's all quite fascinating to me. What a relief in knowing where the pain comes from, where optimism is.

NOTES

1. Y. Ito et al., "Increased Prevalence of Electrophysiological Abnormalities in Children with Psychological, Physical and Sexual Abuse," *Journal of Neuropsychiatry* 5, no. 4 (Fall 1993): 401–407.

2. Many synaptic endings have autoreceptors that respond to transmitter release by presynaptic neurons.

3. Ito, "Increased Prevalence of Electrophysiological Abnormalities in Children with Psychological, Physical and Sexual Abuse," p. 401.

4. All patients are measured for vital signs before and after each session. The physiology tells us a great deal about what feelings the patient is in.

5. Arthur Janov, *Why You Get Sick and How You Get Well* (West Hollywood, Calif.: Dove Books, 1996).

6. R. J. Davidson and N. A. Fox, "Frontal Brain Asymmetry Predicts Infants' Response to Maternal Separation," *Journal of Abnormal Psychology* 98, no. 2 (May 1989): 127–31.

7. Allan Schore, in *Brain and Values*, ed. Karl Pribram (New Jersey: Lawrence Erlbaum, 1998), p. 342.

8. See: Eric Hoffman, "Mapping the Brain in Repression," presented to the California Psychological Association, Annual Meeting, February 23–26, 1995. See also E. Hoffman, "Hemispheric Quantitative EEG Changes Following Emotional Reactions in Neurotic Patients," *Acta Psychiatrica Scandinavica* 63 (1981): 153–64.

9. Ibid., p. 153.

10. S. L. Rauch et al., "A Symptom Provocation Study of Posttraumatic Stress Disorder Using Positron Emission Tomography and Script Driven Imagery," *Archives of General Psychiatry* 53 (1996): 380–87.

11. Davidson and Fox, "Frontal Brain Asymmetry Predicts Infant's Response to Maternal Separation."

12. See D. Derryberry and D. M. Tucker, "Neural Mechanisms of Emotion," *Journal of Consulting and Clinical Psychology* 60, no. 3 (June 1992): 329–38.

13. R. J. Harmon and P. D. Riggs, "Clonidine for Posttraumatic Stress Disorder in Preschool Children," *Journal of American Academy of Child and Adolescent Psychiatry* 35 (September 1996): 1247–49.

7

THE NOTION OF CRITICAL PERIODS

Events are imprinted into the nervous system during what is known as the critical period. Events that happen outside of this period do not have the same dire consequences as those that take place during it. Losing one's parents in an automobile accident at age eight may be imprinted with a force equal to a traumatic event during the first six months of life, but the neurologic developmental effects may not be as severe.

To imprint, a level of high arousal is needed; in other words, a state of emergency that puts the system on alert. The brain begins to change. It can imprint both "love" and "no love." If there is love, the neurons expand, arming the brain against later adversity. Key synapses increase, the brain is stronger and has more inhibitory nerve cells to keep anxiety at bay.

If there is anything that emotional deprivation involves it is in the lack of touch and caresses very early on. When the baby is under stress from a lack of physical closeness, cortisol is released, and when that stress hormone is secreted over time it produces a toxic brain environment that can and does damage certain brain structures in the limbic-feeling system.

Speaking of toxic environment, one of our advanced patients would often feel nauseous and suffer from a burning sensation during her reliving episodes (a primal). Finally, during a reliving sequence of a brainstem-originated trauma she felt a terrible burning sensation all the way down her system. We found out that her mother tried to abort her with something very caustic that obviously did not take. But she had a recurring fixation about living in a toxic environment, fought the good fight against pollution, and finally moved away to a small clean town. Her battle against pollution was a proper one, but the deep motivation was from living in a heavily toxic situation in the womb at three months. That motivation did not necessarily negate her ideas about the environment; it just explained its origins.

There are periods when we must have love to develop properly and others where it is not that important for brain development. Investigators find that there are "critical periods" during gestation when permanent developmental changes could occur. A good deal of work has been done with animals but there is research that has implications for humans. In traumatized animals it was found that any deficit brought on by early deprivation was never made up.[1] That indeed may be the main feature of the critical period: *it cannot be made up.* Damage done early on, animals who were not touched after birth, for example, could not be reversed. But wait! It may not be that bleak.

SYNAPTOGENESIS

In the first eighteen months to two years of life, the synapses are forming between cortical neurons, strengthening or weakening them depending on the extent of trauma. With enough stimulation, simple touching, there is a greater density of synapses in the cortex as pathways strengthen and build integration capacity. Trauma is defined by what cannot be integrated smoothly into the system. It occurs when needs go unfulfilled for any length of time. The timetable dictates the necessity for optimum touch just after birth and for the months afterward. The amount of touch is determined by a sensitive parent who senses what the baby needs, not so much as to overstimulate her, but enough to fulfill her need. The body expresses the lack in allergies, skin disease, infections, and hyperactivity. We can go back to the two-year-old brain and remember things with that brain that we could never do with the adult cortex. When that brain cries it is the sound of an infant. It is in agony from the lack of touch and caress, yet the person has spent a lifetime blithely unaware of it.

We need love to build the synapses to create a brain strong enough to dampen pain. We need a parent who looks into the eyes of his baby, who responds to her moods, is sensitive to her discomfort, and is empathic to her pain and discomfort. That is love. A mother's compassionate look can literally regulate a baby's blood flow to the cortex and impact its development. It does this through the secretion of dopamine, which stimulates the growth of cortical neurons.[2] These projections of altered dopamine cells to the frontal cortex are building a new cortex. The better the flow, the more nutrients and oxygen are transported to the site. The cells are healthier. One measure of how effective and active a brain site is can be through blood flow. For example, in attention deficit disorder the flow to prefrontal sites is impaired. The brain cannot process new information readily, nor can it filter out extraneous stimuli. It is in this way that lack of love sculpts a new cortex by lowering dopamine levels. And it is not only the cortex that is altered. The hippocampus is particularly vulnerable to stress early in life, and its cells can atrophy with enough prolonged trauma.[3] It is not only a hit in the head that can cause brain damage: simple neglect can do it, too. Monkeys who were abused by cagemates had brain damage in the hippocampus not because of the blows but because of the suffering. If we suffer from an inability to conceptualize space relationships, the architecture of a house or a room; if we suffer from memory loss of times, dates, and places, we must look to the hippocampus and what our lack of early love did to it.[4]

During this key period of brain development called *synaptogenesis*, the more dense the synapses the more information the brain can handle. The decrease in synapses, for example, is one physiologic way that a trauma can be imprinted, leaving us with fewer brain cells to deal with adversity. The imprint can be a single learning event that can encompass months of interaction with one's parents, culminating in a feeling like "I'm not wanted." It is an epiphanic moment when the child realizes there is no one to turn to with his feelings. This realization most often happens during a time when the baby is most needy, a time when the brain is crying out for fulfillment, when synapses are crackling, making new connections, producing new networks of brain cells; a time when a lack of fulfillment converts to pain. It is particularly painful during the critical period because it is a biologic need; the system needs fulfillment for proper development.

Rapid synaptogenesis can be considered a key index of a critical period. Severe deprivation interferes with the process of synaptogenesis. Animals who were traumatized and then autopsied had fewer brain synapses. It is during this time that adverse experience, a mother who drinks and smokes, can alter the brain of her offspring. The baby has a less embellished, enriched brain to handle later adversity. It is during this time that given certain genetic tendencies—high blood pressure, migraine, and allergies—the system becomes weakened, allowing those vulnerabilities to be manifest early on in life. A strong brain with adequate synaptic connections may be able to hold back those tendencies. With reduced synapses the stage is set for later learning problems. All this may take place while the fetus is still a fetus and has had no social life.

Compounding the problem is that it can all take place with no awareness by the baby. The baby is simply born "dull." Not being aware in no way affects the impact of the imprint. That imprint is not simply a cerebral memory. It is lodged in a deficient brain. That deficiency *is* the memory, in the same way that a chronically rapid heartbeat due to intra-uterine imprinted trauma is a memory. It is the way the heart "remembers." Some of us have a resting heart rate of sixty beats per minute. Others may find their rate to be over eighty beats per minute. Now we have some idea of how those differences happen, differences in prenatal life. Real memory does not depend on the ability to "remember," to verbalize and conceptualize early events. Memory is evident long before there are words. A rapid heartbeat is a memory of an event that caused the heart to speed up against terror, for example. Now the event is long passed but the fear remains impressed into the system with its hand-maiden, rapid heart rate. The heart doesn't say, "I remember being terrified by my angry father whenever I cried," but it says it forcefully with its lifelong increased heart rate. We can understand when someone says, "I remember my father's rages and his out-of-control tantrums." But it isn't just an abstract mental memory. There is a body that accompanies it that gives the memory a "push."

The *critical period* is that stage of life in which a baby is most vulnerable to certain kinds of input. If a child was loved in infancy but left to fend for himself at age eight, he would not be imprinted with the same feeling of loneliness and abandonment as someone not loved and neglected for weeks just after birth. An eight-year-old can feed himself, reach out to relatives or friends, or perhaps find a surrogate parent in a teacher. An infant is helpless and needs comfort and touch with every fiber of her being. A fifteen-year-old no longer touched and held by his parents may feel hurt by it but he is not going to suffer brain impairment as someone who never was held in infancy. This is the difference between being hurt and experiencing deep physiologic damage. This same deprived infant can be held every day from the age of fifteen on and it will not erase the imprint from the critical period.

It's not because our son Joe hangs out with the wrong people that he's begun to take heroin. On the contrary, he hangs out with those in his same predicament; and that predicament is often the same lack of internal painkillers, with the same impulse-ridden system. Joe is into heavy drugs because he is into heavy pains, and those pains occurred very early in life, before he had his first pal. By and large, the deeper and more remote the imprint the more force it has.

THE FOCAL POINT OF THE CRITICAL PERIOD: THE DOPAMINE CONNECTION

The most important critical period occurs when the brain is forming during gestation. A mother's drinking and smoking, her anxiety or depression will find its way into the fetal system and create havoc. If you alter the availability of a neurotransmitter element during fetal development it will change the number of such cells later on. If you reduce the availability of dopamine (which helps information along nerve pathways), for example, at the receptor site, by blocking the developing receptor there will be a lower number of dopamine receptors after birth.[5] Dopamine is, by and large, an excitatory chemical that makes us alert and vigilant. It is a "hurry-along" transmitter, driving the message toward connection, as opposed to serotonin and the endorphins, which are blocking agents (as well as agents that produce satisfaction and comfort). Dopamine is a "stay-with-it chemical," a key element in tenacity in human beings. When we alter the dopamine levels during gestation we produce lifelong effects on the brain, and that can mean a personality who gives up easily, won't stay with a project once it's started, and cannot see things through to the end. I don't want to unnecessarily alarm parents. I simply want to make them aware of the lifelong consequences of early life. Clearly, one drink will not damage a fetus, but continuous drinking by a carrying mother will. These are not negligible facts.

When dopamine output has been compromised due to early trauma (and that always includes lack of love) we may later find lower dopamine levels in the right hemisphere, which deals with feelings. Because it may be lower, these kinds of individuals (passive, phlegmatic) do not have the neurochemical wherewithal to stay with arduous tasks or difficult relationships; they give up easily because they lack the "stay-with-it chemicals" they need. Here we see how personality starts to form around key events in the womb which shifts the balance of hormones. That is what is critical about critical periods. Their effects last.

I shall cite a number of research studies to reinforce this point because it is not just about dopamine. It appears to be a biological law: that traumatic events in the womb can be exceptionally deleterious and cannot be made up later on. Here is where, for example, slight alterations in thyroid output can begin so that later in childhood we may find hypothyroidism or insulin deficiency. It is in the womb that so many biological setpoints are fixed deviating the system in slight, often subclinical ways that do not become apparent perhaps for decades.

With trauma in the womb, the dopamine levels will be up-regulated (hyper) or down-regulated (hypo), but they will not be normal. Thus, insufficient dopamine stimulation in turn can affect the cortical integration system, which means the person can be overwhelmed later on by the slightest amount of input. There would not be enough cortical capacity possible to withstand adversity. It is not impossible that Parkinsonism and Alzheimer's disease would be the late results of womblife trauma. An excess of dopamine can weaken the gating system by overstimulating and overtaxing its capacities. Janet Giler, a psychologist writing in the *California Psychologist*, notes that when the general external stimulation level is low the person can focus. When a room is filled with noise and stimulation, all focus is lost. She says, "New research indicates that this failure to gate or limit sensory information (and this is one meaning of gating) may be due to increased levels of dopamine."[6] Of course, increased dopamine is not the *cause* of the problem but the result of very early experience.

With too much pain inciting too much dopamine to be secreted (up-regulation) the frontal cortex, which receives dopamine activation, is in danger of fragmenting: "By prenatal administration of pharmacological agents that alter transmitter supply to the emerging dopamine receptor, it has been found that receptor number can be altered."[7] When dopamine receptors are reduced there may not be enough stimulation to keep the frontal cortex alert and active. The prefrontal "mind" can no longer integrate information properly and is easily confused and overwhelmed. Contrarily, an overactive dopamine system may make the frontal area too "busy," overstimulated, and unable to focus and concentrate. The point is that when a carrying mother takes drugs or tranquilizers, the dopamine system may be affected for life.

THE LOSS OF THE ABILITY TO ADAPT

When the researchers just cited altered the transmitter supplies to the dopamine receptors during womblife, the result was a lifelong change in receptor numbers later on. *If this happens after birth, the system will compensate by increasing the number and density of receptors; but if it happens during pregnancy there will be no compensation!* In brief, the die is set in the womb, after birth it is mainly mopping-up operations. It is my assumption that this paradigm may hold for many other biochemical and neurochemical factors. Events in the womb stamp in forever key alterations in hormones, immune functions, neurotransmitters, and nerve circuits. This is no longer simply an assumption, as we shall see; there is research evidence for it. The importance of this is that there doesn't have to be a chemical injection to produce these changes. A mother's mood, hyperexcitability, for example, can produce the same physiologic changes. The fetus can be overstimulated and this can subtly damage the developing neocortex, which is just getting its start in life.

A. J. Friedhoff and J. C. Miller, two important investigators in receptor function, say, "From the adaptive standpoint, when a developing cell, bearing dopamine receptors, senses that there is little dopamine in its surroundings, the system is required to express fewer receptors in order to match receptor number to transmitter supply."[8] The cells adapt to their environment so that when there is less supply, there is less physiological demand.

If the human mother is given heavy doses of tranquilizers, such as Haldol, during pregnancy it will permanently affect neurotransmitter levels in the fetus, and what that can mean is that the adult will never be "quite right"; may never have the wherewithal to repress properly; a jittery, hyperactive, hypermotile type, with the inside and outside in constant activity. It may be that this imprint then requires the now adult to take tranquilizers precisely because the mother did while carrying. The overload of tranquilizers during pregnancy provokes the fetal system to produce less of it since it is already saturated. Now as an adult with less pain suppressing possibility he must seek drugs to help repress pain.

It is not simply supposition that makes me believe in the lifelong effects of early experience. I have seen it in my patients for decades and have written extensively about it. But now others are entering the arena. Friedhoff and Miller reiterate that prenatal drug exposure can result in enduring changes in the system lasting a lifetime.[9] Fetal exposure to antipsychotic drugs has occurred in children of psychotic women, which in turn affected the sensitivity of their receptor systems and made them more vulnerable.[10] More importantly, Rosengarten, Friedhoff, and Miller state: "It is conceivable that maternal neuropeptides, maternal hormones [as a result of psychological states] and maternally transmitted environmental chemicals could mediate such alterations."[11] The chemical changes in the carrying mother due to her moods, say of depression, become corresponding changes in the fetal system. When the mother is depressed so may be the baby. Later on, a mother's continuing depression may dampen the child's feelings because his exuberance is met with a lack of appropriate reaction in the mother. Her "downness" eventually suppresses the baby just by the fact of her emotional state.

A fetus can sense a mother's anxiety while carrying. He is not aware in the cerebral sense of the term; rather he is in the language of malaise, discomfort, and vague tension, in the language of hormone change and altered blood flow. The state of the mother can make the baby uneasy and afraid, and can imprint that fear permanently. The same physiological processes are evident in both prebirth and postbirth times. Many of the current tranquilizers, those used on very disturbed women, alter the serotonin and the dopamine levels of the fetus and can predispose to mental illness later on. A woman who continually smokes or drinks while pregnant can interrupt the output of both transmitter systems in the fetus.

NOTES

1. A. J. Friedhoff and J. C. Miller, "Prenatal Neurotransmitter Programming of Postnatal Receptor Function," in *Progress in Brain Research* (Amsterdam, Netherlands) 73 (1988): 509–22.

2. I wonder if giving small doses of dopamine drops, deprenyl, to depressive, possible low-dopamine parasympathetic patients might help with their energy levels and depression. We will be testing that out in the future.

3. H. Uno et al., "Neurotoxicity of Glucocorticoids in the Primate Brain," *Hormones and Behavior* 28, no. 4 (December 1994): 336–48.

4. B. S. McEwen, "Possible Mechanisms for Atrophy of the Human Hippocampus," *Molecular Psychiatry* 2, no. 3 (May 1997): 255–62.

5. H. Rosengarten, E. Friedman, and A. J. Friedhoff, "Sensitive Periods to the Neuroleptic Effect of Halperidol to Reduce Dopamine Receptors," in *Nervous System Regeneration*, ed. A. M. Guiffrid-Stella (New York: Alan Liss, 1983), pp. 511–13.

6. Janet Giler, "Attention Deficit Hyperactivity Disorder," *California Psychologist* (November/December 1999): 52.

7. Rosengarten, Friedman, and Friedhoff, "Sensitive Periods to the Neuroleptic Effect of Halperidol to Reduce Dopamine Receptors."

8. Friedhoff and Miller, "Prenatal Neurotransmitter Programming of Postnatal Receptor Function," p. 519.

9. Ibid.

10. Ibid.

11. Rosengarten, Friedman, and Friedhoff, "Sensitive Periods to the Neuroleptic Effect of Halperidol to Reduce Dopamine Receptors."

Part II

WOMBLIFE, MEMORY, AND THE IMPRINT

8

IMPRINTING MEMORY

Throughout this work I use the term *imprinting* to describe how events are permanently stamped into the nervous system, with the effects felt throughout the rest of the body. Activating chemicals such as the catecholamines, including dopamine, provide the "glue" for the imprint. Limbic and brainstem structures, where very early traumas are imprinted, are rich in dopamine, particularly when the right hemisphere connects to lower structures. The *locus ceruleus*, a brainstem structure, is one of these structures. The brain needs dopamine for synaptic growth. A deficiency of this hormone leaves the brain less able to handle certain tasks such as memory, motor skills, and coordination. High stress seems to "burn out" dopamine cells over time.

The imprint can occur anytime following the first few months of gestation when a fetus's nervous system is fairly intact. It happens primarily during the critical period when the brain's nerve cells are developing at a rapid clip, when certain needs must be fulfilled.[1] The imprint occasions a sea change in many vital systems, from heart rate to blood pressure, from body temperature to the secretion of painkilling brain chemicals such as serotonin. It is possible to be in pain in the womb and for that pain to be lodged as a discrete memory forever. The fetus makes crying motions in the womb, can wince and scrunch up against attack.

The central early imprinted experience radiates out to encompass all kinds of reactions, visceral, muscular, vascular, etc. The imprint is the result of the "big bang" that happened perhaps around birth or before. At the age of forty we can measure neck tension and stress hormone levels, and find sequelae of that painful explosion. We see the results in blood vessel problems years later or visceral reactions in the secretion of gastric acid. We can treat the far-flung concomitants of the explosion; physical manipulation of jaw tension, for example, but treating these sequelae means that the body will find another outlet, as the explosive force is still at the nucleus of the system. When the early big bang (major trauma) is relived there is often a permanent drop in such things as cortisol levels. That is how we know that the big bang endures for a lifetime and that it is the cause of tension and stress decades later.

Imprinting accounts for a change in the number of synaptic connections, a thickening of certain neurons, and an increase in the dendrites (receiving messages from another nerve cell). In a complicated process all of this accounts for the development of a memory trace as the imprint spreads its tentacles throughout the brain. The force or valence of the trauma becomes the force of the imprint. That energy drives it and disperses to many brain sites. The event is now impressed into certain neurons that connect to other related neurons to form stamped-in pathways. They then have a "complicity"; they understand each other and react to each other more than to other neurons. When they fire together they wire together. They understand the code that binds them, and when similar events occur later on, a disgusted look by someone, or a coldness on the part of a friend, the coded neurons react again to produce fear and anxiety. These codes are the internal representatives that are triggered when similar feelings are evoked. They produce the overreactivity in so-called inordinate reactions to what should be small matters. The work regarding coding by psychiatrist William Gray of the Newton Center in Massachusetts is discussed in the Brain-Mind Bulletin: "In infancy, we experience a basic set of global feelings such as contentment, rejection, anger, fear. Just as the colors red, yellow, and blue are blended into millions of hues, these primary emotions become differentiated through experience into myriad feeling tones."[2] These emotions form a link and code all the elements and similar scenes together. They are coded as neuroelectric waveforms which are elicited by comparable frequencies of new experiences. New experience that has the same kind of feeling or sensation will set off the whole chain of trauma all the way down to birth and before. This is one way that memory traces are set off and are retransmitted. The feeling tones, they say, are "incubated in the limbic system." This is the way that a myriad of disparate experiences are combined under the same rubric. We have found a way to tap into the code.

The imprint is associated with high levels of blood flow, stress hormone secretion, dopamine output, and high metabolic activity of the prefrontal cortex. All systems join in to impress the feeling into lifelong learning. One fine day the child senses he is not loved and is indeed considered in the way; someone to be avoided. The feeling is imprinted without necessarily any thoughts being articulated. He must not make any noise or make any demands on parents who really do not want children. He doesn't even have to think about how to act; the imprint will do it for him. He feels unwanted, in the way, not liked.

A child senses he is not loved. This all may be engendered by parental attitude: the lack of warmth in addressing the child, impatience, irritability, and lack of eye contact. The parents may be as unconscious as the child. The brain senses rejection without any conscious awareness apparent. By the age of three he already knows how to respond, perhaps not rationally, but based on how it responded originally, particularly, when that response was life saving. Worse, the brain begins to be impaired in its growth and function, all because of not feeling loved.

THE LONG STORY OF MEMORY

To *imprint* means to impress a memory into every aspect of our being: in the blood vessels, muscles, nerve cells, and hormones. Each subsystem engraves the memory in its own way—a change in blood platelets, less serotonin-secreting cells, and so on. To accept the notion of engraved memory will change psychotherapy from a therapy of *appearances* (phenotype) to one of *origins* (genotype). For that matter, almost every technique would change once this concept has been incorporated into the therapeutic psyche. It means that memory endures and has a lasting effect on our neurobiology, and can alter the structure of that neurobiology and our later behavior. The approach of medicine would undergo radical change, as well. We would look not only at current stress to explain a heart attack, but into the childhood, as well.

It is the early imprint that deforms perception and provides the channel for later adult experience. Some husbands, after their child is born, come to regard their wives more as mothers than as wives and lovers. The wives may grow frustrated with this change in perception until finally they decide to leave, and the husband is again left without a "mother," as he was when he first married. A person who exposes himself in public until he is arrested does so because he is seeking an emotional reaction that he did not receive as a child from his parents. "Look at me!" "React with me!" "Show some feeling!"—and shock is showing a feeling. He is behaving in this manner because he is living in the past, forced by history and memory to act out early infantile needs. His imprint dominates. Imprints dominate most of us and our behavior. It is critical to an understanding of what symptoms we have. Bereft of the concept of the imprint we are forced into dealing with the presenting symptom as though it were the disease, which most often it is not.

Two of the hormones that block access to the imprint and its repressed feelings are adrenaline and noradrenaline (the catecholamines). They affect the thinking, integrating cortex and help regulate the amount of attention or vigilance exerted by the frontal cortex. When the input is too strong, the cortex works overtime to repress or push back the input. The hydraulic analogy by Sigmund Freud (you push here and it comes out there) was criticized during the early years of psychoanalysis, but it turns out not to be so off the mark. The pressure due to the imprint is there all of the time and must find egress. The energy moves into the frontal cortex for ideation and into the body via the hypothalamus for palpitations. The result: a mystical, hyperactive person who suffers heart symptoms. If enough of the energy can be "somatized" less will be available for thought disorders. The person goes to a cardiologist for the palpitations and to a psychologist for the obsessive-compulsive ideation— and they both can be treated with exactly the same medicine . . . painkillers. Both require tranquilizing and building up of defenses. These are not cures. They are palliatives, but they can work because they are normalizing a deficient repressive gating system that accounts for both ailments.

Recently, there was a story in the papers about a paroled sex offender who was suing because the state refused to give him his tranquilizers to control his penchant for young girls. The state recommended these medications for control of sexual impulses. Why? Implicit here is that pain is the generating source. Tranquilize pain and you block or control the impulse. Yet it is rarely directly acknowledged that pain drives one to act out. What the state has not yet arrived at is that it is necessary to remove the pain, not just control it. It is a small but a very big step.

One of my patients took high blood pressure pills and painkillers; they lowered her blood pressure but the next day she had a migraine. It's the "Appointment in Sumara." (There is an old mythical tale about someone who flees to avoid Death's visit. He decides to go to Sumara only to discover that Death has changed his plans and has decided to go to Sumara.) Wherever we turn, pain is waiting for us. We push it down here and it pops up there. We rush to Europe to "get away from it all," and there it is again. We go to the mountains to find ourselves and what do we find? Pain. Correction. If our defense system is still working we don't find pain, we find mystical notions to quell it. We believe we have just had a magical moment; because it works we feel better.

There are three critical factors in creating an imprint: the quantity of input, response to the input, and the timing of it. All three factors converge to produce a lasting memory that alters our neurophysiology. Let us keep in mind that part of the imprint is the reaction to it, which endures, as well. The pain and its response form a dialectic unity. It determines the tenacity of later behavior: for example, continuing to argue a point that should be over and done with. Other examples include paranoia or severe jealousy with obsessional behavior that has no bounds, the inability to take the pain of rejection, and the need to struggle over and again to be accepted and/or loved. Of course, the most prevalent is the inability to admit we are wrong.

When a trauma is imprinted very early on, even before birth, it is the brainstem that occupies itself with it. It activates, motivates in the precise way that the imprint was laid down: as for example, the twisting and turning involved in breech birth. As the brain and limbic system develop, that precise memory, poorly gated due to its heavy valence of pain, breaks through into limbic structures where it takes on symbolic wrappings. Now the person begins to have nightmares of being turned and twisted in a washing machine (an actual recurrent nightmare of one of my patients until he felt its origins). The anatomical and visceral imprint has now been transformed into images. It is the same memory with the same force as the brainstem imprint which has moved higher in the brain to upper levels of consciousness; that is why the dream or nightmare has such a powerful impact. It is simply a disguise for an earlier occurrence. In general, when a recurrent dream or thought involves sensation—pressure, crushing, choking, or the like—we can be sure that the brainstem is involved.

Imprinted reactions to early lack of love are meant to endure because they establish a template for future behavior, particularly in response to stress. One patient of mine, a hard-driving man, failed in his bid to build a spa and gym complex when he went before the city council. Instead of seeing the futility in continuing, he kept at it, appeal after appeal, all to no avail and at great cost to himself. His reactions were born of the past, and he was not cognizant of the situation because he refused to see it. All he knew and expected was that constant struggle would save his life. His early experience at birth had led to lasting changes in his perceptual apparatus and his neurotransmitter system. He should have stopped himself, reflected on his situation, and considered the consequences of his actions, but he could do none of these because of his fixed template established at birth which said, "Drive on if you want to live. Keep going no matter what the obstacles because death lurks." This is the formula that was behind his drive. To have stopped and given up would literally have meant death. The imprint drove him. Before I have explained fully the birth trauma it will be hard to assimilate these notions; therefore I request—patience.

When imprinting takes place, other nonrelated areas of the brain diminish and over time degenerate. The imprint directs brain development to provide resources where needed; more synapses in specific areas and less in others. Essentially, a new brain is constructed. In reliving early scenes, the patient is "back there." His brainwaves are such that we cannot tell whether the event is occurring now or is simply a memory.

Adults can be permanently affected by the imprint of hypoxia (a low oxygen state) at birth. Being alert and vigilant is a naturally adaptive state for proper functioning, far more so than being energyless. The problem is that many of us are too alert and vigilant due to the high level of internal threat. We find danger where it doesn't exist, or we exaggerate danger because we are already in a hyperalert, fearful state.

When there is a major trauma the hypothalamus is involved. It is known as the "final common pathway" to the internal organs, translating lack of love into physical symptoms. It aids in the imprinting process by the release of corticotropin. This stress hormone activates the sympathetic nervous system. This activation helps to seal in the imprint. It is the activating hormones that provide the glue for enduring memory. They provide the energy for anchoring a feeling into brain systems. They provide the "shock" for the system, making it pay attention and locking in the memory. In dialectic fashion the stress hormones also prompt the secretion of a morphinelike substance to defend us against the conscious awareness of the feeling ("I will never be loved by them"). Thus we release stress hormones that alert and mobilize, and opiates that regulate and suppress that same mobilization, all in one instant. If this did not happen, we would have runaway activation with nothing to attenuate it.

Suffice it to say that we have backup systems to backup the backup systems, all in order to maintain physiologic equilibrium such as body temperature, blood pressure, and mental processes. We need to have security systems to make sure that our inordinate reactions don't threaten our lives.

Generally, the imprint can drive one to find an emotionally cold person and struggle to make her caring and warm. If she is the maternal type, we are fortunate. If not, divorce is in the future. This entire process is done unconsciously because the need and the imprint are unconscious.

We have looked at the imprint and its lifelong effects. Now we shall turn our attention to the kind of universal traumas that tend to be imprinted. Given the kind of birth procedures practiced throughout the modern Western world, the lack of oxygen at birth is one such trauma. It is no doubt strange to think of a lack of oxygen as a lack of love but it is so. Perhaps it is the most important early need in terms of brain development. A child can go a day or so without water but he can only go minutes without oxygen. It is possible to relive that lack of oxygen, which has the most radical effects when it is relived, from stopping migraines to lowering blood pressure and curtailing the need for drugs.

The importance of the critical period and the imprint is its unchanging quality. Once something is set down during the critical period it is there forever, in the sense that we cannot make up for what happened to us during it; except, there may be a way to undo its charge and some of its effects. The critical period and the imprint is truly the leitmotif of this book. It means that what happens to us during later life is less important in terms of personality development than what happened during the early critical period when the brain was forming. We neglect it at our peril; for without an understanding of critical periods and imprints we may never fully understand the onset of heart attacks, strokes, Alzheimer's disease, and other serious afflictions. These are the hidden generating sources of so many later difficulties. Early traumas twist and turn our biology so that it is permanently deviated, too much stress hormone, not enough thyroid, too little serotonin, and so forth.

The critical period is a two-way street. If a mother doesn't have a chance to be a "mother" during this time she will have difficulty being a mother later on. If a baby goat is separated from its mother before it can be licked and then later given back to her, the mother seems at a loss and has "no behavioral resources to anything for the newborn."[3]

Michel Odent discusses other research to emphasize the point: If a lamb is separated from its mother at birth and the separation lasts for more than four hours, half of the mothers would not take care of their babies afterward. But, if the separation took place after one day there was no such problem. The critical period, immediately after birth, had passed. When these mothers were given epidural anesthesia shots to aid in birth they did not take care of their babies afterward. Mothers need their babies during the critical period as well. If they can't love during the critical period they seem to lose some of their capacity to love later on. Mothers, too, in short, can become imprinted with the ability to love or not. If they cannot be mothers when they should be, there is some biological mechanism that prevents them from being good mothers later on. There may be an important lesson here.

NOTES

1. B. Bolon and St. Omer, "Biochemical Correlates for Behavioral Deficits Induced by Secalonic Acid D in Developing Mice," *Neuroscience and Biobehavioral Reviews* 16 (1992): 171–75.

2. William Gray, "New Theory: Feelings Code, Organize Feeling," *Brain-Mind Bulletin* (8 March 1982): 1.

3. Michel Odent, *The Scientification of Love* (London: Free Association Books, 1999), p. 7.

9

BREAKING THE CODE
OF MEMORY

The ability of the brain to perceive and code pain begins just after the third month of gestation when there is already a primitive nervous system. The difference between accessing the coded imprint and recalling an event verbally is that when someone experiences the former, she will be in exactly the same neurophysiologic state as she was originally. This kind of memory cannot be faked. The code of memory may lie in electrical frequencies and chemical composition. Neurons in different parts of the brain share the code and react as an ensemble, a nerve network. Those aspects of the brain not necessary to the reaction to the trauma will fade away or atrophy. The memory becomes "grooved" as the ensemble of reactions can reappear whenever even a slight emotional event takes place. This is because most if not all of our current feelings are elaborations from the most basic sensations organized deep in the brain. Imprinting means not only the creation of new synapses but also the pruning of useless ones. The continual use of a pathway or circuit makes it more likely to be used again and again, thus we are more likely to repeat the behavior. Personality is formed around those consistent reactions. It is my clinical observation that those who suffered from lack of love very early on, perhaps spending weeks in an institution, have impaired social skills, and cannot form attachments readily. This can take place long before the child has use of language. He can be a brilliant psychiatrist and still not be able to relate to others. He may well tend to gravitate to others who are not feeling and who cannot love, as well.

In patients who relive early scenes the entire panoply of memory is reawakened: the smells, sights, tone, and words. It all rises as an ensemble for connection. It is total, not just cerebral; that totality of experience is what makes for profound change.

In a reliving the entire panoply of memory is reawakened and finally connected to the frontal cortex. Sometimes, just one aspect of the memory is evident—rapid heartbeat. A person will suffer an extra beat (extrasystole) or sudden palpitations. They hit when the defenses are weak. But these fragmented reactions are still part of an *overall* memory. Due to disconnection and repression only aspects of the memory get through: the most primitive survival functions such as heart rate and blood pressure. These are basic unelaborated aspects of the memory.

The high level of catecholamines concomitant with the "big bang" (original life-and-death traumas) such as a birth trauma helps disperse the information to the far-flung reaches of the brain—including the brainstem—so that much of the brain can be involved in its own defense. What is attacking is memory and its suffering component. Defense blocks the awareness of suffering. When we feel slighted in the present, the entire brain enters the fray as different aspects of the memory are gathered up by the central nervous system. The assembly of neurons code, store, and react to input in the womb. That is why we can develop a migraine with just a minor irritated look by someone in the present. Or, if the original brainstem trauma was utter helplessness in the face of overwhelming odds at birth (massive anesthesia), then when a person is placed in a similar helpless situation again such as butting up against inflexible government regulations, a normally not-so-terrible event, the unarticulated helplessness rises again. With it comes, perhaps, palpitations or a migraine. The "slight" is anchored in brainstem structures. As the hurt travels down the chain of pain it evokes all of the original related reactions to the first major trauma . . . in this case blood vessel constriction and dilation due to anoxia at birth.

Thus, a doctor is treating a migraine in a patient of forty while the very early generating sources is forty years old. It is no wonder origins are so hard to find. If someone else starts out to find the origin it will never be found; only the sufferer can find it. And he can never do it willfully. It becomes contradictory, trying to get below the cortex using the cortex.

When doctors perform an analytic blood-testing procedure on a fetus, introducing a needle through the skin, the catecholamines rise considerably in reaction to pain. Is a fetus in pain if it reacts but can't put it into words? Of course. Its stress hormone level rises some 600 percent in reaction to the needle puncture.[1] And it reacts! . . . forever. The stress response is now coded and stored permanently. The catecholamines catalyze the imprint before the baby is born. It is therefore possible to be marked for life even before we see our parents for the first time. Our reactions to our parents in infancy may be blunted, not by their behavior but because of womblife.

As neurobiologist Lise Eliot has found, when a mother is under stress and has high catecholamine levels her offspring is more likely to suffer cleft palate. Catecholamines restrict the blood flow to the fetus and thereby lower its oxygen level. It is also possible that chronically high maternal catecholamines may deregulate the setpoints so that the baby then has a different level himself throughout his life. He may indeed be more excitable, for example; have less tolerance for frustration, be more irritable and impatient. Because, as I pointed out, the endocrine system is a *system*, higher cortisol and catecholamine levels can alter the testosterone levels of the baby. We know that stress lowers the level in men, but I believe that a stressed mother lowers the level in her male offspring. The result may be a slight feminine male child. Now add a distant, remote father and the result is predictable. (See chapter 18 for a fuller discussion of this point.)

Lise Eliot has pointed out that the catecholamines react differently in adults and babies: "Whereas catecholamines mobilize an adult for action by increasing heart rate and enhancing blood flow to the muscles, they have an opposite effect on young babies, decreasing their heart rate, slowing breathing activity, even paralyzing certain movements."[2] C-section babies do not get the catecholamine surge that vaginal-delivery babies have, and that makes a difference in whether there will be breathing problems later on. Eliot reports that vaginal birth leaves the baby with a greater feeling of well-being, perhaps due to the higher metabolism rate.

A very recent report on the long-term effects of early trauma was made by researchers at Washington University School of Medicine together with the British Columbia Children's Hospital and Arkansas Children's Hospital.[3] They say in part: "Pain and Stress reactions have been shown to induce physiological and behavioral reactions in newborn infants, even those born prematurely." Fran Lang Porter, lead investigator, goes on to say, "There is evidence that these early events not only induce changes, but *that permanent structural and functional changes may result*" (emphasis mine). It has taken some thirty years for research to catch up to our clinical observations but more and more information leads to the conclusion that there are indeed enduring changes in our systems, including the brain system, as the result of early trauma. The researchers are coming to the conclusion that infants and fetuses can perceive pain and that those infants who are circumcised (something I am against in infancy when the baby is being hurt for no reason apparent to him) need painkillers. Premature infants, they report, who were subject to various traumas during pregnancy and delivery were less responsive as babies at eighteen months of age. Circumcised boys reacted more strongly later on to the pain of a vaccination than uncircumcised ones. And what they find is something that I have stressed, "There is evidence that memory for pain can be recorded at a biological level."[4] All this means is that events are registered on the physiological level before recall-memory is possible. It again explains how certain vulnerabilities are set down in the womb that make some of us react strongly to stimuli and others who do not react at all. A kind of lifelessness can be imprinted at birth so that all later reactions are dulled. In very depressed patients we see this dulling, called *diminished affect*. It is usually not because the person has no feelings; rather, those feelings are repressed.

Regarding stress in infants, UCLA professor of neuropsychology Allan Schore says, "This psychoneurological mechanism may mediate the effects by which exposure of an infant to emotional trauma results in sensory-affective, motor, emotional instinctual recording of the experience that are inscribed in the neurotransmitter patterns of the limbic system. This can lead to permanent deficits in reading the emotions of others."[5] In other words, the memory of a trauma can be observed in the changes in neurotransmitter systems of the brain. The imprint, or early trauma, alters neurotransmitters, the messengers that either facilitate or impede important information—such as pain—to top-level cortical sites that make us aware of our feelings.

Another outcome is an underregulated cortex and, later, as a result, manic states. Both depression and manic states also involve a high level of energy. Depression, after all, requires effort to keep the repressive system intact. Manic activity means there are leaks in the gates. It is not as though manic and depression are two different diseases. They are often both dealing with the same imprint. Only in the case of depression is there effective repression. In manic states the repressive system is defective or "leaky," driving the person into frenetic activity. They often alternate in the same person. As repression gives way to an exploding force, the manic individual writes reams about nothing at all, shops without restraint, and talks a "blue streak." That exploding force may be anoxia at birth.

We can give these states all sorts of fancy diagnoses, bipolar affliction, but it is still pain and trauma. Much better to investigate how effective the gating system is. Criminals, as I discuss later, have leaky gates, which accounts for their impulsiveness and acting-out. Their crime sprees can sometimes be considered manic-induced. But manic is not a disease; it is how we react to central problems. We have treated too many manic individuals to think differently.

As the load of their pain is lessened the impulsiveness and manic activity also lessens. The effectiveness of one's gates, as I discuss in the chapter on gating (chapter 14), is largely dependent on the birth process. A struggle-fail birth where massive anesthesia shuts down the newborn's system will more likely lead to depression—"I give up. I can't try anymore." The manic may have had a birth where massive struggle was necessary to get out, and it succeeded. Activity is stamped in as a survival mechanism. The original trauma sets that activity in motion. He runs from the imprint and runs because of the imprint. Those gates may have been erected at birth, when a trauma interfered with the development of the newly forming prefrontal brain cells, or in the womb. It can happen if a mother has abused Valium or other painkillers. As I pointed out, when the fetal physiology detects painkillers introduced into its system by the carrying mother, it "decides" not to produce its own. The result may be a permanent deficit in painkilling ability.

When elevated, the stress hormone response can permanently alter other hormone systems. Men who complain of chronic anxiety are up to 600 percent more likely to suffer sudden cardiac death than those without a history of anxiety. Those who are depressed are three times more likely to die if they suffer a heart attack.[6] We will see in a moment how early those reactions begin. Suffice it to say that the same imprint that produces anxiety can also cause cardiac arrest later on. The heart and guts (butterflies in the stomach) are coded as an ensemble. They are not separate diseases but part of the same syndrome. It is hard to be anxious and not have the heart work overtime.

Research has indicated how this coding may take place. A study by B. J. Young and others, investigating how memory is coded, measured single neurons in the parahippocampal region of laboratory rats after the rats were subjected to specific odors. In the presence of each odor, every related neuron fired simultaneously and the memory was *encoded* and preserved in the parahippocampal region. The researchers hypothesized that this area may encode memories in a different manner than in the hippocampus itself.[7] It seems that each neuron holds a piece of the code. Being left by a mate at age thirty may trigger an old feeling of abandonment at age six months. The fact of being left may trigger the old fear and a vague malaise. A depression may follow whose roots are a mystery.

There is new evidence of the importance of the cerebellum in coded memory. Many decades ago a neurophysiologist named Karl Lashley tried to find the "engram" or memory trace in the brain. He wasn't all that successful in his efforts. But now it seems that one important part of that memory trace may lie in the back lower part of the brain, something that looks like a miniature brain, the cerebellum.

When I point out that our patients are in the "there-and-then," rather than the "here-and-now," I mean that past and present are indistinguishable in terms of how the brain reacts. Sometimes stimulation of the cerebellum produces the same patterns as if an old traumatic event were happening now. The memory is clearly being partly held in the cerebellum. Paul MacLean of the National Institute of Mental Health (in a private communication) suggested we take a look at this structure as key. In any case, the best weapon against imprinted pain is memory. Reliving memory separates past from present so that one is no longer acting-out one's history in daily life.

Once adulthood is reached, the imprinting process cannot be entirely reversed because too many years of specific deviated behaviors have passed that are now embedded in the system. It is as if you initially learned the wrong strokes in tennis and are now trying, with difficulty, to correct them. The code keeps dredging up the same agglomeration of cell assemblies to produce the same deviated behavior (incorrect strokes) no matter what the will to do otherwise. The imprint forges certain nerve pathways that endure. As Schore points out, "Imprinting experiences have been shown to produce long-term electrophysiological effects on the spontaneous neuronal activity of different regions of the brain."[8]

READJUSTING THE BIOLOGIC SETPOINTS

Imprinting may also establish new long-term setpoints of basic biologic processes: e.g., the amount of endorphins and serotonin secreted and basal metabolism rate. *Elevated stress hormones, for example, are part of the code that is still responding to the memory as though it were present.* Memory keeps these setpoints fixed, and the biologic processes seal in the memory. Put differently, these alterations are the way memory is fixed. If we can manage to change imprinted memory we can stop the flow of energy deregulating certain setpoints. And we can. In my practice, our hypertensive patients experience a permanent drop of an average of 24 points in blood pressure after some eight months of therapy. The average body temperature of my patients is 97.5 degrees. This is not a negligible difference, since research indicates that for every one-degree drop in body temperature, there may be an additional ten years of life. Why does this happen? Memory is finally connected to frontal centers for integration. Why did the body temperature go up? Memory. The body is working harder to repress and is creating heat. It is continually reacting to internal danger. Feeling the danger no longer requires the system to react to it. Hence a systematic drop in many vital signs.

Keeping feelings inside eventually will take its toll on one's health. Repression is a constant force that wears the system down, resulting in, possibly, a shorter life span. In my observations, deep repression of early catastrophic pain can lead to catastrophic disease, not the least of which is cancer. There is some preliminary evidence that trauma in the womb results in some kinds of cancer to the offspring. Heavy-drinking mothers are at greater risk to produce cancer in their offspring. The earlier the imprint, the more likely the devastating result years later.

An article in the *New York Times* joins the groundswell of new information correlating later disease with trauma in the womb. "Evidence is accumulating, though the research is still in its early phases, that the periods before and soon after birth, childhood, and early adolescence are much more important to breast cancer risk than had been appreciated," stated Dr. Karin B. Michels, epidemiologist, of the Harvard Medical School.[9] The article goes on to state that a baby, exposed to harmful substances soon after birth, may be critical for later disease.

Having just explained why feelings need expression, I note an article in the *London Sunday Times*.[10] In it statistics are cited to explain why it is best *not* to express feelings. (It all seems so English.) They claim that research shows that "venting your spleen" leaves you more tense. Of course, if you are just abreacting, or simply discharging the energy of feelings. That is not expressing your feelings. It is releasing their energy. The authors state that it is better to control anger by doing something calm instead. The *Los Angeles Times* in a major story echoed the same sentiment. The *Los Angeles Times* piece considers anger as a "self-destructive habit."[11] It is considered addictive by them as is any drug addiction. They reported on a blood pressure study in which expressing anger caused a rise in blood pressure. We found the same in our own research when anger is a deliberate, conscious act with no context and no descent into a more primitive brain. When our patients smashed the walls of our padded rooms *in context* they uniformly had a lowering of blood pressure and heartrate. We know when it is abreaction by the sporadic rise and fall of key vital signs. It is, of course, no accident that serotonin levels are lower in aggressive personalities[12] (since they are less effective at repressing).

DAMIENNE: FILL ME UP

This statement "fill me up" has been one of the stories of my life, for me the double meaning is quite profound, both in my alcoholism and the lack of ever receiving what I needed.

I was officially branded an alcoholic at age fifteen although I had been suspended from a Catholic girls school at thirteen for being continuously drunk in class and skipping school to hang out in bars. At one point I'd taken a whole week off school while my mother was out of town, to hang out with the boys who lived next door. We drank all week. The following year (at age fourteen) I was asked to leave after being caught drinking and smoking at a school dance. For my fifteenth year I was sent to a Seventh Day Adventist boarding school (according to my mother I was uncontrollable). I was sneaking out at night to drink with the older boys next door, attending parties after lying to my mother about my whereabouts. I would say I was going to the movies when in fact I was going to nightclubs with my friends. My mother was of the opinion I needed "Discipline." Her punching me out hadn't worked, her constant threats to send me to live with my "fuckin' father" who'd beat me into shape hadn't worked, and trying to ground me for weeks on end was totally ineffective.

During that year I made no friends, I was one of those bad kids, a "troublemaker." I swore about everything (including church). I kept bottles of alcohol and packets of cigarettes hidden in my mattress and other places so the dorm deans wouldn't find them during the weekly room inspections. I got a part-time job at the horse stables down the road, but that meant I had to work Saturday mornings. The school forced me to quit after three weeks because I had to keep the Sabbath (Saturday) sacred. I was devastated. It was the only thing I had that made me feel good. The end of first term I was suspended for drinking and smoking on the train going home for the holidays. I can still recall my mother standing in the kitchen yelling at me that I was nothing but a "useless drunken little bitch" while slapping my face. This was nothing new, I'd grown up with these words and her abhorring me was only too obvious, as far back as I can remember.

Back at school for second term I got caught by the police spraying graffiti about the school on the walls of the public toilets in the city square. I had also started taking the motorbike from the school farm to sneak into the city on Friday and Saturday nights to go to the pubs and clubs. The other kids thought my behavior was obscene. To make matters worse all I talked about was how mean and cruel my mother was. I went to the dorm dean once after my mother had given me a hiding in my room (an impromptu visit) only to be told that I really did deserve it. Unfortunately for me I just couldn't fit the mold of being a "good Christian girl." I had tried really hard at times, but never succeeded.

I went home for a five-day midterm break. While home I agreed to help my mother's best friend's husband clean up his yacht. That night I got really drunk with him and he raped me. I wrote a letter to one of the girls at school telling her my fear of now being pregnant. I never sent the letter and I returned to school having told no one, I was too ashamed. My mother asked me home for a weekend a month later. I was so excited my mother wanted to see me. My mother took me to lunch at one of her favorite cafés, but when we went to sit down my mother's friend and my stepfather were already seated. I'd been set up; my mother had found the letter I thought I'd buried in my drawer. I was questioned and then blamed for what this forty-year-old man had done to me: I got drunk and led him on, I was fifteen. I went back to school and was then expelled at the end of second term, only this time for attempted suicide. I couldn't cope anymore with the loneliness and hurt I felt. No one liked me, no one understood, no one would listen. If they did they didn't believe me. I didn't want to die, I wanted someone to care and to help me. No one did. The doctor couldn't believe that my mother wouldn't come to the hospital and then told him I was just attention seeking.

From the hospital I returned to the Seventh Day Adventist boarding school, only to be told by the principal that the school would no longer put up with my disruptive behavior and I was an "attention-seeking little bitch." Even he did not know what my mother could do with me. His advice was to "put her in a girls home."

I went home to my mother, who hated the sight of me. She had a new man in her life, one of many since my parents' separation three years earlier. My drinking got steadily worse. Now no longer in school but at home with my mother full time, I couldn't bear it.

At sixteen my mother kicked me out of the house for my drinking and smoking, and because she also found a contraceptive pill in my drawer. I had gone on the pill after the rape and had become very active sexually. A friend of mine took me in and I stayed with her and her alcoholic father while attending the local high school, at which time my father came and asked if I wanted to live with him and continue to try and stay in school.

I moved in with my father and started going to the local college (my fourth high school) but every day I would take a thermos to school filled with either gin and tonic, Southern Comfort and lemonade, or whatever I could lay my hands on. By lunchtime I was usually fairly well intoxicated. Now living with my father, my life was a nightmare. (He was a serious alcoholic, like Mom said.) Every weekend I would go up to the local rugby club and watch the games; afterward I'd get drunk and have sex with any of the players who wanted it. The attention felt so good.

After being suspended from yet another school for drinking and carrying alcohol on the school grounds, and my father hearing of my extreme promiscuity, I received a severe beating. The doctor thought my skull had been fractured. Thankfully this was not the case. I ran away from home and decided to try and get a job to fend for myself. I was now completely on my own and accountable to no one. I was alone. I gained and lost three different jobs over the next eight months, from either being hungover, late, or not showing up at all.

What I will share with you now is for me the most devastating, in terms of the price I have paid, for my alcoholism.

At seventeen I became pregnant, which at the time meant very little to me. The father and I would meet at our local bar every day after work and drink till closing. I would wake up in the morning and have a beer for breakfast to feel better (hair of the dog so to speak), then at lunchtime I'd go to the bar for a drink. I was also smoking fifty to sixty cigarettes each day and marijuana when I could get it. The father kicked me out when I was five months pregnant and I continued to drink up until two weeks before the birth. I was eighteen with a newborn son to now care for, although my mother had several prospective "rich" people come to meet me to adopt my baby, even a couple from Australia. I refused to give him up.

By the time my son was three months old I was drinking heavily again; so much so, that one night I went to a party and got so drunk that on my return home I heard him crying, so I picked him up to feed him (I was still breast feeding); I walked halfway across the lounge room and dropped him from chest height. I walked over him and sat down in a chair and left him screaming on the floor. I was totally oblivious to what I had just done. Thankfully he was unhurt physically.

Having gone back to my mother's house immediately before the birth, I left again when my son was seven months old. My mother had been telling our family doctor what an "unacceptable person" I was, while I had been seeing him for my depression, my drinking problem, and telling him about the abusive treatment I was getting at home. I wasn't allowed to go out. At home I cooked, cleaned, and did all of the washing for the entire family while trying to look after my baby and paying $100 a week board for being allowed to stay at home. I felt like I was worse off than Cinderella had ever been.

I was taken in by a Salvation Army shelter for battered women. While there I would leave my son with the other mothers and go out drinking. By the time he was twelve months old I was pregnant again. I was stunned. I couldn't care for the child I already had and didn't really want. What the hell was I going to do with another one? At nineteen I decided to have an abortion. Once my decision was made and I'd set up the appointments, I felt nothing about it. Even when the doctor came to see me after the surgery and told me very angrily that I had been over the twelve-week term, and that he'd had to pull "it" out in pieces, I felt nothing. That night I went straight to the club and got drunk.

As my son got older my self-abuse and destructive behavior gained momentum. I would leave him at home on his own at night while I went out drinking. In the mornings I either couldn't wake up or couldn't get out of bed to care for him. He would stay in wet and soiled diapers for many hours. If he could get them off on his own he would crawl around in the filth.

Along with my drinking I had uncontrollable anger and fits of rage. By the time my son was four years old I had already been severely abusing him physically and emotionally. One particular evening after drinking all night I could no longer cope with my son's ceaseless demanding; I beat him with a plastic baseball bat. I finally picked up a phone and asked for help.

Over the next few years I had "intense psychotherapy." Once a week I saw a psychotherapist who tried to teach me to put my different memories onto imaginary bookshelves because they were no longer part of my present life. I saw a parenting counselor once a week, who tried to teach me better parenting and that I didn't have to do to my son what had been done to me. I went to group therapy one night a week and role-played different situations with other people, but we had to keep our feelings in check so as not to upset others too much. I enrolled in anger-management weekend courses regularly, but was never allowed to get angry. It was about controlling my anger, learning to be positive, and doing nice things. This infuriated me, but I kept going because I thought they were right and I was the problem.

I tried really hard to stop drinking. Sometimes I'd be able to quit for several months. I thought I was getting better. I would still have a few drinks several nights a week but I wouldn't get obscenely drunk. The difficulty was that after months of what was abstaining for me, I would hit the bottle worse than ever. My son would have to go into foster care while I drank twenty-four hours a day, seven days a week, for periods of up to six months at a time. The therapy made me worse. After three years of trying to "put my past behind me" and failing over and over again, I literally exploded. I beat my son so badly I had to call an ambulance. I thought I had killed him. By the time the police arrived he was playing with the paramedics, badly bruised and shaken but nothing broken. I still raged but now I took it out on the people trying to help. I had no idea what was happening to me. My son went back into foster care and I went back on the bottle.

All my relationships were abusive and ended in failure. I can't remember all the one-night stands I had. I just kept looking for attention. I would actually pride myself on being able to outdrink even the seasoned drinkers, through which I would get a lot of attention.

On May 14, 1996, I met the man I am now married to. He introduced me to Primal Therapy. I read *The Primal Scream* from cover to cover in two days and within the week had skimmed another two books written by Dr. Janov. I was going to do this Primal Therapy.

I have now been in Primal Therapy for almost two years and at this moment I haven't had a drink at all for ten months, even then it was one night, and no drinking for six months before that.

Two months prior to starting therapy I started taking antidepressants because I wasn't coping, but I continued to drink; I felt no effect from the drugs. Then I ended up in the hospital with a condition called Pseudo Tumor Cerebri (an overproduction of spinal fluid creates immense pressure on the brain). Not only could I not cope emotionally, now my body was reacting to a lifetime of built-up pain. Everything was too much.

The neurologist told me I would not be able to start the therapy for at least three to four months, maybe six. I was shattered. I was half a world away from my home, desperate for help, and they tell me I can't get it. I was on drug therapy for my illness as well as my emotional state, facing a regimen of lumbar punctures, and feeling utterly hopeless and helpless. I had to send my son home on a plane because I was unable to care for him, physically or otherwise, and my husband was starting his three-week intensive at the center.

During my husband's three weeks he needed to spend as much time as possible in isolation, which meant I had to be isolated, too. By this time I felt like I was going crazy. I would call the center every day and they'd just talk to me, sometimes for hours, so I didn't feel so alone. My drugs had been changed again and the dosage increased, but sitting in motel rooms on my own at night I would still drink up to three-quarters of a bottle of gin for relief. Thankfully I was able to start the therapy the following month.

For the first twelve months of therapy I was severely overloaded and couldn't function on a day-to-day basis. I had no gating system and no defenses to hold back or cope with the flood of pain that was overwhelming me. Initially I needed a lot of assistance from drugs because I couldn't turn the feelings off. I had also been told that if I continued to drink as well I would have to be institutionalized. There was the possibility of brain damage from mixing the drugs and alcohol. At one point I was on a combination of Haliperidol, Valium, Temazepam (for sleep), and Clonidine, and at times I still needed to drink. (According to my therapist, it would take fewer tranquilizers to knock out an elephant.) It was only through the constant therapy and huge support from the Primal Center that I was finally able to understand and change my life.

The insights have come through reliving many and varied memories which revolve around my mother and her treatment of me all through my childhood, as well as the events surrounding my birth. Being born was the beginning of my hellish life. My mother had a cesarean section after a thirty-six-hour labor during which I was being strangled by the umbilical chord and in a breech position. I was taken straight from my mother and placed in I.C.U. because I was having difficulties breathing and my mother had a severe adverse reaction to the anesthetic during the cesarean; she was also taken to I.C.U. to recover.

I remember arriving at the Primal Center one day for yet another session. I was feeling nervous, agitated, irritable, and just really uncomfortable. My therapist took my vital signs measurements which were really high: blood pressure 160/110, temperature 99.3 degrees. In the room I started talking about how hot and awful I was feeling along with being scared that I was never going to make it living in L.A. I couldn't work or function properly because I was always either crying or raging. I also had to try and look after my son, when all I wanted to do was throw him up against a wall. The therapist asked about my son. I was so angry that I had to look after him and could barely look after myself. Nobody had ever looked after me. Why did I have to look after him? It wasn't fair and it pissed me off. The therapist asked me what I would do to him if he was there. I started pounding the wall with my fists, yelling and crying at the same time. "I hate you, I hate you, I hate you." I then started to cry uncontrollably and there was physical pain in my stomach along with feeling like something was whipping me. I start clawing at and trying to climb the walls of the room, screaming in terror, trying to get away from my mother. I am back there and listening to her yell at me, "You fuckin' little bitch." I can feel the alkathene piping burning the backs of my legs as she hits at me over and over again, tearing away the skin. Still screaming and trying to get through the walls, all of a sudden I can't breathe and I start to panic. The therapist encourages me to "stay with it." I'm starting to feel a piece of my birth. I can't breathe and my body arches backward. My neck keeps stretching as if it's being pulled backward. This is killing me! I break out of it and go straight back into being terrorized by my mother. The therapist touches my shoulder and says it's okay. In order to reassure me I'm not still in the past, he tells me, "She can't hurt you now." I sit up and start telling him about the memory I had. As I do I begin to see how the feeling connects through my entire life.

The connections (insights) happen in response to the complete process of the therapy. It begins with how I am so emotionally angry in the present at my son because he needs and is asking me to care for and look after him. This is also seen in my body by the presence of such elevated vital signs. My elevated vital signs are an indication of the fight contained within my system between the feeling needing to be expressed and defending against that expression. The experienced therapist knows that buried underneath the anger I am expressing in the present there is a specific memory somewhere in my past of an unfulfilled need which is causing my overreaction now. By encouraging and, most important, allowing me to fully express this overreaction I can travel backward to the time the need went unmet. During my session I realized that I needed help to stop my mother from hurting me anymore but I was completely alone and had to survive her constant abuse. I was fighting for my life when I just needed to be helped and protected and I wasn't. Following this time reversal the feeling goes even deeper to my birth. Again I am in trouble. I can't breathe and the sensations of something strangling me are terrifying. I needed help but I was completely alone and felt like I was dying. The pain through all of this is too much, I am fighting for my life. The end result is the recognition that my son's need to be helped and cared for is the mirror image of what I needed and never received.

Primal Therapy acts like a conduit connecting my painful past with my present actions and feelings. It is with this connection into consciousness that I can heal; the connection means I have felt the feeling so it is no longer trapped within my system. This can also be seen at the end of my session. When the therapist again measured my vital signs, the results were 130/85, temperature 98 degrees—a substantial decrease in vital functions showing that the pressure on my physical system had also been alleviated. Herein lies the major difference between Primal Therapy and all other practices. A primal feeling is one that is linked through the entire system. Crying, hurting, and anger are the emotional components; the physical sensations of pain such as I felt in my stomach and my body's memory of the beating, combined with my birth. These memories are then brought into my consciousness. The key to this is the recognition that "feeling" is a neurobiological state.

Primal Therapy has changed my life in absolutes. It is due to the fact that I now have the ability to release the pain and heartbreak, and empty these feelings from my system rather than to forget or pretend they are no longer a part of me. I have learned that I must relive the traumas in my past in order to feel what my childhood system could not cope with at the time. To have felt that much pain as a child could have killed me or rendered me psychotic. With this in mind I have been able to go back to memories of times when my mother would hurt me, and I felt that she hated me, but now I can feel the absolute agony of being alone, unloved, and neglected. Having emptied tiny pieces of these feelings from inside there is now room to allow good feelings in, such as hearing from other people that they like me and that I'm a kind and generous person. I can feel and believe that this is true. I am no longer the little girl who was alone and abhorred, which in turn alleviates my need for constant alcohol consumption because I'm not trying to fill up the emptiness I feel or hide from my misery because a part of it is gone.

It is difficult to describe the impact of a feeling. I thought I understood after reading Dr. Janov's books. I actually didn't have a clue until I started the therapy. My feelings are contained in my mind, my body, my personality, my whole being, and because of this, crying and talking about everything is not enough as other therapies had me believe. I have spent my life reacting to my past. I believed I was an awful person and no one could possibly ever love this hard-assed bitch that was always on the attack. I didn't realize that in fact I was still living as a terrified little girl just trying to protect myself and not wanting to let anyone hurt me anymore. I no longer walk around like a rabid dog, trying to keep everyone away and always overreacting to situations that threaten me. I can differentiate between the reality of someone saying something that hurts and the feeling that comes up from my mother that they actually want to half-kill me. It means I am starting to build a life based on being an adult woman and not having my history dictate how I live that life.

I also now have the ability to see and hear my son's needs, I can listen and give to him, which I was never able to do before Primal. He, too, became both my whipping post and a void filler. To now hear and enjoy his laughter, to hold him when he's scared without telling him to grow up because I can't handle it or let him cry when he's sad without telling him to shut up because I don't want to hear it, is to me an almost miraculous feat.

Now I have the ability to "FEEL" what went wrong so long ago and heal from the inside out. It cannot be done any other way.

NOTES

1. "Fetal Plasma Cortisol and B-Endorphin Response to Intrauterine Needling," *Lancet* 344 (9 July 1994): 77–81.

2. Lise Eliot, *What's Going on in There?* (New York: Bantam Books, 1999), p. 99. I highly recommend this book.

3. "Infant Pain May Have Long-Term Effects," *Medical News and Alerts* (16 August 1999).

4. Ibid., p. 3

5. Allan Shore, *Affect Regulation and the Origin of the Self* (New Jersey: Lawrence E. Erlbaum, 1994).

6. See the related work of Ichiro Kawachi of the Harvard School of Public Health.

7. B. J. Young et al., "Memory Representation within the Parahippocampal Region," *Journal of Neuroscience* 17, no. 13 (1 July 1997): 5183–95.

8. Schore, *Affect Regulation and the Origin of the Self*, p. 180.

9. Jane Brody, "Risk for Cancer Can Start in the Womb," *New York Times*, 21 December 1999, p. D1.

10. S. Farrar and Y. Membery, "Bottling Up Emotions Is the Healthiest Option," *London Sunday Times*, 9 May 1999, p. 5.

11. "It's a Mad, Mad, Mad, Men's World," *Los Angeles Times*, 7 June 1999, p. S1.

12. R. A. Clarke, D. L. Murphy, and J. N. Constantino, "Serotonin and Externalizing Behavior in Young Children," *Psychiatry Research* 86, no. 1 (19 April 1999): 29–40.

10

THE TRIGGER EFFECT

A patient of mine, Joe, was awakened at 7 A.M. by a telephone call. The person on the other end said, "Oh, sorry. Wrong number," and hung up. My patient then fell into a depression. He didn't know why at first. In our sessions I let him experience that depression, a process I call *feeling a feeling*. My patient felt, "No one is interested in me." In his mind, the caller immediately knew he was not who she wanted. This took him back to his childhood, where tragedy and his family's financial concerns took precedence over his needs, leaving him feeling completely left out. His parents were preoccupied with making ends meet and coping with the death of a family member. He discovered that he was depressed during most of his adolescence for the same reason.

Receiving the wrong-number call triggered that hidden feeling. My patient wasn't being rejected but he believed he was. The feeling had sprung to life in his brain and was altering his perception. Fortunately, he was able to address it by feeling it, connecting it to the frontal cortex, and dispelling part of it. But how do these feelings get imprinted onto our system? Why do they linger, and where?

In our sessions Joe revealed that he wanted a woman who would give him her total attention to the exclusion of everyone else—an impossible need to fulfill. This helped explain his string of failed relationships. He

wanted an attentive "mother" so he would never again feel left out, a role
no one could ever fulfill except his own mother, now deceased. She could
have fulfilled that need only during the critical period.

If she came back now and loved him fully, it would be too late. It
could attenuate but not reverse the imprint. This patient had to feel as
an adult what he never really felt as a child: that no one was interested
in him. They cared only about themselves and their problems. He has to
go back in time to a more primitive brain and to experience with that
brain what he could not experience or feel at the time.

This patient's act-out was to find a mother/woman. And when
someone hung up abruptly on him, he was plunged into the real feelings
he harbored all of his life: no one wants me. Instead of allowing himself
to feel the feeling (my mother doesn't want me), however, he repressed
it and therefore became depressed. He had the help of many chemicals
that kept him unaware of that simple yet agonizing feeling.

Examining certain principles of brain function can help us understand why we become depressed, why we are anxious, why we can't sleep
or get along with others. What's the brain got to do with it? Can you get
well without changing the brain? I think not. Feeling better involves
more than just ridding yourself of an aching back or sore muscles. You
need to get well everywhere, because the memory is everywhere. Our
tendency has been to fragment the patient and treat her piecemeal. Too
often we take a migraine and try to make *it* better, or high blood pressure
and try to make *it* better, or a phobia and try to make *it* better. We treat
each symptom as though it didn't belong to a whole person. Specialists
become experts in symptoms and not of causes.

Conventional psychotherapy has been impregnated with the belief
that you get well in your mind—in your thinking, prefrontal cortical, logical mind—that you can *think* your way to health. I believe it is impossible to get well in that way, based on sound neurologic principles. We
may *think* we are getting well, but that is not the same as *being* well. The
brain is quite capable of deceiving itself. What is "well"? If it were simply
a matter of what we think about ourselves, then all the religious conver-
sions, the born-agains, the epiphanies would be just as valid as any psychotherapy, and the claim of a cure in many sects would equal that of any
psychotherapy.

A patient told me that as a young, hyperactive boy he constantly acted-out in class and was unable to sit still and concentrate. When he was eight, his parents decided to send him away to boarding school so that he could learn "discipline." One day he sat in the principal's office across from his mother. He had no idea what he did wrong. He looked at his mother's angry eyes and knew he would never again get any help from her. It was the ultimate rejection. He was not aware of his constant movement and the inability to sit still. It began almost at the beginning of his life.

The boy was then sent to a psychologist for evaluation. The Rorschach test was presented to him. After each image, he pleaded with the psychologist to tell him if he was giving the right answer. No response. No acknowledgment. He felt terrified because he believed that if he gave the wrong answer, he would never be allowed to go home. As it was, he wasn't allowed to come home for years. He couldn't ask to go home, for he felt there was no one to ask. His parents rarely visited him at boarding school.

Later, as an adult, he needed constant attention and assurance. Whenever his wife left to run an errand, he became anxious and felt rejected. He was convinced she was seeing someone else. The relationship ultimately failed. (The prestigious George Miller Award in psychology from the American Psychological Association was presented in 1998 to a woman who claims that childhood events involving one's parents do not follow us into adulthood!)

JUST GET OVER IT!

Why couldn't this person just "get over it" and move on with his life? He needed his mother so badly that everything became twisted in his mind. Does the brain actually become twisted? Is it reversible? Yes. What we previously have believed to be a genetic legacy actually may originate from what happened in our nine months of gestation. Our experiences in the womb may account for much more than we imagine, from drug addiction and alcoholism to psychosis and sexual deviation. In this book I will cite a number of research studies that reinforce my point. Take, for example, a pregnant woman who is chronically anxious, drinks four cups of coffee a day, smokes, and never stops dashing around. Her speedy biology may be affecting her fetus, flooding it with impulses, excitation, and stimulation that accumulate and threaten the newly developing, integrating centers of the baby's brain. Later on, the child is assigned many chores, is not allowed to rest, and is pressured to get top grades in school. She chronically feels overwhelmed, not only by the chores but also by all of the stimulation she received during gestation, which did indeed overwhelm her, not conceptually but biologically. These factors built up and provided her with the true sensation of being in over her head in the face of the smallest tasks.

This process is a physiologic imprint low in the brain that only later will be given a name by the now mature cortex: "over my head." Until that cortex kicks in there will be the interminable act-out of not being able to handle anything complicated. The person must act-out to produce a balance in the system—homeostasis. The system can only take so much input. This kind of person is already just at the threshold of being over her head. Let me reiterate: act-outs are part of the homeostatic mechanism. They should not be tampered with until we know what the underlying forces are. Too much of today's therapies, both physical and psychological, are tampering devices. They attempt to correct the compensating mechanisms rather than the forces that require compensation.

New evidence from ultrasound photos indicates that the fetus actually makes unmistakable crying motions in the latter part of pregnancy. This is particularly evident in mothers who smoke. The baby is suffering—a silent scream. If he is cranky after birth and has colic we now know why. He had a terrible nine months. If we were forced to sit still while someone blew smoke in our face for nine long months it would be a heavy trauma. The organism has no choice but to shut down against the onslaught of the oxygen deprivation. Just like the plant discussed at the beginning of this book which could take only so much sunlight, the level of repression or inhibition must rise to meet the threat.

Rarely does a man say to himself, "I want to be taken care of." Rather, the need is immediately acted-out with no conscious-awareness. To him, it just "feels right" that he should be taken care of; his behavior matches his unconscious need and seems logical. The past is prologue. He says, "Bring me a pen." She responds, "Get it yourself. I'm not your servant." Now the argument begins. She is reacting to forever being told what to do by her father. He is acting-out his dependence because early in his life no one was at home to take care of him. His father and mother worked outside the home. His needs conflicted with those of his parents. It may have begun at birth, when his mother was sick and remained in the hospital. He had no one to take care of him then, nor anyone afterward. He needs to be taken care of, and that is what he can only see— the need. What is devilish about this is that if we were to say, "You are acting out a need to be helped by your parents," he wouldn't have the slightest notion of what we are saying.

The need doesn't change, only the target. The person is caught in a time warp, and is angry because his girlfriend won't be his mother. The act-out is as unconscious and automatic as the need.

Around age two, the circuit of feeling is complete: brainstem-limbic-thalamus-orbitofrontal cortex. In the best of all possible worlds, this is the route feelings take. In most instances, though, feelings do not travel this route. Instead, they are blocked and reverberate in a closed neuronal loop for a lifetime; bedwetting, chronic anxiety, depression, and sexual compulsions are all effects of the feeling. The point of the reverberation is that we are at all times vulnerable to being triggered off. The neuronal circuit is just waiting for a trigger. In the case just discussed a simple phone call, a wrong number, set off a depression because the reverberating feeling was, "No one is interested in me." Here his depression was beginning to be resolved by connection to the real feelings and scenes in the past. Connection stops the reverberation, hence lessens the vulnerability for depression. Depression and anxiety are not specific diseases; rather, they are how feelings are treated. Good repression equals depression. Bad repression equals anxiety. The same death feelings (anoxia) may be lurking in both cases but the depressive is enveloped by the feeling and gives into it, while the anxiety person runs from it.

Because what I am writing about does not follow prevailing psychological theories, it is important to keep an open mind to all this. Particularly, since genetics is now holding court in the current zeitgeist. If we neglect nine months of life in the womb, the birth trauma, and the first months of life we no doubt have no choice but to ascribe adult problems to genetics. It is, in effect, saying, "There is nothing we can do about any of this. It is all predetermined." It is not! Or perhaps it is but it may be predetermined not by genetics but by the imprint. And we can do something about that.

The only other alternative in treating these disorders in the current

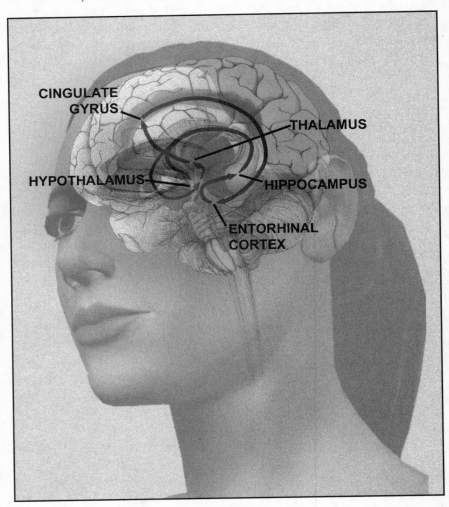

Fig. 5. Possible Circuit of a Reverberating Feeling

practice is to discuss the problem. This is skipping evolutionary steps. It is trying to rid a brainstem imprint with ideas. It is an unending task, and the reason why analysis takes years.

The early pain this individual experienced becomes a reverberating circuit; the feeling, trapped, cycles through the brain system in an unending reverberation. It will do so until connected. UCLA professor of neuropsychology Allan Schore describes how feelings reverberate in the brain. What Schore is suggesting is a possible neuronal loop for this reverberation which keeps us tense and anxious. It is the reverberating circuits that take up space in the unconscious and keep brain circuits overactive.[1] (Please see the work of Post in this regard.[2])

The reverberation process is a constant reminder of our unfinished business. Ample research shows that repeated similar events, such as neglect or lack of attention, early in life strengthen certain pathways, producing the means by which feelings about these events may be triggered in later years.

I have discussed the reverberating circuit and the importance of the nine months of gestation. We see how we can be so easily triggered by even benign events. The more disturbed the person, the more the reverberating circuits are laden with pain, the less it takes to trigger it off. Thus, in psychosis no stimulus is needed. One of my disturbed patients was walking by a parking lot kiosk and was sure that the attendant was laughing at him behind his back. He was eating a sandwich and was convinced that the attendant didn't want him to eat while walking.

Let us now go on with womblife and see why it is so important. I will cite a good deal of research to support my views but I must admit that I had these views decades before the research came along. Observation of patients is a valid form of research so long as there are few preconceived notions to color perceptions. I simply noted what I observed and from that developed a theory. I did not establish a theory and then superimpose it on my observations.

ANOXIA: AN IMPRINT FOR LIFE

In explaining oxygen deficit at birth and its effect on the brain system, I expand on ideas from my previous work, *Why You Get Sick and How You*

Get Well.[3] The experiment I discuss here is the most important research we have ever done to verify the existence of imprinted memory. It can and should help change the face of psychotherapy because it is strong evidence of memory's imprint and how it guides our lives.

The research in blood gases was carried out at the UCLA Pulmonary Function Laboratory in association with director Dr. Donald Tashkin and his associates, pulmonary scientists Dr. Eric Kleerup and M. B. Dauphinee. It was filmed. Two patients were wired for, among other things, oxygen and carbon dioxide levels. They were then taken through a simulated primal. During the simulation both patients became dizzy and had "clawed hands," typical of hyperventilation syndrome.

We took frequent blood samples with an in-dwelling catheter during the subjects' reliving episodes (every two to three minutes for one and a half hours) and during voluntary hyperventilation. We measured blood oxygen and carbon dioxide levels, as well as core body temperature, heart rate, and blood pressure. The simulation and the reliving were quite similar in terms of strenuous physical activity and deep, rapid breathing.

During the simulation, the blood carbon dioxide and oxygen levels were what one might expect. There were clear signs of the hyperventilation syndrome after a little over two minutes of deep breathing, including dizziness, tingling hands, rigidity of the extremities, bluish lips, loss of energy such that the subject could barely exert himself, and great fatigue.

In the reliving of oxygen deprivation at birth, however, there was no hyperventilation syndrome. Despite 20 to 30 minutes of deep, rapid, locomotive breathing, there was no dizziness, puckered lips, or tingly hands. The UCLA researchers could not account for the lack of hyperventilation syndrome: "There has to be some other factor at work," they offered. I believe that factor is imprinted memory.

Why did being in the birth memory inhibit the hyperventilation syndrome, and what importance has that for the origin and cure for human suffering? We know that the locomotive breathing we witnessed in the primal is organized deep in the brainstem most likely by the medulla. It seems probable that the locomotive breathing is part of the imprinted memory of anoxia or hypoxia. There was a real need and impulse to breathe even when it wasn't possible during birth. When that memory is triggered in later life, the original associated breathing emerges.

In the UCLA study, we had accessed, almost directly, the medulla and other brainstem structures, something unheard of in the psychological literature. This kind of access has been called the Holy Grail by a number of neurophysiologists. One piece of evidence of that access to lower-brain levels is the lack of hyperventilation syndrome. Only if one is in the memory can it be avoided.

Deep breathing, when done by an act of will in our simulation, is regulated higher in the brain, in the cortex. It is a higher-level *decision*, not a deep-level imprint. It is the higher-level brain participation that makes for hyperventilation. Being enveloped by the imprinted memory, however, made the deep breathing automatic and did not lead to fatigue. The whole system, brain and body, was back there in the memory. Not thinking about the memory; being immersed in it totally.

During a difficult birth, the fetus's back and abdominal muscles grind, producing enormous energy and lactic acid. Reliving this experience as an adult will involve precisely the same muscles along with an enormous lactate output. This is what my colleagues and I found in our research at the UCLA pulmonary laboratory. Memory is exact in every aspect. If it is accessed in a feeling it must be exact in every psychophysiologic domain.[4]

Today there are schools of deep breathing, such as holotropic breathing, which claims to solve any number of problems through deep-breathing exercises. It is nothing more than magical thinking. Deep breathing avoids the question "why?" It can temporarily ease the tension and a symptom, but it has nothing to do with memory. The minute "why?" is neglected, we are forced into spurious and specious procedures.

Let me be clear about the UCLA experiment. The subject's system is responding to cells crying out for oxygen decades ago. It is truly the silent scream, just as our bodies are screaming out for love, even while we have a loving wife or husband at home.

In a different recovered memory syndrome, when the patient *relives* a trauma such as incest, psychophysiologically instead of *recalling* it with her cortical apparatus, all of the original reactions will emerge intact. That is how we can verify if the memory is real. To recall is to rely on words and ideas, a cortical event. To remember is to uncover a deep-seated, wordless wound and to experience it again just as when it happened; it has the same stress hormone release and brainwave patterns. It is the difference between a total physiologic state, an experience, and an ideational exercise by the prefrontal cortex. Pain is not set down as an idea but as an experience.

Incest can be a completely wordless memory, as is anoxia during birth, as is the lack of close human contact in the first weeks of life. In the course of conventional psychotherapy the incest might not be remembered at all by the patient until she has access to and can liberate deeply registered hurt. I have seen the hands of a patient locked with wrists bound together as she relived being held tight by her mother's boyfriend during a sexual attack when she was eleven years old. As each aspect of the incest was relived over and over again, the same wrist position had been evident.

OXYGEN DEFICIT AND STRESS FOR LIFE

Oxygen deficit at birth forces the fetus to produce high levels of stress hormones, the catecholamines (adrenaline and noradrenaline). These hormones prepare the system for flight or fight from danger; in this case, the danger of death through anoxia, and later through the equal danger of the *conscious-awareness* of it. The event and its conscious-awareness are precisely the same danger with the same hormone release and vital-signs rates. The brain treats the danger in the same way, mobilizing the fight or flight response as if it were happening now. It is literally happening again, this time, however, the patient is older and stronger; the brain will not shut down immediately against the experience.

The catecholamines accelerate heart rate and help shunt blood away from peripheral organs and toward key organs such as the heart and lungs; the system is preparing for combat. The immune system whips into action and produces certain immune cells, such as natural killer cells, to fight against feeling as if it were a deadly virus. The stress hormones not only are helpful during birth but also help adjustment after birth. The catecholamines help the absorption of lung fluid at birth and also help clear the alveoli (air sacs) of the lungs, allowing them to remain open. Cesarean babies tend to have far more respiratory problems later in life because they lack the necessary compression at birth.

Some of my patients reliving birth will bring up a cupful of fluid the minute they are in the sequence. Their clearing mechanisms were evidently faulty. These patients explain that some inner button seems to have been switched on so that the fluid just pours out, and they uniformly report that they feel as though they are drowning. Each time they relive that event they experience the same flow. It is obviously integral to the memory. Fluid production is yet another way the body remembers; which is why I insist that memory is not the same as conscious, effortful recall. In recall *the experience* is lacking.

In our stress hormone studies, entering patients seem to be still responding to early imprinted trauma. Studies with infrared cameras on our patients found better blood flow in the peripheral vessels after one year of therapy.

It has recently been reported that hypoxia in lamb fetuses activates brainstem (subceruleus) neurons. This hypoxia interferes with the breathing function of these animals and may be implicated in later breathing problems, not excluding asthma.[5] The implications for humans is evident—brainstem imprints.

In a study with fetal sheep, it was found that minimal depletion of oxygen *over time* caused impaired development of brain structures including the hippocampus and cortex. It was not just one event of insufficient oxygen, but rather a deprivation over time, something that might happen to a carrying mother who smokes heavily or who lives in a polluted city atmosphere. Rats not handled just after birth also showed diminished cell development in the hippocampus.[6]

The growth of the frontal cortex takes some time after birth. Anoxia hinders cortical development, and this can hinder catecholamine output, which can result in poorly controlled impulses and/or lifelong tension and anxiety. We see this in therapy with patients who have first-line, brainstem intrusion; this is an aspect of the birth trauma shooting through during a reliving of a childhood scene. There is coughing, gagging, an arching back, and loss of breath. As the patient returns to very early events the fault lines in the brain begin to show up. This can result in poor control over preverbal memories.

Allan Schore points out that a loved child has the cortical ability to uncouple arousal of the system, transferring sympathetic stimulating impulses to a parasympathetic slowing metabolism; she is able to slow down cardiac acceleration and put the system at rest.[7] A loved infant, in short, has the brain wherewithal to stop inner agitation, can put down anxiety, and keep the heart rate at comfortable, healthy levels. The orbitofrontal cortex is part of this uncoupling mechanism.

An article in the *Journal of the American Medical Association* reported, "The hazards confronting the fetus mount to a climax during the hours of labor. Birth *is the most endangering experience to which most individuals are ever exposed.* The birth process, even under optimal, controlled conditions, is a traumatic, potentially crippling event for the fetus"[8] (italics mine).

Lagercrantz and Slotkin, two researchers on the birth process, indicate that "Nearly every newborn has an oxygen debt akin to that of a sprinter after a run."[9] Catecholamines prepare the system to combat anoxia by facilitating breathing. They speed up metabolism; hence the hyperactive child who was deprived of oxygen at birth. If the child could tell the teacher why he could not stay in his seat he might offer: "I suffered anoxia during my time in the womb because my mother smoked, and I suffered anoxia at birth because they gave her strong anesthetic. Now my system is still suffering from it, speeds up to fight off the memory, and pushes me out of my seat to keep me running away from the memory. I will happily sit still if you will take away that memory." We have had good success with young children (the few we have taken); they really can sit still after their primals. It doesn't take much to change them radically. There are no reinforced patterns to deal with. They can go to their childhoods easily because they are already there.[10]

Sometimes during a low-oxygen birth, the catecholamines rise to such levels (two hundred fold) that if the newborn were an adult, there would be a likelihood of a stroke.[11] It is my belief, having seen the enormous pressure that reliving demonstrates, that the imprint of hypoxia in humans may be one important contributing factor to later cerebral strokes. If we understand that at the age of sixty the memory of low oxygen is still there, still in force, then the reactions of the infant may indeed become the reactions of the sixty-year-old, and a stroke.

In a study of seventy-five newborns, it was discovered that oxygen deprivation during birth did not lead to brain damage if there were *not* previous distress in the womb.[12] Fetal distress was the major contributing factor in neurologic damage. So it turns out that the birth trauma is not the whole story. There is an important background of nine months of fetal life that sets the stage for how the birth trauma is reacted to. To deny this is to deny the fact that a fetus has a nervous system that can code, store, and respond to stimuli.

At birth we need oxygen and nutrients to make axons, the con-

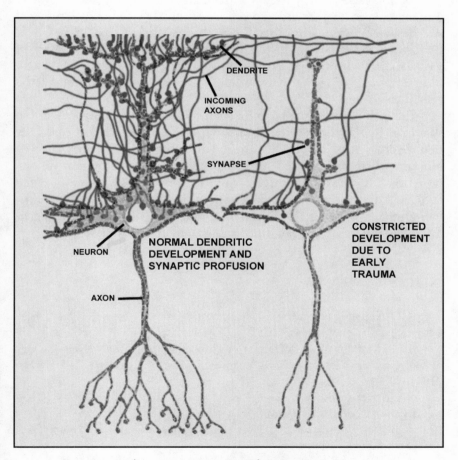

Fig. 6. Early Trauma Impoverishes Brain Connections

necting rods to nerve cells; and we need oxygen for the development of dendrites, the branchlike sprouts that accept input into the neurons. Early trauma hampers neural development so that we literally have less brainpower to deal with life later on. When we have anoxia at birth or even later during a drug overdose or suicide attempt involving barbiturates, the damage is likely to be in the hippocampus and possibly other limbic structures. The result is poor repression and constant pain.

As discussed, adult patients with migraines have almost invariably suffered oxygen loss at birth. In reliving birth they sometimes turn red and desperately try to breathe. When they relive the oxygen lack over time, their migraines either diminish or disappear.[13] In any number of vascular problems, we can look to oxygen deprivation at or around birth. Migraine may be one of many examples of the far-flung effects of the primal "big bang."

The lack of oxygen at birth imprints a life-and-death urgency in the system to live. It is often translated later on as a life-and-death urgency to have drugs, for example.[14] Drugs such as heroin are excellent brainstem blockers where the life-and-death imprint is impressed. So it is no surprise that heroin is addictive; and it is no surprise to us who have treated addicts that so many of them have serious traumatic brainstem imprints. Heroin makes up for the deficiencies in inhibitory neurohormones occasioned by the trauma. It helps normalize the lower-brain system.

NOTES

1. Allan Shore, *Affect Regulation and the Origin of the Self* (New Jersey: Lawrence E. Erlbaum, 1994), p. 297.

2. R. M. Post, "Transduction of Psychosocial Stress into the Neurobiology of Current Affective Disorder," *American Journal of Psychiatry* 149 (1992): 999–1010.

3. Arthur Janov, *Why You Get Sick and How You Get Well* (West Hollywood, Calif.: Dove Books, 1996).

4. Post, "Transduction of Psychosocial Stress into the Neurobiology of Current Affective Disorder."

5. S. Breen, Sandra Rees, and D. Walker, "Identification of Brainstem

Neurons Responding to Hypoxia in Fetal and Newborn Sheep," *Brain Research* 748 (1997): 119–20.

6. See A. Barbazanges et al., "Maternal Glucorticoid Secretion Mediates Long-Term Effects of Prenatal Stress," *Journal of Neuroscience* 16 (1996): 3943–49. See also: T. J. McDonald and P. W. Nathanielsz, "Bilateral Destruction of the Fetal Paraventricular Nuclei Prolongs Gestation in Sheep," *American Journal of Obstetrics and Gynecology* 165 (1991): 764–70.

7. "An environmentally attuned prefrontal cortical system which can rapidly uncouple arousal and switch off sympathetic (activating) cardiac acceleration and switch on parasympathetic (slowing down) cardiac deceleration, . . . acts as a cortical system which regulates autonomic responses to affective (emotional) cues." Allan Schore, *Affect Regulation and the Origin of the Self: The Neurobiology of Emotional Development* (New Jersey: Lawrence E. Erlbaum and Associates, 1994), p. 225.

8. Abraham Towbin, "Organic Causes of Minimal Brain Dysfunction," *Journal of the American Medical Association* 217, no. 9 (30 August 1971): 1213.

9. Hugo Lagercrantz and Theodore Slotkin, "The Stress of Being Born," *Scientific American* 254, no. 4 (April 1986): 100.

10. We have had a four-year-old reliving being abandoned by her mother at age two.

11. Lagercrantz and Slotkin, "The Stress of Being Born," pp. 100–107.

12. Hanns C. Haesslein and Kenneth R. Niswander, "Fetal Distress in Term Pregnancies," *American Journal of Obstetrics and Gynecology* 137 (1980): 245–51.

13. It helps to imbricate the biological evidence with those statistical and neurologic findings. One way we know this is by looking at the brains of our patients who are very busy repressing pain. When the pain is removed in our therapy, the brain is far less busy, with slower frequency and lower amplitude (see my book *Why You Get Sick and How You Get Well* for a discussion of brainwave results).

14. A. Barbazanges et al., "Maternal Glucocorticosteroid Secretion Mediates Long-Term Effects of Prenatal Stress," p. 3943.

11

WOMBLIFE
Prelude to Real Life

The most important stage of child-rearing occurs during the nine months of pregnancy. The events during that time seem to have permanent effects because they are imprinted into a naive and vulnerable nervous system.[1] We have research through autopsies on psychotics, but it would seem that all manner of deviated behavior and symptoms can be traced first to prenatal events. I will spend some time on the lifelong effects of the birth trauma, something I have written about for the last thirty years. The current psychological literature is mostly about the new "ego-psychology." Having abandoned delving into childhood events because it yielded so little, the analysts turned their attention to the here-and-now. It is mostly about taking presenting symptoms and treating it separately as THE problem. Last night there was a television news program about a new approach called "Exposure Therapy." The obsessives, for example, who really believe that every bump they go over in their car is a dead body, were treated by exposing them to bags of dirt and having them drive over them while being reassured by the therapist copilot that there was nothing to be afraid of. There *is* something to be afraid of, only it is not evident. It came from an experience at six months compounded by many other later experiences. If we neglect history this is the kind of nonsense we are forced to adopt and call it "therapy." When my uncle's kids fell off a horse, he made them climb back on, saying, "See, there is nothing to be afraid of." The reason this kind of "therapy" is tolerated and given sway is that it doesn't require much probing. It is quick and to the point and something a parent might understand and do without calling it "Exposure Therapy." I point out elsewhere that the reason the depth psychologists abandoned probing childhood was that it yielded so little. It wasn't the probing, however. It was the fact that it was "talking about or even crying about" instead of reliving. It did not take neurology and evolution into account. It did not emphasize or even acknowledge the imprint. It did not see that early events were coded and stored in the brain and needed to connect with frontal integrating mechanisms. Ignoring all that means doing what the patient is forced to do once she is repressed—focus on the present; believing that the problem is outside instead of inside. So, "My husband doesn't give me room to breathe" is taken at face value instead of understanding that it may have roots in anoxia at birth. It is true that the husband may not give her room to breathe but her wanting a divorce may be due to an inexorable force from within. Besides, who could dream that this statement by a forty-year-old could harken back to birth or to a smoking mother when the fetus was at minus three months? Without the proper tools to explore all this it is understandable that these facts are ignored. It is no different from trying to understand what is at the bottom of the sea without the submarine explorer. We now have the "explorer."

Love begins in the nine months of womblife. Following a healthy diet, abstaining from cigarettes or alcohol, and living a calm, steady life are the first steps to positive fetal development. *It is not just fetal development; the stage is being set for the rest of our lives.*

To find out what happened to us in the womb and at birth, we need to learn the language of the brainstem, where these prebirth and birth records are kept. Figuratively speaking, we have to be a salamander again. As we observe patients reliving very early events with an ancient brain system we are witness to the evolution of our own brain over the decades.

Key nerve tracts that carry pain signals from the spinal cord to the lower centers of the brain are laid down in the nervous system between the second and fourth months of gestation. This takes place before the development of the inhibitory neurotransmitter tracts such as the endorphin network, which becomes operational around the fourth month.[2] K. S. Anand has been studying pain and fetal life for some time. He reports: "Nerve tracts carrying pain signals from the spinal cord to the lower centers of the brain are almost fully developed by 35 to 37 weeks."

Jean Lauder, who has investigated the development of nerve cells and their axoms, writes, "Neurotransmitters may be released from the tips of growing axons and sculpt the morphology of neighboring axons and target cells."[3] She states that during development, neurotransmitters can be considered morphogenetic (structural) signals, a function of their evolutionary history. They say, "Change structure or die." A change in structure helps regulate the transmitter. What is clear here is that the message traveling along nerve pathways can alter the structure of the connecting axons of the neurons. It is one more way that the brain structure is altered with the influx of pain. The structure of the neuron and its tentacles must change to accommodate that message of pain. The change in structure is one more way that the pain is regulated and controlled. Therefore, change is life saving and in some way maintains the overall integrity of the brain. This is the meaning of "dislocation of function."

A study by two Finnish scientists, M. Huttunen and P. Niskanen, investigated children whose fathers died either while the mothers were pregnant or during the first year of the child's life.[4] The offspring were examined over a thirty-five-year period using documentary evidence. Only those who lost their fathers while in the womb were at increased risk of mental diseases, alcoholism, or criminality. Clearly, the emotional state of the carrying mother was affected and that had lifelong, deleterious effects on the child. The results of this study suggest that the emotional state of the pregnant mother has more long-term effects on the child than the emotional state of the mother during the year following birth.

Jean Lauder points out that whatever increases neurotransmitter levels significantly, as those associated with chronic stress, would be expected to have an important impact on later brain development.[5] What happens to us in the womb is absolutely crucial to neurotransmitter production. It determines how much we will suffer emotionally later in life. If a pregnant woman is abandoned by her partner or husband in the first few months of pregnancy and suffers anxiety or depression, this can be transmitted to the fetus through hormone changes.

Hormone changes in the mother affect neurotransmitter development in the fetus and according to Huttunen and Niskanen, "define the organization of brain pathways."[6] They state that "alterations in maternal, fetal and neonatal biochemistry during critical periods (of development) may irreparably alter the circuitry and thus postnatal behavior of young animals."[7]

This is critical because it is a barometer of the child's and the adult's effectiveness at shutting down pain and dealing with obstacles and adversity. It means that a weakened repressive system cannot shut out all the impinging impulses from below that surge upward to the cortex, and the failure can mean poor sleep with the inability to focus and concentrate . . . as well as attention deficit disorder. We cannot concentrate when all sorts of old memories are surging upward, fragmenting the frontal processes. Study after study demonstrates that "neonatal handling produces physiological and behavioral changes that persist into adulthood." In animals, handling is one way the animal feels love. In a number of studies, handled rats could withstand later stress better than those that were not handled.[8]

TO BE TOUCHED IS TO BE LOVED

We can extrapolate from these studies that caressing newborn children not only produces the kind of transmitters and receptors necessary to handle later adversity, but also remains with youngsters as a positive imprint. With early trauma and lack of love the brain system is constantly in a deficit mode of its serotonin supplies. It is no wonder that later tranquilizers will be necessary to boost those supplies artificially. The brain needs to normalize, so it is not surprising that after taking Prozac a person may feel "normal" for the first time.

The authors of the cited study indicate: "Other brain structures, particularly the . . . neocortex, seat of rational thought, have yet to become fully developed. . . . [They] lay down a set of emotional lessons based on the attunement and upsets in the contacts between infant and caretakers," which become "wordless blueprints for emotional life."[9] The "emotional lessons" that are taught are lifelong.

The lack of attunement of moods between mother and infant counts as lack of love and affects brain development. The child is joyful for a moment and the mother doesn't react accordingly. The child is sad and the mother (remember, "caregiver") is alienated and indifferent. The child cries for comfort and the mother is irritated and angry. At the age of three the child has nowhere to go to express her feelings and needs. It is not that the mother denies the child's needs directly; she simply isn't there emotionally to support the baby. I am not discussing momentary moods on the part of a parent. It is the chronic day-in day-out behavior that is critical.

When a mother is under stress during pregnancy, there is an increase in the steroidal stress hormones (glucocorticoids). This in turn decreases the number of receptors in the hippocampus. Suffice to say, stress is not conducive to feeling. Research such as that of Barbazanges indicates that prolonged steroid output is one of the major causes of brain defects in offspring and can adversely affect the later output of stress hormones in the baby.[10] Mental retardation or sleep disturbance can be the result. Based on animal research, this in-utero alteration can leave the individual far less able to handle anxiety and stress. A down-regulated hippocampus is likely to cause memory deficiencies. Are your childhood memories sketchy or nonexistent? Do you have trouble remembering where you put your glasses, or remembering a phone call, or have difficulty with spatial concepts? More important, are you easily overwhelmed by events, tend toward hysterical outbursts or complete emotional withdrawal? Are you afraid of life? Of change? Look to what happened while you were in the womb. When prolonged early stress hormone release compromises the hippocampus, all of the above may result.

MENTAL ILLNESS IN THE WOMB

It would seem that the origins of some severe mental illnesses are in the womb due to dislocated limbic development. Alzheimer's disease, for example, in the elderly, begins in the hippocampus and spreads to corresponding frontal cortical cells. A study of psychotics found that the cause of severe mental disturbance may lie in the second trimester of pregnancy.

In one autopsy study of schizophrenics, disarrayed neurons were found in the limbic system. The neurons were radically imbalanced. There may have been a mental imbalance later on precisely because there was a severe neurologic dislocation in the womb. To put it another way, traumatic events early in pregnancy may disrupt the development and proper order of limbic cells. Eventually, this will warp the psychological development of the individual who cannot function normally with a limbic system in disarray. In psychotics some of the limbic cells are actually upside down. So not only is a fetus affected by a trauma in the first few months of gestation, but that trauma disorganizes the limbic system neurologically.

There is some preliminary evidence that the fingerprint ridges change with different events in the womb. This was found with homosexuals and in a study of babies eight weeks after birth.[11] Fingerprint ridges begin to form after the second month of gestation. Here is what Peter Nathanielsz, who writes on womblife, has to say about this: "If at the critical period of development around the tenth week of life (in the womb), the finger pad swells for any reason (trauma), the ridges are drawn out into a circular design (whorls) and when the tip is slim and flat, the ridges are more like arches."[12] We don't know all the reasons that the finger pad swells but when taken together with other information (cited in chapter 18) it offers additional evidence for womb events and later homosexuality. Because I do reverse it from time to time I do not think it is predetermined genetically. More likely, womb events, the same events that may make different fingerprint ridges, may also alter sex hormones, leaving a vulnerability. Thus, when there is a certain family configuration, an absent mother for a small girl, plus this vulnerability, there may be homosexual tendencies—a need to be loved by a woman. It is logical to believe that trauma in the womb is not confined to finger pads but also encompasses hormone systems. We do know that high-stress hormones in the carrying mother can alter the sex-hormone balance of the fetus. Later on, I am going to discuss in detail how heart disease in later life can be related to the birth trauma and life in the womb, how strokes at fifty can be the logical denouement of events at six months of gestation. We will see how the size of the placenta when you were born may determine how long you live, and how the psychologic attitudes of the carrying mother can determine whether the baby will have serious disease later on. Nathanielsz points out that a very large placenta has been correlated with high blood pressure later in life.

The word "dislocation" is one I often use. In the case of schizo-phrenia the dislocation took on literal form in the brain cells as I noted hippocampal cells were often found upside down.[13]

It has been found that high levels of stress hormones in the blood of baby animals inhibits the development of new adult brain cells in the hippocampus.[14] We can postulate from this that the same process may be observed inside the womb when the fetus's stress hormone level is high. It does not develop the hippocampal cells properly, which deficit may result later in poor memory, poor repression, and difficulty in new learning. In brief, if the system is overexcited very early on in gestation it never can smoothly develop limbic structures dealing with feelings later on. This is how a very anxious mother can produce a very anxious baby, one who cannot properly inhibit or repress. We attribute this to genetics when in fact it may be due to events in the biochemical rapport between mother and baby. The way a fetus and mother "get along" is in matching biochemistry.

It has been noted that the small size of the abdomen of the baby at birth is highly correlated with high levels of cholesterol later in life.[15] Here is how Peter Nathanielsz explains it: "Babies who develop in a sub-optimal environment in the uterus develop clever tricks to protect the development of their brain. If the placenta is not functioning properly or if the mother is poorly nourished, it is likely that the availability of oxygen and essential nutrients in the baby's blood will be less than optimal. In this event, the baby preferentially sends blood to the brain, cutting down the amount of blood going to the gut and liver."[16] The result of all this is a normal head size and reduced abdomen as the system tries to protect the essential—its brain.

At the risk of repetition, I must point out that this is not a onetime affair; it is an enduring, lifelong consequence, both in the physical sphere and in the emotional-mental domain. Correlative studies have found that, with low birth weight the risk of heart attack later in life is much greater. Yes, childhood does count but the vulnerabilities are established long before we settle here on earth. It is not simply low birth weight;

rather low birth weight may be an indicator of trauma that will ultimately affect the cardiac system.

It seems that wherever we look we find lifelong effects of prenatal
and perinatal trauma in behavior disorders.[17] It is obvious by now that
womblife profoundly affects later adult life and in a host of ways. Childhood cancer researchers Gold and Gordis suggest that the chain of
events leading to cancer can start in fetal life.[18] This is my clinical observation, as well. Deformation of cells leading to cancer later on may well
take place in the womb and not become evident until age fifty. That is
why understanding origins of catastrophic illness is sometimes not so easy
to do, but is terribly important if we are trying to prevent this disease.

In a Danish study, three thousand women were asked whether they
had been under stress while pregnant.[19] Seventy women reported some
stress and had a weak social support group. Their children, on average,
were born with a smaller head circumference, a specific effect on brain
development. (Smaller head size has been correlated to later mental illness.) They also had a lower birth weight.

Recent studies indicate that birth trauma is a major factor in later
suicide attempts in adulthood. Lee Salk has studied birth and suicide
extensively. His work at Cornell University Medical School and the
work of researchers at Karolinska Medical Center in Stockholm,
Sweden, verifies the effects of birth trauma on suicide.[20] A trauma at
birth, registered deep in the nervous system and brainstem, continues to
influence our behavior until it drives us to suicide decades later. In this
way the imprint directs behavior until it becomes antisurvival.

How does a birth trauma make us want to kill ourselves later in life?
It is the sensations that are imprinted. When no amount of effort will
help the fetus get born, when anesthesia to the mother enters his system
and shuts down all effort, what is stamped-in is the physiology of defeat
and despair. This later becomes elaborated when the child is up against
insuperable odds, where the parents are strict, implacable, and
unyielding. Despair is compounded. Later on when his mate leaves and
refuses to come back, he is filled with despair and the feeling that
nothing he can do will change anything. It is then that he becomes suicidal. He is hopeless as he was at birth and cannot see alternatives
because in the original trauma there were no alternatives. It is part of the

imprint. This is the meaning of suicidal depression when hopelessness and despair are lined up on all three levels of brain function: frontal cortex, limbic, and brainstem. When one of my patients was not allowed by her husband to go out with her girlfriends she tried suicide. It didn't seem like such a drastic event, but in therapy she learned that her tyrannical, controlling mother and her difficulty in "getting out" at birth conspired to anchor in a deep depression. She felt that she "couldn't make a move"—a statement that was expressed on all three levels.

The physiology of approaching death is stamped in and later "death as a solution to agony" is the imprint. Suicide (death) comes immediately to mind of the person who is having difficulties because in the prototypical situation death lurked as an immediate option. The feeling, "You have to die" has become transposed from the imprint, "You are going to die." Thus again, the current situation, confronting an employee, becomes anxiety producing because the hippocampus, under stress, harkens back to the original trauma with its original consequences . . . death lurks. Without that primal foundation the reaction might be of slight apprehension about a confrontation.

In the Salk study, one of the major traumas contributing to later suicide attempts was respiratory problems at birth. Sixty percent of the subjects in the study had three major risk factors: lack of prenatal care for the first twenty weeks of pregnancy, respiratory distress at birth, and chronic disease in the parent. We can be sure that one central culprit was anoxia.

SUICIDE AND BIRTH

In a study by L. P. Lipsitt of the Child Study Center at Brown University, a dramatic relationship was found between suicidal tendencies and problem births. It is nearly always the parasympathetic, down-regulated imprint that is the culprit. The system is literally "down," no energy; everything seems too much and the odds are so overwhelming that one falls into the "resigned" mode. As we shall see, it is the "down" imprint at birth and before that lays the groundwork for later depression because all those feelings I just mentioned are part of the original imprint. A drinking or drugging mother overwhelms the adaptive capacities of the fetus. A mother heavily tranquilized or anesthetized leaves the baby "feeling" overwhelmed, literally unable to struggle to save its life, so that later it is finally articulated as, "What's the use?"

For mothers who had two or more birth problems, the risk of later suicide for the offspring was five times greater. The key meaning of the Lipsitt study is that trauma, once imprinted, follows us throughout life and can affect us enough to deny our lives.

It may seem that what I am saying is that we are all helpless victims of the early imprints. Is there nothing we can do about it? The whole point of this book is to point out what we can do about it. The truth is that at least knowing what our imprints are can help us combat them in some measure. We cannot eradicate them by any act of will but we can try to control them and change our behavior. I wish I could say it differently, but the imprint is all-powerful. If one is resigned and despairing all of one's life since birth, including childhood, no simple decision to cheer up is going to change that. We cannot "get over it." We cannot get over our physiology nor our brain circuits. The frontal area of the cortex where decisions are made is not designed to be stronger than our survival mechanisms lower in the brain. Is it hopeless? No. There is something each of us can do about it if we want to. If we choose to live as we are then so be it. It is all a matter of choice. What I am doing is offering choice. We don't have to be victims of our childhood.

In the meantime, we can stay off drugs or chocolate cake. We can take painkillers and blood pressure medication. But all of this is palliative, not curative. The state of psychotherapy today is palliative. It needs to be changed.

Recent research by A. R. Hollenbeck, another specialist in fetal life, documents how any drug given to a carrying mother will alter the neurotransmitter systems of the offspring, especially during the critical period when these neurotransmitter systems are forming in the womb.[21] He states that administration of local anesthetics, such as lidocaine (to aid the birth process), during sensitive (critical) periods in gestation is capable of producing enduring changes in the offspring's behavior.[22] Brain chemicals such as serotonin and dopamine can be changed permanently when an animal undergoes birth even with a local anesthetic. This again affects the gating system.

In another study, Hollenbeck found that pregnant women who were exposed to an anesthetic, as opposed to those women who were not, had babies who weighed less. This low birth weight may be indicative of alterations in the baby's physiology which in turn can affect later behavior.[23] Most evidence points to the fact that local anesthetics cross the placental barrier and affect the newborn. They are more sluggish than nondrugged babies and do not root for the nipple as readily. It can be the beginning of a generally passive personality. Neurosis begins somewhere.

When the uterine environment in animals is altered by introducing cocaine, neurotransmitter production is altered in the newborn and affects the brain in a long-lasting manner. Levitt, Reinoso, and Jones, who have studied development of brain cells in fetal life, indicate: "The cellular milieu of the developing nervous system prenatally thus serves functions as critical as environmental stimuli postnatally that promote synaptic development and refinement."[24] The chemical environment during gestation is just as important as the social environment after birth, indeed, more so.

The work of other scientists investigating fetal life, J. M. Cermak et al., showed the same result.[25] Long-lasting changes in the repressive-inhibitory system are brought about when the uterine environment is changed by even a single nutrient. In this case, the nutrient was choline, which permanently enhanced memory retention in the offspring. Choline is an essential element in the signaling process within cells. It is essential to brain development and aids in the inhibitory process of cells.

Research in Sweden found that when a delivering mother was given opiates or barbiturates at birth there was a much greater chance of later amphetamine addiction in the offspring.[26] What many of the new studies of addiction neglect, however, is the nature of the birth, whether it imprints a phlegmatic, passive personality who later may need speed, or a more aggressive, excitable person who will later need downers.[27] The kind of birth dictates to a large extent whether there will be a cocaine addiction versus a painkilling one. Whether, in short, the biologic need is to soup up the dopamine system or aid the inhibitory-serotonin system. Down-regulation before and during birth through the use of tranquilizers can dictate a cola or coffee addiction later in life. The body goes on compensating for the intrusion of drugs in the womb for the rest of our lives. It is as if we are constantly trying to reset the deviated setpoints.

Sleeping pill or quaalude addiction may act directly on an overactive reticular activating system. That reaction depends on whether the prototypic personality is hyper (sympath) or hypo (parasympath). In brief, the early ingestion of drugs by the carrying mother may sway personality into certain grooves. Constant use of tranquilizers by the mother could well lead to "speed" addiction later on of the offspring. In this case the setpoints for adequate activation are set low in the womb so that later the person needs some kind of stimulant. That is why one can drink three Cokes before bedtime and sleep like a log.

I have discussed some of the relevant research regarding womblife, and how some of our biological setpoints are fixed during the time in the womb. A certain lifelessness may be the result of heavy tranquilizers taken by the carrying mother which find their way into the fetal system. A hyperactive mother may imprint that state into her baby so that later, after birth and in adolescence, the child will need downers to feel "normal" or relaxed. I shall now continue with this discussion regarding diminished oxygen during birth, something that is often the result of heavy anesthesia given to the birth mother. If there were a universal unconscious it would be the hypoxia and anoxia we often suffer during birth. It is behind so much smoking and drinking. My anoxic patients are nearly always the ones who smoke heavily. It is a life-and-death experience when the baby is first coming into the world; an organism with a naïve brain and a great vulnerability. It is engraved into the system with an incredible force. We have only to observe the reliving (often filmed) when the patient turns red, struggles for breath, and seems to be dying. This is not a theory I concocted; it is an observable fact, day in and day out. No one could possibly suggest such an event.

WOMBLIFE AND LATER ILLNESS

Prenatal life can determine the rest of one's life in the most profound of ways. Deviation of the hypothalamic-pituitary-adrenal axis (HPA) can suppress immune system function and cause immune deficiencies later on. According to M. Weinstock, who has studied the HPA circuit, "Prenatally stressed human infants show the following long-term problems:

Attentional deficits, hyperanxiety, disturbed social behavior, impaired coping in stressful situations, and a general dysregulation of the hypo-thalamic-pituitary-adrenal axis."[28]

I want to reiterate the importance of the critical period, usually the period where the brain and its synapses are developing rapidly. If we drink coffee for a few days all we might feel is "hyper." But if a carrying mother drinks 4 to 5 cups a day over several days during the critical period of synaptogenesis in the fetus, the possibility is there for an imprint which will change the setpoints of the baby for a lifetime. The agitation is impressed into the fetal system and endures. It is why I believe that a child with a subterranean stream of terror due to the birth process and its anoxia can be subject to sudden infant death syndrome. The fear of being alone in the dark at six months combined with the archive of terror, lodged in the brainstem locus ceruleus, may be too much for its young heart. The babies can die of a heart attack or stroke because they cannot take that much terror.

Very low birth weight is highly correlated with later heart disease.[29] David Leon, of the London School of Hygiene, has found that being born skinny heightens the possibility of diabetes in later age. It may be that in the womb the insulin and glucose setpoints were altered by trauma. The simple fact of a vain mother starving herself while pregnant to keep her figure can be exceptionally harmful for the fetus. Perhaps all this infor-mation is, as they say in France, "drowning the fish." I am only focusing on what has been so neglected. Need starts in the womb. The techniques now exist to allow us to probe to those depths.

It is possible that pain laid down in the first months of gestation can produce an underlying dysregulation that appears in infancy and child-hood in the form of somatic ailments (asthma, allergies) or psychological traits (sullenness, aggressiveness, constant crying, fidgeting, hyperac-tivity). The newborn baby can be in pain whether he feels it or not, whether he is aware of it or not, or whether he has words for it or not.

As I write this I realize how hopeless it may seem to some readers. Is everyone neurotic? I don't think so, but it is true that many of us are com-pletely unaware of what is going on in our unconscious. Is it important to know? Not if you are happy with your life as it is. It is important from an objective standpoint because of the vulnerability of the system to premature illness and death. It is important to know if you are hampered by the need for drugs and painkillers. Or if you have compulsions that are out of control, or have symptoms that will not go away. No birth is absolutely perfect, nor is every prebirth life ideal. But I am emphasizing that which has been neglected. It is not a matter of being a perfect parent. It is a matter of knowing what the consequences are of not touching and holding one's child. A mother who was chronically depressed while pregnant may now understand some of depression's effect on the child. The child's behavior and symptoms won't be such a mystery. I am proposing signposts, marking where one should detour. It is my experience if the parent is a loving soul, even with making many errors with the child, yelling at him when he misbehaves, for example, the child has a good chance at life. If we go on thinking that gestation has only a negligible effect on the infant we may think it is fine to smoke and drink when pregnant. Also, for those physicians and therapists who are faced with strange symptoms on the part of their patients they may have a handle on the causes.

The seeds of heart dysfunction, palpitations, irregular heartbeat, atherosclerosis, high blood pressure, cancer, autoimmune disorders, depression, phobias, panic, and anxiety disorders may be sown before we are ever able to say one word. Chronically high cortisol levels have been found to bring about atherosclerosis in adult life. Indeed, it is most likely that the pains we store without words are the ones to cause the most damage later on. Catastrophic pain mediates catastrophic disease later on. It is counterproductive to try to get a patient to discuss a past feeling that has no words. It simply drives the feeling further away.

PUSHING THE ENVELOPE

We must push the envelope back to womblife if we are to understand and treat all manner of later disorders. Just when some of us caught on that birth trauma affected us for a lifetime, now we must consider prebirth events as even more important in shaping our lives. We "don't get over it, nor do we grow out of it."

In animal experiments with fetuses in the last week or two before birth, a stressed mother adversely affected the serotonin output of the off-spring. The long-lasting effects of early stress to later development has been documented by David Peters of the University of Ottawa, Canada, with Ross Ader, S. M. Barlow, and R. Chapman.[30] Peters found that stress impaired the later development of key inhibitory neurons and interfered with synaptic connections. He writes: "Studies have shown that adult behavior in rodents can be significantly influenced by prenatal events."[31] What much of this means is that early trauma to a mother can make changes in the offspring. These changes are first and foremost a reduction in the inhibitory neurochemicals that combat pain and anxiety. So much evidence now demonstrates that a mother who suffers late in pregnancy has an offspring who is not "combat-ready." He becomes the child who is fear-ridden, cannot shut out distractions, and therefore cannot properly do his studies.

Inhibition/repression begins in the womb; it is only at a few weeks (approximately twelve) after conception that we find the beginnings of the production of inhibitory neurohormones. How could we ever gain access to those early memories? We can ride the vehicle first of feelings and then of the sensations below those feelings to their terminus in the brainstem. How do we know when we have arrived there? Right now we don't because the sensations may be vague, most likely amorphous, and have no concepts or scenes attached to them. But we can know empiri-cally by clinical observation.

ON BEING OVERWHELMED IN THE WOMB

A carrying mother full of anguish over her husband's loss of a job may be hyperagitated. She drinks three cups of coffee a day, smokes furiously, and is generally nervous. She is overstimulating the fetus, whose environ-ment is now an agitated one. To reiterate, when that fetus becomes an adult, he or she may feel overwhelmed under even the slightest pressure. Just getting dressed for an evening party may cause him or her to change clothes over and over, trying to decide what to wear.

He: Can you please stop trying on dresses and pack your suitcase so we can get out of here?

She: Stop pressuring me. It makes me want to give up and stay home.
He: It's not pressure. The plane leaves in one hour.
She: (cries) I can't do it! It's all too much for me. Just let me stay home.
He: Hell no! Go see your shrink.
The Therapist: There is nothing so overwhelming about getting dressed. Let's go over it step by step. (Well . . . getting dressed for a party may be simply a trigger for the old intrauterine trauma hidden in the unconscious. To call it an overreaction or even neurotic is to miss the point.)
She: He doesn't understand. I feel so overwhelmed by everything. I'm so tired of it all.
He: (to his doctor) She doesn't understand. She won't do anything unless I press her. And she won't do anything if I do because she then feels pressured.
The Doctor: Let's look at it this way. Maybe you can be a little more patient.

They are both talking in the present about a problem from the past. The cortex is trying to have a dialogue with the brainstem but it doesn't speak English, or any language, for that matter. It is only later in life that she is able to label this sensation-feeling as something specific in her history: being overwhelmed by too much input. This is no different physiologically from being pressured by too many demands in childhood. In the first case the input is neurophysiologic; in the second, it is social input from the parents. The social, emotional input is built on the neurophysiologic experience of birth and before, producing a much heavier feeling. The sensation of being overwhelmed by input in the womb is the substrate of her anguish. As an adult she can put a name to it, it can be diagnosed, but it has a reality even without a name. Getting dressed is but the focus of her feeling, not the central problem. She carries around "overwhelmed" with her every day of her life.

In a self-fulfilling prophecy, this woman starts to tackle a problem and then wants to give up right away. The feeling of defeat has happened when her mother received massive anesthesia at birth (which entered the fetus). She had to give up. There was no choice. The past in the present makes her feel the same way now. This feeling was then compounded when her parents overloaded her with chores, homework, and a barrage of demands. How do we treat it? We start in the present discussing the suitcase and the dresses. We eventually go back (not in one session) to how she felt when her mother made constant demands, and then weeks or months later she will drop into a birth cycle. The difficult part is the timing. When is she ready to go deeper? We look for the clues and let her body decide.

CHRONIC FATIGUE IN THE WOMB

Sometimes the patient comes in exhausted. The battle is all too much. One woman had been diagnosed with chronic fatigue syndrome. She relived the real battle that had been too much for her at birth, and much of her fatigue went away. She was constantly fighting against over-whelming odds in her brain. Perhaps I make it sound like a patient comes in, has a feeling, and leaves cured. Not so. Reliving the original battle in her case took many months.

One patient of mine had a feeling of "Daddy, let up on me. Give me time, please!" She was overwhelmed by her tense, impatient, and demanding father. After she felt this feeling for one hour, she slipped into the pure, wordless sensation of being anesthetized at birth. After connecting the feeling, it was put into the past where it belonged. To get her to *talk* about her feelings was exactly what we did not want to do, for that would surely lead her away from the early wordless memory; but words are often the way in. The therapist would be engaged on a cortical level when the sensation is down deep in the patient's brain. It would be a dialogue attempting to bridge millions of years of evolution.

One of the signs of early preverbal material coming to the fore is the nightmare; the limbic system absorbing the energy and terror from the brainstem, adding its share of images to the mix to produce a really scary dream . . . being crushed or suffocated by a dark stranger, for example. Still later on that very same force moves to the frontal cortex where ideas are twisted to accommodate the imprint. "Everything seems so confusing, so upside down." Confusion is often the response when immersed in deep, remote events because there was very little frontal cortex operating at the time to clarify matters. Confusion can become prototypic—in the face of complicated instructions, as for example, finding a strange street, or repeating a phone number, the cortical mind blanks out and confusion reigns. If the patient goes back and relives events at one year of age, before there were sentences, then there will surely be no sentences in the reliving. The brain is inexorable in its wisdom.

NOTES

1. E. G. Jones, "Scientists Link Faulty Distribution of Certain Brain Cells to Schizophrenia," *Los Angeles Times*, 16 May 1996, p. B2.

2. K. S. Anand, "Growing Sensitive to Infant Pain," *Insight* (8 February 1988): 52–53 referring to K. S. Anand.

3. J. M. Lauder, "Neurotransmitters as Morphogens," *Progress in Brain Research* (Amsterdam, Netherlands) 73 (1988): 365–88.

4. M. Huttunen and P. Niskanen, "Prenatal Loss of Father and Psychiatric Disorders," *Archives of General Psychiatry* 35 (1978): 429–31.

5. Lauder, "Neurotransmitters as Morphogens."

6. Ibid., p. 171.

7. Ibid.

8. J. W. Smythe et al., "The Interaction between Prenatal Stress and Neonatal Handling on Nociception Response Latencies in Male and Female Rats," *Physiology and Behavior* 55, no. 5 (May 1994): 971–74.

9. Ibid.

10. A. Barbazanges et al., "Maternal Glucocorticoid Secretion Mediates Long-Term Effects of Prenatal Stress," *Journal of Neuroscience* 16 (15 June 1996): 3943–49.

11. See: Peter W. Nathanielsz, *Life in the Womb* (Ithaca, N.Y.: Promethean Press, 1999), p. 14.

12. Ibid.

13. Schizophrenia is a complicated subject. It is not possible to do it justice here, except to point out a few salient points. For example, in a study of psychotics it was found that the left hemisphere was less dense than the right side. It was believed that there is a left hemisphere dysfunction in schizophrenia. See: E. Cantor-Graae et al., "Link between Pregnancy Complications and Minor

Physical Anomalies in Monozygotic Twins Discordant for Schizophrenia," *American Journal of Psychiatry* 151, no. 8 (August 1994): 1188–93.

14. G. Kempermann and F. H. Gage, "New Nerve Cells for the Adult Brain," *Scientific American* 280, no. 5 (May 1999): 52.

15. Please see all of David Barker's research and writings, including *Mothers, Babies and Health in Later Life* (Churchill Livingstone, 1998).

16. Nathanielsz, *Life in the Womb*, pp. 11–12.

17. I refer to a very large study by B. Pasamanick in regard to behavior disorders (see B. Pasamanick, "A Child Is Being Beaten," *American Journal of Orthopsychiatry* 41, no. 4 [July 1971]: 540–56; idem, "Letter: Maternal Nutrition and Low Birth Weight," *Lancet* 2, no. 7937 [11 October 1975]: 704–705; idem, "Letter: Ill-Health and Child Abuse," *Lancet* 2, no. 7934 [20 September 1975]: 550), in cancer (see "Brain Tumors Among Those Children of Mothers Who Took Barbiturates during Pregnancy," the work of E. Gold and L. Gordis), lymphoma, and diabetes. G. T. Livezey et al., "Prenatal Diazepam: Chronic Anxiety and Deficits in Brain Receptors in One-Year-Old Rats," *Brain Research* 334 (1985): 361–67.

18. E. Gold and L. Gordis, "Increased Risk of Brain Tumors in Children Exposed to Barbituates," *Journal of the National Cancer Institute* 61 (1978): 1031–34.

19. H. C. Lou et al., "Prenatal Stressors of Human Life Affect Fetal Brain Development," *Developmental Medicine and Child Neurology* 36, no. 9 (September 1994): 826–32.

20. Lee Salk, as reported in the *Lancet*, 16 March 1985.

21. A. R. Hollenbeck et al., "Anesthesia Exposure to Unborn Suggests Future Health Problems," *Science* 16, no. 2 (1985): 126–34.

22. Ibid.

23. Ibid.

24. P. Levitt, B. Reinoso, and L. Jones, "The Critical Impact of Early Cellular Environment on Neuronal Development," *Preventive Medicine* 27, no. 2 (March–April 1998): 180–83.

25. J. M. Cermak et al., "Prenatal Availability of Choline Modifies Development of the Hippocampal Cholinergic System," *Faseb Journal* 12, no. 3 (March 1998): 349–57.

26. K. Nyberg, "Opiate Addiction in Adult Offspring through Possible Imprinting after Obstetric Treatment," *Acta Obstetrica et Gynecologia Scandinavica* 301 (1990): 1067–70. Read more on the subject: B. Jacobson et al.,

"Obstetric Pain Medication and Eventual Adult Amphetamine Addiction in Offspring," *Acta Obstetrica et Gynecologia Scandinavica* 67 (1988): 677–78.

27. I discuss this in chapter 5 on sympathetic and parasympathetic nervous systems.

28. M. Weinstock, "Does Prenatal Stress Impair Coping and Regulation of the Hypothalamic-Pituitary-Adrenal Axis?" abstract, *UCLA Louise M. Darling Library Biomedical Neuroscience and Behavioral Reviews* 21, no. 1 (January 1997): 1–10.

29. See the work of David Barker, Southampton University, England, who has studied this extensively.

30. D. Peters et al., "Effects of Maternal Stress during Different Gestational Periods on the Serotonergic System in the Adult Rat Offspring," *Pharmacology, Biochemistry and Behavior* 31 (1989): 839–43.

31. A. J. Friedhoff and J. C. Miller, "Prenatal Neurotransmitter Programming of Postnatal Receptor Functions," *Progress in Brain Research* (Amsterdam, Netherlands) 73 (1988): 518.

12

THE BIRTH TRAUMA
How It Directs Our Lives

The notion of birth trauma may seem completely fanciful, whimsical, or mystical to outsiders; I also found it hard to believe at first. Years ago I told one patient that if he ever again mentioned that he relived birth, I would discharge him. I observed it in patients for two years before I came to accept it, mostly because I had discussed it with neurologists who told me such a thing was impossible.

Birth trauma is a true experience and a measurable one. Due to its heavy valence of pain, it is also the most dangerous event to undergo in untrained hands. Rebirthers beware! If one defies the evolution of brain function, and attempts to probe an ancient brain long before the person is ready, one will get out-of-sequence pains from deep in the brain that surge to the top and overwhelm the cortex to produce strange ideas and mysterious symptoms. The result for the patient is inevitably confusion.

At the other extreme lies traditional insight therapy, which rearranges the cerebral furniture, often leaving a seething caldron of agonizing feelings and sensations churning below, never to see the light of day. We may say that patients often weep openly in psychoanalysis; they certainly did when I practiced psychoanalytic therapy. But it is the cortical, adult brain "crying about," not the baby brain crying like an infant. You need that baby brain to be involved, and ultimately the fetal brain;

219

the reason—to have the *experience* of the past, not just the recall. Again, you can only heal where you are wounded. If the wound is at one year of age, that brain must participate.

If someone goes through a birth sequence and even cries like an infant it is surely a fake experience. Patients from some twenty-four countries have gone through it, yet I never heard a word from any of them; none could use their arms and legs. It is never suggested or planned. It happens when the patient is ready. The sounds of crying differ from the ten-year-old to the newborn infant. They are clearly organized in different areas of the brain. We know we have tapped into infant memories by the sound of the cry which can never be duplicated by the patient after the session. As we shall see, connection is a sine qua non, for good neurologic reasons.

IS THE UNCONSCIOUS DANGEROUS?

Unfortunately, the theoretical zeitgeist is that delving into the deep unconscious is dangerous. It is an outgrowth of nineteenth-century religious philosophy that espouses the belief that we are all inhabited by demons that must never be unleashed. There are no demons! We are inhabited by needs and pain from their lack of fulfillment. They are knowable. At the start of life the need is for oxygen.

The deeper and lower we go into the brain, the less malleable it is because we are dealing with basic survival functions. Conversely, the higher we go in the brain, the more flexible it is. That is why ideas can "go crazy" (i.e., can fabricate the most strange of notions). Our task is not to bring ideas back into the norm, but rather to normalize the overpowering feelings that are driving those ideas into paranoid channels, for example. Of course, this is what most psychiatric practitioners are doing without acknowledging it. They use tranquilizers to normalize feelings, then talk with the patient to help address the ideas. "After all," a doctor might say, "you know no one is sending messages from Europe through the TV to cut off your breasts." This was the delusion of one of my patients. She believed wholeheartedly that she was receiving such messages and would not be dissuaded from the idea. In our sessions we never addressed the idea. Instead, we dealt with her feelings. "They want to dis-figure me to make me feel ugly," she said. That delusion had as its base: "I feel unwanted. I must be ugly to be so unwanted." The message, she thought, was being sent to make her feel ugly and therefore unwanted, or unwanted and therefore ugly. This was related to how her parents had treated her.

The bottom of that delusion was a feeling of being unloved. If someone doesn't want to be with us time after time the obvious conclu-sion is that he or she doesn't like us; and so we feel unliked. If that person is the sole human being on earth whom we depend on for life, suste-nance, caring, protection, and love, then the slightest rejection is cata-strophic. We cannot develop our brains by ourselves. We need the care-giver's input. His or her love governs our brain. His or her rejection deforms our brain.

We traced the unwanted feeling in the patient just discussed to birth where she was suffocating and in danger of dying; this was interpreted, in light of her mother's later attitude, as "she didn't want me to live. Of course, years of experience of parental coldness and indifference pro-duced the full-blown feeling. The impetus and force, however, the force that stretched the frontal cortex to the limit and beyond, was birth. We don't have to guess about this. We measure the brainwaves and vital signs of patients approaching the birth trauma and find skyrocketing indices. The experience of the birth trauma is what it is, but later experiences will be interpreted differently. Its force will be funneled into what kind of trauma is undergone later on. Here it was made part of "she doesn't want me to live."

Ideas grow complicated, but feelings do not and are thus much sim-pler to treat. Take cancer researchers who smoke or doctors who drink too much. No matter what ideas the prefrontal cortex is aware of, the feelings and needs take priority. First, the person must find a way to make himself comfortable. Then he can get on with his life. The subconscious has reasons of which the cortex knows not. Because ideas are flexible and infinite, the conventional therapist is forced to enter a never-ending labyrinth of beliefs. He is then in the position of a deprogrammer, trying to dissuade a person from her ideas. All of this is unnecessary and inef-fective.

Is it necessary for individuals to delve into an agony they already have lived? Why put the patient in pain? The pain was never fully lived. The brain wouldn't let it happen. It refused to react to the lack of love, for example, so that reactivity was blocked. The event was only partially lived. Another part was kept in storage, in the dark. Here lies the key to feeling—reactivity. It is the reaction to overwhelming feeling that has been repressed. There is an internal governor that limits reactivity for two reasons: (1) to prevent the vital signs and vital functions, blood pressure and heart rate, from arching into dangerous levels, and (2) to keep the internal pressure away from the cortex so that it is not overwhelmed and fragments. We see what rebirthers liberate in their therapy and how it often drives the person crazy. Sadly, the person is often not aware of it. Rather, she believes she has had an epiphany and has reached cosmic consciousness. The hallucinogenic drug LSD also releases deep pains and diminishes the frontal cortex's ability to integrate. Again, we see the bizarre ideation that is mistaken for some kind of mystical experience.

Like many aspects of human behavior, the way in is the way out. To get out of pain, you have to go into it. Yet many current approaches, from acupuncture to massage, from dream analysis to bioenergetics, from behavior therapy and vitamin counseling to "the patch" (for smoking), try to solve symptoms without any pain.

Who doesn't want a painless way out of suffering? To do so, however, ignores biologic laws. There is no magic. We have had experiences that change our neurobiology, and we need to address those experiences if we are to normalize. Elsewhere I discuss the salivary cortisol measurements we took of our patients. There was a significant drop in those levels after several months of therapy. This means that the person is under less stress and has less tension driving her. This is one way we normalize.

Should we "let sleeping dogs lie"? We can't because on one level of the brain we're feeling it all of the time. On that level nothing is sleeping. That is why the stress hormone levels are so chronically high. Meanwhile, we visit one doctor for these symptoms: high blood pressure, allergies, hyperthyroidism, colitis, compulsive gambling, high blood pressure; and another doctor for phobias, obsessions, perversions, and alcoholism. Yet, often there is often a single pill, a tranquilizer, that can treat all of them. Pain is the common substratum in many of these cases. Of course, there are genetic tendencies, environmental issues, etc., but pain must not be neglected, particularly, imprinted pain; more particularly, the pain before we meet our parents formally. It is a relief not having migraines every three days, not having to overeat, or being controlled by sexual impulses. It is a relief not to have constant anxiety attacks, not to have to live on blood pressure medication or tranquilizers and antidepressive pills. It is replaced, in short, by an extraordinary feeling of well-being. The person finally comes alive after feeling his deadness, because he is *feeling*. Feeling is a small price to pay for that freedom. When the pains finally exit there is this wonderful feeling of being alive—"alive" because we are able to *react*. This is not some utopian idea. It is an observable fact.

Too often we feel that we are not getting anything out of life precisely because we cannot fully react. Everything inside has been dulled by repression. We look at children who are so alive and we may wonder where we lost that ability. We don't grow out of that enthusiasm, that joie de vivre. We lose it over the years as we become strangers to our feelings.

The more remote the pain the deeper the repression and the greater the liberation when it is felt. We know a patient is reexperiencing the sensations of birth trauma by the way she breathes. Her utterances have a different tone, a different energy, and a different cadence. We notice this in the birth feelings of Dierdre.

In the following case history we will note how Dierdre became immobilized by her feeling of hopelessness. She was so immobilized that she could no longer help herself, because that was the original imprint where she could not help herself and could not react. She had the old familiar feeling stemming from birth, "feeling stuck." We note her progression from crying about her problems in the present to brainstem imprint intrusion—coughing and gagging. From there she descended into a "conscious-coma," as described by many patients—"I am in the room but I'm not in the room." She cried about missing her mom and the physical need for her touch. Then she went into a state of silence and dolphinlike movements. She had trouble breathing, and felt as though she were dying. She came out of it with the insight that she did everything she could and lost hope for warmth and help. She felt the origins of being and feeling stuck and of the attitude that she couldn't help herself. She began to see how she acted-out her hopelessness through her life, being a reactor instead of an actor. There was no chance to fight at birth when death approached.

DIERDRE

What has reliving primal feelings done for you?

Why do you go through the whole process? Take just one example out of my life since I am in Primal Therapy. I have been for the last seven years a foster mother for two children and I was told to go to a trial where the judge was about to decide whether the children have to visit their biological parents or have to go back to them. I felt very bad. My mind was racing, I felt despair and hopelessness. I felt I was being forced into something I didn't want to happen. My thoughts were ending every day with the hope to finish this whole situation by committing suicide.

I went to a Primal Group. I told the therapist how hopeless and despairing I felt, and that I felt that I was totally alone in this situation and that there was no help for me. My heart was broken. I believed that I was going to lose everything I've had in my life and that I couldn't do anything about it. I felt angry, too: anger against the judge and the children's services.

Nobody could help me, I couldn't help myself anymore—I felt totally stuck, didn't know what to do, and didn't understand anymore what was going on. I yelled at everybody. How dare they even consider letting those parents who did horrible things to my foster children visit the kids or even have them back? I started to cry. I was helpless and defeated. My body felt more and more weak. I felt hopeless. I felt the fear of losing the children. I felt that everything I ever did for them and everything I ever did in my entire life was worthless. While my crying got louder and deeper, I started to cough. My crying sounded different and came more out of the depths of my guts. I felt my whole body being involved with pure pain. The coughing got stronger and I felt a need coming up, the need for being helped. I asked them, louder and louder, to help me and my voice changed. It got higher.

Then I lost the connection to the therapists and to the room where

I was in, and inside I felt very little like I was a child again and suddenly I realized that all my hope for help was focused on my mother. I wanted her to hold me, to comfort me. I followed my impulse of being held with going into the arms of my therapist: but I missed my mom and I cried very deep and sounded like a child would cry. And while I was crying I realized that my mother wasn't there, not then when I was a child and I felt huge anger coming up toward my mother combined with an immense amount of need for her. I demanded help from her to soothe my pain, but she didn't come and while I was still begging for her to be there I realized that I lost my hope that she ever would come to me. I gave up.

Memories flooded my mind about situations in my childhood, where I needed my mother, but where my need got denied, again and again. My feeling grew bigger; my entire body got involved in it. I coughed again, this time much stronger. A very strong knowledge of not being helped came up and I felt myself in total rage, which was expressed through my whole body. Combined with the rage I felt a pure need to be comforted, to have body contact and touch from my mother and I wanted her to be together with me. Painful screams came naturally out of my mouth with a power I never would have imagined. At the same time I recognized it as always being there but never being expressed. My mouth got wide open and I could not move my body at all and no sound could come out of my mouth anymore. And in silence my body started to move again but with rage. I needed to get out of this unbearable situation where I had no longer the comfort and the support which I desperately needed.

I obeyed the pressure to do something that I didn't want at that moment to do but which I needed to do in order to survive. I lost completely control of myself and for what I originally wanted (to stay further in the comfort and warmth of my mother). I felt the pressure that something was holding me back and didn't allow me to breathe anymore and I moved with an intensive force like a dolphin; knowing I had to fight against dying. My lungs were hurting, my entire body felt sore. I felt totally alone. It seemed like I was waiting for something, waiting for a long time. But nothing happened. I lost the hope for help, comfort, and warmth. And I fell back into agony because I had lost everything.

And while I still was reliving this feeling I acknowledged with relief: that this is the same powerful feeling that interferes with my reality. My feeling and my mind started to connect in this situation and I understood that it was my birth and the immediate time following it where I did everything I could do to survive. I wanted to live, but I felt that I lost everything because of this—to be together with my mother, the hope for support.

I stopped asking for help, I lived alone for the rest of my life. And I understood that I needed to go back and feel this old pain of having lost the warmth of my mother forever to understand why I couldn't reach out for what I needed. This feeling grew bigger because my mother didn't support me during my childhood in situations where I needed her help. I developed the behavior of being a totally independent person.

Those feelings have guided me my whole life in difficult situations and led me toward wrong decisions where I lost mostly everything because I was always acting out my hopelessness—that after I did everything I could to get born I didn't get what I needed and I stopped hoping for anything more. Now I am able to do something in this situation. I want to fight for what I believe is right to do. I don't just give in. I go and ask for help when I cannot do it alone. After I felt the primal feeling I didn't feel suicidal at all anymore. I felt like something inside of me gave me the strength to focus on my problems and not on old feelings from the past.

After a long time I started to talk about how much this feeling after birth is similar with the feeling I had in the present when I was informed of the trial and that I have to fear losing the children; and having to do things I don't want to do. It was so much the same. I felt suicidal because my birth was life threatening and I felt also that my need was dying, and as it died, I died with it. And while I was talking I cried again as an adult, but with relief from the knowledge that now there is help. I can ask my friends, lawyers, and some employees of the children services and I don't have to fall in agony again. Now I can do something.

I have changed very much. I have friends, and I want to keep my friendships. I look differently at what I am doing and I have started to be more satisfied then ever with me. I am in the beginning of a new relationship and can receive openly the gentleness of my partner. I have started to consider myself as important enough to want to choose what I really want to do and to give myself enough time before I make decisions in difficult situations. I don't give up easily when I don't get what I want right away, and I am open for advice from other people. I am trustfully looking forward into my future because I know that I am not in the grip of the trauma of my birth and childhood anymore. I can choose and I can trust my nature—I am an active person who can also rest. I look forward to meeting the me I am to become because I found a way to stop my past from making me what I wasn't.

13

THE STRESS FACTOR
Building a Different Brain

Adult rats that had experienced vigorous licking and grooming as pups were more exploratory and curious than to those that had not been licked and groomed.[1] They also possessed an "abundance of brain receptors for a class of anxiety-reducing, pain-killing substances called benzodiazepines."[2] There are other receptors that are involved including the neuropeptides, oxytocin and vasopressin. (Discussed fully in chapter 17 on oxytocin.) These are important in bonding behavior from parent to child and vice versa. The key point, which I shall make over and again because of its importance, is that very early touch is central to developing a healthy brain.[3] Irrespective of the neurojuices involved, it is clear that lack of love changes the chemicals in the brain and can eventually change the structure of that brain. Like the little sapling that has been warped in its childhood, the warped brain deviates thereafter.

Rats stressed prenatally showed high anxiety in postbirth behavior. If they were stressed in the womb they showed a stress syndrome after birth. These seemingly benign facts have immense implications, for they indicate that intrauterine events have a lasting effect afterward in life. But some of these effects can possibly be vitiated by events just after birth. Rats handled right after birth showed diminished output of the stress hormone corticosterone.[4] In a number of studies, the hormone glucocorticoid is implicated as important in mediating the stress syndrome. Stress in animals such as tree shrews was found to reduce serotonin receptors,[5] something that has been found in numerous animal studies. These studies reveal that the absence of a mother soon after birth leads to increases in stress hormones, with damage to some cortical cells and hippocampal sites. The news is good and bad. The earlier we experience love, the stronger our serotonin-endorphin secretion and the better we feel and behave later on. Contrarily, the lack of early love weakens the repressive system and makes us physiologically less able to handle stress later in life.

With deprivation the system remains continually under stress because there is an electrochemical sign inside that flashes "unloved" on and off. That sign gives a string of orders: secrete this chemical, stop that one, reduce this hormone, increase insulin, change the blood platelets, change the natural killer cells of the immune system.[6] These deviations are the compensating mechanisms for alien intrusion. The natural order of things is love. The lack of love is an alien force. It is unfulfilled need that sets off the alarm.

Researchers have described fetal stress syndrome. This is no different than combat stress syndrome. A baby who doesn't sleep well, is unhappy and uncomfortable, has all the signs of post-traumatic stress syndrome (PTSS). The only difference is that we cannot "see" the origin of the baby's stress as we can in combat fatigue. The baby has been in a battle all her own, trying to get born despite being strangled on the cord. She doesn't have the words yet to tell anyone about her ordeal. She can shake and have a severe startle reaction but few adults can read those cues properly. It is a battle to stay alive for the fetus who is choking and suffocating against the smoke a mother inhales. And it is not possible for the fetus to remain "sane" and in comfort when the mother is taking in alcohol which changes the brain of the fetus.

Not only are high stress levels in a carrying mother accompanied by cortisol secretion, but prolonged cortisol output also damages the baby's hippocampus, which is in charge of laying down new memory. As a result, the adult won't be able to articulate his feelings or remember very well.[7] When hopelessness sets in early, as for example, trying to get born and not being able to do anything about getting out, there are corresponding high levels of cortisol which wreak havoc and destroy brain cells.

NOTES

1. "Child Sex Abuse Leaves Mark on Brain," *Science News* 147 (3 June 1995): 340.

2. Ibid., p. 167.

3. See: C. S. Carter, "The Integrative Neurobiology of Affiliation," *Annals of the New York Academy of Sciences* 8070 (15 January 1997): xiii–xviii.

4. Monique Vallee et al., "Prenatal Stress Induces High Anxiety and Postnatal Handling Induces Low Anxiety in Adult Offspring," *Journal of Neuroscience* 17, no. 7 (1 April 1997): 2626–36.

5. G. Flugge, "Dynamics of Central Nervous 5HTIA Receptors Under Psychosocial Stress," *Journal of Neuroscience* 15, no. 11 (November 1995): 7132–40.

6. See also: T. R. Insel, "A Neurobiological Basis of Social Attachment," *American Journal of Psychiatry* 154, no. 6 (June 1997): 726–35.

7. See M. A. Smith et al., "Stress and Glucocorticoids Affect the Expression of Brain-Derived Neurotrophic Factor and Neurotrophin-3 mRNAs in the Hippocampus," *Journal of Neuroscience* 15 (1995): 1768–72.

14

THE GATE-CONTROL THEORY

Our gating system turns the feeling of great early pain into its opposite: no feeling. To understand how this happens, we must look at the work of Drs. Ronald Melzack, author of *The Puzzle of Pain*,[1] and Patrick Wall, who developed the gate-control theory of pain.

Melzack and Wall used transcutaneous electroneurostimulation (TENS) to support their theory that a gating system exists in the midbrain. They implanted an electronic device high up on the spinal cord. The patient could then push a button on a transmitter and flood the area with electrical impulses to shut off a great pain such as that of cancer. These impulses are neutral, yet they send information to the gating system to inhibit and repress pain signals. In short, overstimulation by a powerful electrical force can lead to shutdown or gating. The force need have no content. It has to have a certain impact beyond which neurons will no longer respond. This is exactly what happens to electrical input that does have an emotional content, "They don't like me." If the meaning/feeling inherent in that content is exceptionally painful, there will be an automatic shutdown. An inundation of electrical impulses stimulates the gating system into action. There is then an effective disconnection between lower-level pain and higher-level appreciation of that pain. As emotional pain grows more excruciating over the years, an

231

in-built antisuffering mechanism sees to it that we do not suffer inordinately—the gates.

When there is too much accumulated pain over time, however, the gating system crumbles and we then need outside help. The meaning of "crumbles" is that there aren't enough chemical/neurohormonal supplies to keep early trauma out of conscious-awareness. The defenses don't work. The person is then awash in fears and terror or rage, for example, so that there is inadequate concentration, focus, and mental tenacity. Electroshock therapy can help with gating and repression because the system does not produce enough serotonin (and other internally manufactured painkillers) to keep the pain down. Shock therapy, with electrical input directly to the temples and therefore to the brain, creates a massive input that stays in the system. It also produces higher levels of some of the inhibitory chemicals to keep feelings in their place. I have witnessed patients reliving their shock therapy exactly as it happened. When a

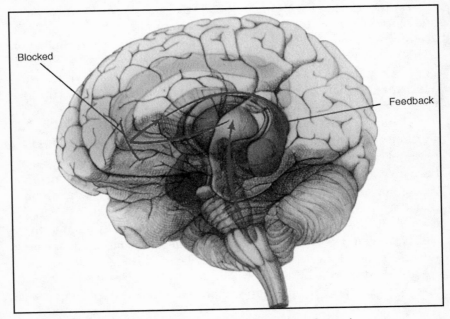

Fig. 7. Feelings are blocked on their way to the frontal cortex.

rubber tube is placed in the mouths of these patients during a session, they clamp down and grimace just as if they were receiving the shock. (We have filmed this.) What goes in must come out eventually, whether it is electrical impulses from a machine or from an emotional trauma. Shock makes the person ahistoric; someone cut off from the past. It is the same shock and memory loss whether it arrives as a result of an automobile accident or from incest inflicted on a child in the very early years.

The gate-control theory has been recently modified by Melzack. It is now about neuromodules but what I have observed in Primal Therapy still lends support to it. Patients reliving a birth sequence in my sessions have shown forceps marks on the forehead. Those marks never manifested themselves before because they had been gated away, stored as a memory. I have seen and heard the wails of a baby come from forty-year-olds reliving early trauma that cannot later be duplicated by them willfully. During a feeling, patients can maintain the fetal position for up to an hour. The tension that infuses our bodies arises because we are gating away massive amounts of primal energy. My patients call this energy "primal fuel."

Clearly, there are no little gates in the brain. Shutting down takes many forms: the secreting of serotonin-endorphins, the neurons going silent and not sending the message, and others. Whatever the form, however, there is the equivalent of a door shutting away feelings. The result is lack of access. We can no longer open the door by any willful act. But we can slip into the room where the feelings are hidden and rummage around if we have the keys to access. One of the keys is the hippocampus, which seems to scan our history and offers access to part of it.

Having a parent sent to a mental hospital, losing a sibling in an accident, being sent to a foster home or boys school at a young age, suffering incest, and other traumas all flood the brain with electrical impulses that amount to a shock. It is information overload. It can also happen just in the day-to-day sterility of a household where unphysical parents never hold or talk to their child. That information overload is cumulative. I have noted earlier that this mechanism reaches back to plant life. It is literally hundreds of millions of years old.

Information doesn't have to be in words, particularly when the trauma or lack of love occurred long before we had the capacity for words. It can be in chemicals that overload the system in exactly the same way as constant parental yakking or too much physical jostling overloads a child. It is all overstimulation. One of the chemicals involved is the stress hormone cortisol.

Morphine is an example of a higher gating action at work. A person in the throes of a heart attack will have a shot of morphine and suddenly feel comfortable. When the drug wears off, he hurts again. We produce that same morphine in our brains to render ourselves "comfortable," even though the pain and its cause still lie deep in our brain. Morpheus, the Greek god of dreams and sleep, has dulled our sensibilities and made life gray. In becoming insensitive to ourselves, we become insensitive to others. We don't see their pain; we can't empathize or feel for or with them.

Gates preserve our internal reality in pure form. They are benevolent, part of our survival mechanism. We therefore never lose reality, we only lose touch with it. The more we get in touch with those emotions the more

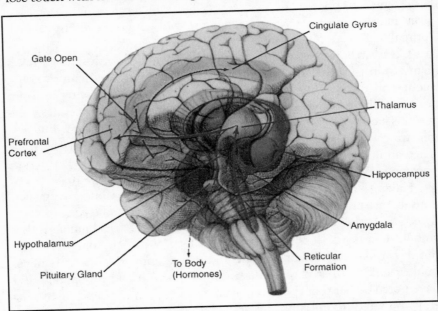

Fig. 8. A general overview of the key structures involving feeling in the brain.

sensitive and human we become, because human beings are feeling beings. To lose part of our ability to feel is to lose part of our humanity.

Each aspect of the gating system seems to have a specific tolerance. The brainstem (what I call "first-line") gate—the receptors that handle trauma—may, by way of example, have a capacity of ten. Other gates may have a capacity of five or six (that is, the neuroinhibitor density is lower in these areas). A trauma such as losing a parent at a young age may overwhelm the gate with a valence of seven or eight. The lower gating system clearly seems to be adapted to much more powerful input. Or, the accumulation of pain over time may ultimately debilitate the gating system, bringing on chronic anxiety or tension.

What we sometimes see in our patients is a fragile gating system due to compounding of pain all along childhood. This is the kind of person who cannot separate out feelings. She will come into therapy and have a feeling about childhood soon mixed with all kinds of birth trauma. Compounded pains produce a melange that prevents the person from having one single integrated feeling. What is required at this point is tranquilizers or painkillers that will push down heavy valence pain, bolster the gates against brainstem stimulation so that the person can integrate feelings which are less remote and less laden with suffering: one feeling at a time. We use drugs as a means to aid in feeling, to allow the patient to deal with lesser valence pain higher in the nervous system, and not as ends in themselves. To use drugs without a dynamic understanding of how the brain functions is to believe in magic. The belief that somehow medication can solve emotional problems—that drugs can actually cure someone of being unloved and neglected most of her childhood; that drugs can cure someone who grew up in a cold foster home or someone who had a violent drunken father—is to fall into the abyss of mysticism. Drugs aren't going to do anything but keep us *unaware* of reality. *It is not and cannot be an end in itself.*

THE FEAR OF DEATH

One patient of mine has been plagued by fears of immediate death most of his adult life. He had a terrible birth experience in which he was stuck in the birth canal. He then had neglectful parents; a mother who was psychotic (insane). As a result, he was never able to build a defense or gating system. In each of his primals the "death" feeling from birth would surge up and literally drive him bolt upright within seconds. He felt suffocated, turned red, and clutched his chest as if he were going to have a heart attack. He felt himself drowning, with thick fluid filling his lungs which spilled out onto the mat. We used small amounts of Zoloft (and sometimes clonidine) initially to bring him into the feeling zone; clonidine holds down brainstem imprint activation, while Zoloft increases serotonin levels and thereby enhances gating[2] (explained fully in the following chapter). As he experienced that feeling over and over in our sessions, the fear began to diminish. The "death" memory was right below conscious-awareness for most of his life. We have to be clear what we are pushing down with the drugs that we prescribe.

Many of those who took numerous LSD trips have come to my sessions with what I call "blown gates." Facilitated by the hallucinogen, their gating systems opened up but were never able to totally close again. One patient told me that after dropping acid he came close to a death experience at birth. Soon afterward he joined a cult. In many of these cults the first order of business is to take care of death; one reason is that the hallucinogen has liberated very early death feelings. These people are looking for ideation to restore their blown gates. In most cults death either is denied or is welcomed as it leads to a better "life." After many months of therapy the patient then can begin to feel what LSD unleashed—the near-death experience at birth. The difference now is that it can be integrated; there is an operational frontal cortex to help out.

A patient who was the victim of incest did not consciously discover that fact until she was two years into Primal Therapy. She had begun talking to herself on the street and felt she was "losing it." She also felt she was going to die. In her unconscious, feeling the feeling was tantamount to death. Remember, a traumatic feeling close to consciousness elevates the vital signs into danger zones. This woman came into therapy not knowing what was wrong. Over many months she relived aspects of the incest until one day she faced it head-on in horrific agony. Even the pieces of the memory had been gated away, so she could remember only the most innocuous aspects first: fear of the dark as a child, fear upon hearing footsteps coming down the hall. In later primals she saw a threatening shadow in the room; still later, she felt the sensation of something big and sharp between her legs. Finally, nearly a year later, Daddy!!

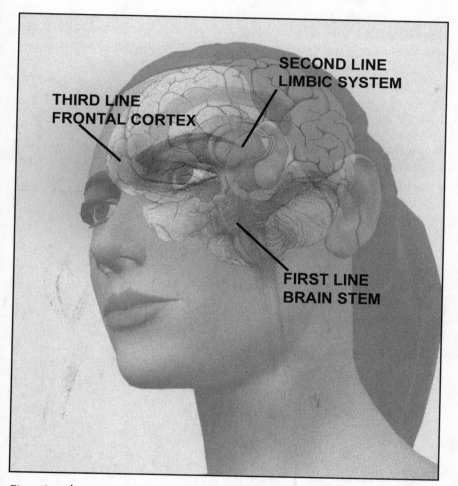

Fig. 9. The Tripartite Brain: Brainstem (First-Line), Limbic System (Second-Line), Frontal Cortex (Third-Line).

THE ROLE OF SEROTONIN IN GATING FEELINGS

For the past two decades researchers have focused on such receptors as serotonin without understanding that pain receptors proliferate or diminish in the face of trauma. We had been looking at only one side of the equation and have neglected why serotonin is being secreted or diminished. Serotonin helps keep imprinted impulses in check, except when they are too strong. There are at least fourteen different kinds of serotonin receptors. This neurotransmitter dates back some five hundred million years and is found in the most primitive of animal species.[3] Great deprivation during and just after birth damages this system and creates hyperactive, impulsive children who have trouble learning.[4]

Researchers looking into all manner of diseases find an alteration in serotonin and assume that a genetic change in serotonin levels is the "cause" of the disease. Some types of medication for migraine target sero-

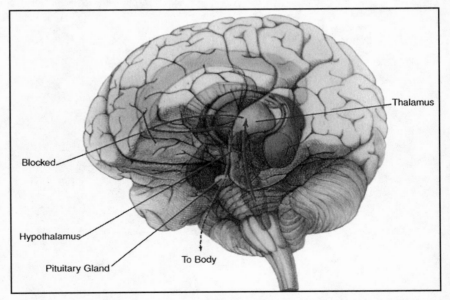

Fig. 10. Feelings are blocked and rerouted through the hypothalamus to various organ systems.

tonin receptors. But the cause is not always genetic; we have overlooked life in the womb.

Recently it was reported that bulimia may be caused by a genetic defect in L-tryptophan, the amino acid precursor to serotonin.[5] "These findings suggest that lowered brain serotonin function can trigger some of the clinical features of bulimia nervosa in individuals vulnerable to the disorder."[6] What has been left out of the equation, however, is how the imprint may permanently reduce serotonin function, and how this may lead to later symptoms. In bulimia the imprint is a pain that may need to be quelled by food. We have to be careful not to ascribe to genetics something that has its roots in our lives, albeit, very, very early lives.

Endorphins, serotonin, and gamma-aminobutyric acid (GABA) all serve ultimately as neuroinhibitors. GABA is a true inhibitor whereas serotonin has other functions including mediating comfort. In one way or another they help the cortex inhibit excitatory messages arriving from the limbic system. When any kind of pain is prolonged, GABA supplies seem to be exhausted, allowing pain to rush toward cortical consciousness. Drugs such as Gabatril take up the slack and help lock away the pain once more. As Dr. Frank Wood, my consultant, points out, "The sensations of satisfaction in life are not simply due to the suppression of unpleasantness, but also of activation of good feelings."[7] On the other hand, when my patients use tranquilizers to suppress pain, or even direct painkillers, they feel better.

Dr. Laurence Tecott of the University of California, San Francisco, investigating serotonin, disabled the receptor for the serotonin precursor in mice. The animals became fear-ridden, huddling next to the walls of a maze, too scared to explore new objects.[8] In this study, as in so many others, animals that cannot repress their fears due to defective serotonin output may represent the equivalent of humans in states of anxiety. Fear seems to cause paralysis and caution, dampens curiosity, blocks spontaneity, and in humans can lead to bulimia and/or anorexia.

One example of how animal research helps human inquiry was a study by J. Altman and G. D. Das, of the Massachusetts Institute of Technology (MIT).[9] They described how there was new neuronal development (neurogenesis) located in the hippocampus of adult rats. Later, based on this finding it was then located in the same area in humans.

Animal research can teach us about human beings. We need to study animals for clues to human behavior, and we need to study humans for clues to human behavior.[10] Something isn't true just because a research study says so, witness the conclusions about bulimia in the study above. We don't have to guess about childhood pain or the birth trauma. With the right tools we can see it and measure it in a clinical setting. After having seen several thousand reliving episodes of infancy pain I could never be persuaded that it doesn't exist.

Expressing how we feel—sad, angry, happy, ecstatic—is the most natural of things: it is important to express all of these feelings. There are also statistics to show otherwise. Statistics can be twisted to counter the most natural of human tendencies. There is a new therapy contending that you wave a wand (I'm not kidding) to the right and left in front of the patient's eyes and it can drive away anxiety. This therapy has accumulated a mountain of statistics to "prove" its case. Some noted scientists are adherents. To think that one can drive away a lifetime of neglect with a wand, a lifetime of being left alone without love, is completely mystical and mystifying for me. Yet, there are the statistics.

A study by Steven Locke examined how a group of individuals dealt with problems. The good "copers" had high levels of natural killer cells; the bad "copers" did not.[11,12] Ordinarily, the serotonin gatekeepers stop the message of hopelessness from rising too fast and too easily to frontal centers. But their troops get diminished when the battle goes on for a long period of time. The message is kept at home, so to speak, so that the "neighbors" (the nearby neurons) never find out.

I have just discussed some of the chemical messengers that impede pain information to higher centers. The effect of this is to keep pain out of awareness. That is why so many of us feel "wonderful" while we carry around an intolerable load of pain. The human brain is designed to keep us unconscious so we can get on with our lives. It wouldn't do if we were rolling around the floor in agony all of the time. This is what happens to my patients who finally have access to their unconscious. We make sure that they are in pain in the session and not afterward. We want them to structure up after the session so that they do not leave in pieces. In those mock primal therapies too often the patient abreacts and does leave in pieces. We too often get blamed for this.

Now we will see how repression is universal and reaches back to the earliest times in phylogenetic history; even fish, it seems, can repress. They have the same drug specificity as mammals so that the capacity to put down noxious stimuli has a very long history.

ORGANIZING THE NEURAL TROOPS

The history of gating and repression reaches back to microscopic pro-tozoa, and even to plant life before them. Evolution has favored the use of whatever helped us survive throughout millions of years. It is some-what surprising that we use plant derivatives such as poppies (heroin) to dampen our pain. Solomon Snyder and others have observed that there is as much opiate binding in primitive fish and sharks as there is in mon-keys and man.[13] "The opiate receptor of these primitive fishes displayed the same drug specificity as the opiate receptors of mammals, indicating that few if any changes in the chemical structure of the receptor had occurred in the course of vertebrate evolution."[14]

During the course of evolution, the brain has produced receptors for dif-ferent kinds of internally produced painkillers or opiates. Repressors or inhibitors attach themselves to these receptors to help gate or block pain and feelings. When trauma sets in very early on, unnecessary receptors are elim-inated while others are enhanced, and connections from one brain circuit to another are uncoupled and recoupled. The brain becomes a lean, mean, fighting machine, directing resources toward whatever threat is present.

Thus, as I pointed out earlier, brain cells are engaged in the Dar-winian struggle of survival of the fittest. The strongest neurons survived, as well as the most effective, internally produced painkillers. Receptors become more and more refined over time. They are also effective before birth, since they are found even in the placenta.

ALPHA SPROUTING: BUILDING A DIFFERENT BRAIN

In 1996 I went to the pain clinic at Johns Hopkins Hospital in Baltimore, Maryland, because of chronic, intense throat pain due to several surgeries. The doctors explained that it might be caused by "sympathetically maintained pain." When there is damage to tissue, the related nerve cells begin what is called alpha sprouting, a proliferation of microscopic pain receptors that deal with excessive pain. The receptors are part of a protective survival mechanism. When the body is injured, the sympathetic nervous system activates neurohormones such as noradrenaline, which lock into the receptors to continue the feeling of pain. The pain in turn activates the system, telling it to protect itself, thus forming a feedback loop where pain repressors are secreted. Sometimes the pain is stronger than repression.

The principle of alpha sprouting is crucial. When there is severe physical damage the system produces more alpha receptors or other types of pain receptors to handle the excess. My assumption is that early birth trauma or serious early abandonment produces the same kind of sprouting. We know, for example, that alpha 2 adrenergic receptors are increased in depression and schizophrenia.[15] The mobilizing chemicals (catecholamines) ultimately affect the number and responsiveness of the alpha receptors. What calms these pain receptors? Medication that works on the suppression of brainstem stimulation.

It is the sympathetic nervous system that processes trauma, keeps us on the alert, and maintains a state of pain. And, vice versa, it is pain that keeps us alert, often too alert, so that we cannot relax. When stored and imprinted primal pain is brought to conscious-awareness, excess pain receptors become superfluous. Feelings of anxiety no longer signal vigilance because the gates have been opened and the pain becomes simply a memory, shorn of its power.

Pain reverberates around the limbic system and brainstem, trying to find a way out. Once it is out, the body can rest. That is why at the end of one year of Primal Therapy, the levels of salivary cortisol (stress hormone) in our patients drop considerably. By allowing the event or feeling to enter conscious-awareness it can be fully reacted to and then the system can rest.

As I pointed out earlier, the gaps between neurons are filled with chemicals that either impede or accelerate the message. The message isn't put into words until it reaches the top-level frontal cortex. This doesn't happen until many months after birth when the cortex is more mature. When the impulse of pain is too great the neurons fill the gap with an inhibitory neurotransmitter that stops the message. The nervous system already "knows" when other nerves can't take any more. The point is that the infant's pain can be repressed at the age of two weeks or even minus two weeks.

Physiologically, pain receptors seem to proliferate commensurate with the amount of trauma to body tissue.[16] Our evolutionary ancestors developed the ability to react quickly to danger in order to survive. As a result, our ability today to shut off pain in order to deal with the world is crucial. And we become alert to the *possibility* of hurt. We can anticipate. Too often we anticipate a doom that has already taken place, only without access we believe it is external.

Often, when an imprinted sensation is very strong, its energy travels to the frontal cortex, but due to repression it cannot hit its target and instead travels to areas associated with feeling. This may prompt the person to exclaim, "I have to get out of this house or to get out of this marriage." He just has to "get out," period. Ironically, the sensation is unable to connect because of the force of pain that connection would mean. "No one wants to help me" and "They only want to hurt me" can get their impetus at birth. Then later when parents really do not want to help the person, the feeling is compounded. Then decades later when the husband doesn't offer to help carry the groceries the anger by the wife is inordinate. "You never want to help me!"

When we learn of the sudden, unexpected death of a friend, we cannot integrate it. It cannot penetrate. The gating system allows only so much painful information at a time to reach conscious-awareness. Later, we begin to accept more and more of the loss. It is doubly true of the infant. She doesn't have the intellectual equipment to even begin to understand what is going on in her family.

Gating may account for differences in personality between siblings, say two boys. Both are hugged and kissed by their parents, but one may have experienced massive pain early on—such as a period of parental neglect—hence equally massive repression. This brother may be more distant and unapproachable, whereas his sibling may be more confident and open and feel more accepted by others. Or, more likely, the trauma of birth is quite different for each resulting in a different prototype. One may be more outgoing than the other (literally at birth), and is more easily hugged and kissed.

One way we can measure gating is to observe the results of a patient on tranquilizers. How many are needed for the person to feel relaxed and comfortable, and how strong do they need to be? If strong sedatives such as alcohol or stimulants like coffee leave one unmoved, chances are that the gates are so strong that nothing gets through, not even caffeine. It is odd but understandable that someone can drink strong coffee and then fall asleep. This is someone who may be a parasympathetic, down-regulated person, or someone so well defended that coffee cannot do what it is supposed to do, keep us alert. For those who need stimulation due to an underregulated system, coffee may be a normalizing factor.

A person who can "hold his liquor" is another example. Even a strong anesthetic like alcohol cannot make the person drunk or even sleepy, because very little information is arriving at conscious-awareness.

This is why some of my previous suicidal patients could take enough painkillers to kill a horse, and not even fall asleep. The brain was so activated by pain it would take an enormous dose just to calm the person. We see this activation in our brainwave research.[17] Perhaps we can begin to understand what are known as "paradoxical reactions" in medicine, where you get the opposite of what you intended with a certain medication. There is a major lawsuit going on now with a pharmaceutical company because it is claimed that their tranquilizer caused someone to kill himself. The argument is that this tranquilizer is dangerous and can provoke self-destructive behavior. It is not the drug. It is the reaction to it, and that reaction depends on one's history. What drugs such as Prozac may do in some cases is bring the person down into the primal zone where he can feel. The old sadness and hurt starts to come up with all of its hopelessness; the person has no idea what is going on; his childhood becomes his current life as he can no longer distinguish between the two and he becomes suicidal. We need to be careful about labeling this drug or that as "bad" without taking into consideration the host body that the drug is penetrating.

We now come to Samantha's story. What it points out, above all, is the great relief there is in knowing that when she is anxious she can delve into the why of it. Her anxiety states are no longer a mystery. There is now a way of finding out what's wrong. Just taking the mystery out of it is such a good feeling; no longer to be attacked by some unknown demon that stirs us up for no apparent reason. No longer to be immersed in a depression that seems to come out of nowhere, for which psychologists term it "endogenous depression," meaning something from inside. That isn't much of a help. *What* from inside is it?!

SAMANTHA

I came to Primal Therapy because I was extremely anxious, always feeling that there was something wrong with me, but not knowing what it was. Whenever I had to do anything new or difficult at work I'd become very tense and have irrational fears that something terrible was going to happen to me. I would feel completely helpless and become very dependent on my husband, wanting his help and advice but never feeling that I was able to get the reassurance I needed. I would also lie awake at night obsessing and worrying over something that I had to do the next day at work.

My feelings always seemed too extreme for the situation. I often felt a strong sense of impending doom. I also began to realize that I had never been able to face up to the reality of my sister Gloria's death. At the age of twelve I was involved in a horrific car accident in which she was killed. My sister and I were very close and we shared a room for most of our lives. Suddenly I was left totally alone. It was such a shocking experience that I was unable to really feel the impact of what had happened to me and to grieve for my sister. Just prior to coming to therapy it began to dawn on me that there was something very wrong in the way that I had reacted. I had the sense that there was a little time bomb ticking away inside of me.

Since starting therapy I have been able to cry and to really grieve over Gloria's death. I have relived the terror of being alone after she died and finally acknowledged the reality of her death. Feeling the pain has brought relief—it was a secret locked away. Before I didn't have anybody that I could really talk to. The only way I could hang on to my sister was to keep everything inside. Because I couldn't talk about what happened and how I felt, it was like she didn't really exist. The realization of this hit me when I tried to talk about Gloria in group one day. I felt intimidated by everyone and I didn't want to share any information with them. My feeling was that she was all mine if I only kept her inside. Eventually I began to talk and to cry and it dawned on me that I didn't want to let her go.

Subsequently I had a session in which I remembered how my mother used to come into my room at night after my sister died. She would talk and cry with me about Gloria but I always found it difficult. I felt uncomfortable and guilty because I sensed it was for her needs. It felt wrong and I stopped crying. After a while I would pretend to be asleep so that she wouldn't come in. I remember lying under the bedclothes in terror feigning deep breathing, while I heard my mother standing at the door. The only way I could keep my sister for myself was to suppress my tears and to be completely alone.

I have also been able to relive the terror that I felt when I came round in the back of the car after the accident. At the time of this event I felt completely frozen and unable to react. But in one particular session I was able to take on board the full reality and horror of being enclosed in a shattered car with broken glass everywhere. My mother was screaming hysterically and I was aware that there was something very wrong with my sister. I was able at last to move and scream and to feel the terrible reality that I had sensed at the time—that I had lost her. Much of the terror and loneliness that I felt after Gloria died was compounded by similar feelings from my birth. All my life I have felt crippled by feelings of "I can't do it" and "I'm going to die."

These feelings made no sense in relation to my present reality. It is through Primal Therapy that I have been able to find their source and to gain some relief. Now I understand what is going on with me. My parents told me I had a good birth. I was born naturally, with no drugs, and the labor was about eight hours. Over time I have been able to feel the reality of being stuck at birth and the terror of being completely alone. I pushed and pushed to get out and did not get any help from my mother. I have reexperienced the hopelessness of feeling that I will never get out and the panic as I find that I am not able to breathe properly. I have often gone into sessions uttering the statements "I can't do it" or "I don't know what to do" in response to problems in relationships and everyday life. Now having relived my birth I know where these feelings come from and how they affect my life. Feeling this pain has brought me considerable relief and has allowed me the space to be able to cope more readily with everyday life. I feel much more able to do things now. I no longer lie awake at night worrying about how I will get through the next day. I have a greater understanding of who I am, what I want. I know that I can do things on my own. The biggest difference for me now is that if I feel bad I know that I have to sink into the feeling and find out where it's coming from—this brings me relief and then I feel better.

PENETRATING THE GATES OF REPRESSION

The placenta is not just a "barrier"; it is a gate that allows new elements to enter and alter fetal development. The taking of tranquilizers by a carrying mother can alter the receptor capabilities in the fetus. Later, how genes express themselves will be in accord with that early input. Both child and adult may have difficulty repressing; the result can be chronic anxiety, sleeplessness, and an inability to concentrate and function. This happens because the fetus is flooded with tranquilizers, far too heavy a dose for such a little body, and the environment dictates to the little system not to produce its own tranquilizers. The result may be a lifelong deficit as the setpoints in the womb have been altered for a lifetime. And then what? The adult now grown up is deficient in indigenous and endogenous drugs and must seek out external tranquilizers. All this depends upon the critical period when setpoints for serotonin and other inhibitor/repressors are being organized.

Levitt writes, "Experimental studies in animal models reveal that early environmental influences in utero can modulate cell fate choice and neuronal growth. Modification of the determinants can have long-lasting consequences."[18] Environment of the cells prenatally "serves functions as critical as environmental stimuli postnatally that promote synaptic development."[19] How intact the feeling brain becomes will depend on factors that existed while living in the womb.[20]

Give a child a good birth (if at all possible, no drugs to the mother)[21]

248 THE BIOLOGY OF LOVE

and a good first three years, especially a good first three months, and a major part of the job of child rearing is done. Why? Because the brain chemicals are there to help the child to deal with adversity. Unfortunately, those parents who are not loving or caring enough to give their fetus the best possible chance at life go on compounding the pain year after year so that the child never develops the chemical wherewithal to handle a lack of love. As an adult he suffers. Sometimes, however, it is just lack of education that makes parents produce unhealthy conditions for the baby. The baby, with the onslaught of a smoking mother, who goes on a weird diet in order to look thin and attractive, and is making the baby feel unsafe. Her womb environment is unsafe, something that will be felt all of the baby's life, albeit unconsciously.

The adult will have this underlying stratum of fear that will appear in various forms, from phobias to the fear of trying anything new. A drinking mother is creating an unsafe world for her baby; unarticulated, it will be articulated later on in reaction to Y2K where there is an inordinate cataclysmic reaction to it. It may trigger the "unsafe world" feelings from in the womb. There is the feeling of impending doom from this memory; a doom locked into the lower reaches of the brain that bubbles up to make the cortex think that the doom is imminent; and it is, it is coming up from below, now projected to the world outside.

The world as "unsafe" derives from the womb where the world of the fetus was unsafe. It is then compounded by a childhood in chaos where the child never feels secure, protected, and safe. The adult is now riddled with deep-seated fears, most of all the almost constant fear of death; everything will seem like the end of the world to a person who has undergone this kind of early life. One of my previous psychotic patients nailed shut his apartment doors next to his neighbor because he felt so threatened, so unsafe. His childhood was terrible: one parent left, the other one was drunk all of the time. It compounded his lack of safety and his final delusion that danger was everywhere. One can say, "Why is it that one child can handle the divorce and the drunken parent and the other cannot?" The answer may well be in the substructure of fear that lies deep in the nervous system that produces a fragility. The simple fact that during one pregnancy the mother took tranquilizers, and during another she did not, can make all the difference in later personality development.

A good birth requires that the mother avoid anesthetics during labor, have a delivery room that is not freezing nor loaded with very bright lights, and above all, that the baby be put on the mother's tummy immediately and the cord not be cut prematurely (there is still much oxygen in that pulsing cord). He is entering a new planet with new sights and sounds, all he knows at that point is the comforting touch of the mother. She is the whole world to him, just as her womb was the "whole world" to him earlier. She starts him off with taking good care of herself while carrying and then follows up with soft caresses, keeping him near. This has to go on for months and years to help the baby feel secure and loved. It also means producing a healthy brain. Physical presence and touch are a sine qua non.

If insurance companies and HMOs wanted to save a great deal of money and stop human suffering, they would launch a campaign for the LeBoyer birth. So many later expensive diseases could be avoided with proper birth procedures, to say nothing about avoiding so much mental illness and the cost of hospitalization and psychotherapy.

The division of the brain into three sections is important for how we diagnose patients, which has nothing to do with how they are diagnosed in the conventional therapy world. Too often, therapists take a behavior, call it something special, and make it a diagnosis. Consider, for example, obsessive disorder. The patient says, "I keep having to check the locks" and the therapist tells her it is an "obsessive-compulsive" disorder. What has happened is that everyday descriptions have been translated into psychologese without any progress in diagnosis. Much better to diagnose in terms of brain functions and deep, generating causes, because that makes a difference in how it is treated. The usual analytic diagnoses makes little difference in therapy except for what drugs are used with the patient. Otherwise, it is insights and more insights offered to the patient.

The case history of Rita is instructive in the relationship between vital signs and psychological states.

ABOUT RITA

This morning I saw a patient who came into the session with a body temp of 95.3. I was sure that our gauge was faulty so we tried another one and found the same temperature. This fact alone provided me with a frame of reference for the coming session, which, in my opinion, involved deep hopelessness, a parasympathetic dominant state. Rita started the session in deep despair and felt how hopeless her life had been; no mother for months after birth, a father who was angry and distant, and a brother and sister who detested her coming into the world. Lately, she had two car accidents and felt there was no more use going on. The whole thread of her life was the hopelessness of ever being loved. She felt, "Who could ever be interested in me? I'm so unlovable." We never suggested at any time what the feeling might be but I've rarely seen a deeply depressed patient on the verge of hopelessness with a high body temp. This patient left in two hours with a temperature of 97.5. Why the rise? Because she felt the hopelessness as an infant. Originally, it was physiologic; later to be translated into an idea—hopelessness. That imprinted feeling is something she carried around all the time. Experiencing it left her less mired in the feeling: the dialectic, feeling hopeless in order to feel hopeful. Why? Because, she said afterward, "I have put it in context when I was very young. It is no longer my current state of being." Her feelings did that for her. Her current despair led her to feeling alone in a crib in a dark room as an infant with no one coming, an angry father who yelled the minute she cried, and no one anywhere to whom she could reach out. There was nothing she could have done. Until the present she could hardly function, feeling hopeless about school, every job she had, and every broken relationship. It wasn't just the early imprint; it was the compounding of it year after year.

With an electronic thermistor (thermometer) placed in the rectum we have measured (and filmed) early hopelessness in a patient during a session where the body temp went from 98.6 to 94.8 in about twenty minutes. This, even though the patient was physically active. When I say that reliving is an unfaked event this is what I mean. Not only is there no act of will concerning body temp but the patient is not aware that there is a drop. No one would know how to make that drop in temperature. In no case is this temperature discussed with the patient until after the session.

Fear or terror during an incest trauma increases adrenaline, makes the heart pound, and raises blood pressure, producing a major release of cortisol. This then causes an imbalance in the brain, largely in the hippocampus, where there are then memory lapses, anxiety, and an inability to control (repress) emotional outbursts. It can result in attention deficit disorder where frontal repression is inadequate to separate out extraneous pain impulses from early childhood. In an article about traumatized children by Martin Teicher, Department of Psychiatry, Harvard Medical School, he noted that there were fewer left hemisphere nerve-cell connections in these cases . . . hence there was less repression and control by left cortical neurons.[3] When these children were given a medication that blocked brainstem activation they did much better. In short, there was less inhibitory work to be done. The implication of Teicher's work is that early trauma may interfere with left cortical processes in a physiologic way so that we have fewer left brain connections to control impulses.

First-line sensations are the least accessible and the most agonizing, therefore they are the least believable. When we feel the sensation of being strangled, of a crushing feeling on the chest, we can look back to the original, gated sensations associated with early first-line trauma. Because it is the level from which memories are the most difficult to retrieve, it is generally the last level to be reached by a patient in therapy. We can hear in the pattern of crying, the sporadic sobs, and the loss of breath when brainstem imprints are involved. This allows us to know whether the emotional scene being relived is first-line driven or whether there is first-line, brainstem intrusion. We can also tell by the body language: arching of the back, fetal position, and the appearance of a "fetal face."

The body is well suited to deal with the trauma of birth, if indeed there is a trauma. After the fifth day of life on earth, there is again a return to lower opiate levels. Birth can be enormously traumatic when it doesn't go right, given the evidence of massive release of painkillers while it is going on.

It is in reliving the first-line that hormone output may be stabilized.

We know that thyroxin (secreted by the thyroid gland) begins its manufacture at about twenty weeks of fetal age.[22] Stress from the mother can be transmitted to the fetus, making slight alterations in thyroxin setpoints. Later on, in childhood or adulthood, one can see beginning tendencies toward either oversecretion or undersecretion. Patients who were hypothyroid, listless and lacking energy, gaining weight too easily, are often far less hypothyroid after reliving and connecting traumas on the first-line. Small amounts of thyroid hormone given even to my "normal" patients (on the low end of normal) seems to help stabilize emotions. Thyroid hormone acts as a neurohormone in the brain and is converted into its active form in the locus ceruleus of the brainstem. The more epinephrine that is secreted the more the conversion to active thyroid. In depression, where there is low norepinephrine there is also low thyroid hormone output. The symptoms of this are lethargy, low body temperature, and resignation. The thyroid gland has everything to do with body temperature. What we are learning is that the noradrenaline system is highly connected to the thyroid. They share information together so it is not unlikely that when there is imprinted pain it directly affects the thyroid system. This is probably why in cases of depression, giving thyroid hormone sometimes helps ease the symptom.

To the average person, the notion of first-line may seem like believing in the tooth fairy. It is, however, a physiological and measurable event. For years I got up in the morning and went out for coffee, a seemingly normal act. But in my own birth primal I felt the urgency to get out and recognized the vague anxiety I had each morning that was relieved only by "getting out."

Another matter that was resolved in my primal was that I always hated to "go back" when I forgot my keys or left something behind. It was an effort to turn around. The feeling was, "If I go back to that agony, I will die." This was out of an imprint of anoxia at birth. One of the reasons that impulses rule is that the control system against feelings is faulty. Birth anoxia can interrupt the cortical-medulla connections and affect breathing. I dwell on anoxia because many births arrive with the mother heavily anesthetized; that ultimately means partial loss of oxygen for the newborn. This is why I recommend against anesthesia during birth if at all possible.

In the drugged birth, the mother is administered an anesthesia to ease labor pains. The drug passes through the placental barrier, providing a dose several hundred times too powerful for the baby so that neither the mother nor the baby can react normally to facilitate the birth process.

THE ADMINISTRATION OF DRUGS TO THE MOTHER AND DAMAGE TO THE BABY

After administration of drugs, the mother's uterine contractions grow fewer and weaker. Worse, drugs block important neural messages so that the sequence of contractions from back to front is also altered. This means that the baby is less apt to be propelled forward in a smooth way. Most often, it is squeezed and mashed by the out-of-synch contractions— a bit like going through a compacting machine. The uterus therefore acts like a contracting chamber where its movements are strong enough to crush but not rhythmical or forceful enough to smoothly propel the baby down and out.

Next, the baby's head cannot properly align itself at the top of the canal. This means that the amniotic fluid, which the contractions push forward forcefully, is forced into the baby's mouth, lungs, trachea, and stomach. She is being both crushed and asphyxiated, and, in essence, drowning. Because the baby too is drugged, her respiratory system is weakened (anesthetic drugs interfere severely with respiration), and she does not have the muscle strength to move to where it hurts less— namely, the proper position for birth.

If the baby were not so heavily drugged it could act instinctively to aid in its own birth. It could flex its muscles so as to push out; it could assume a torpedolike, well tucked-in position for maximum propulsion; and it could make its body a single unit—chest and belly one entity. With drugs, the body is in a "loose" and fragmented position so that, for instance, the hands and arms are trapped. While trapped it is running out of oxygen. It is this oxygen deficiency that we see so often in our patients. The patient I see now turns bright red for over a half hour during the anoxia primal. With anoxia the heart of the baby can skip beats, the blood pressure can rise or drop in radical fashion, and in some ways there is a mild stroke from which the baby can quickly recuperate but which may leave certain neural deficits leading to a stroke later on.

Fetuses swallow amniotic fluid in the placental sac. It is reabsorbed back into the gut. When this process is interfered with—for example, when the mother is taking tranquilizers or painkillers—there may be drowning. I have seen so many patients reliving birth who seem to be drowning.

KEN

I came to Primal Therapy because I could not stand the constant pain I experienced every day of my life. An overview of my early life reveals the sources of my inner torment.

I have a lot of the usual stuff: a shitty birth; separation from my mother immediately after birth for several weeks in an incubator; deprivation of my mother's breast after only two weeks; infantile illnesses, including allergies; heavy medication early on; belt whippings; and absolutely no physical contact from my father beginning after month one. Most of this was gnawing at my insides while I was largely unaware of it. It would bubble up in the form of overintellectualization, daydreaming, depression, anxiety and, occasionally, a suicidal thought.

My first seven years were spent with my father, mother, and my little sister. On the surface, we were the typical American nuclear family. My dad was a construction worker and we moved about once a year following company projects. He was high-strung, ambitious, aggressive, and angry. In contrast, my mother was a mellow, apathetic, unenergetic, and extremely unstimulating person. Their personalities were severely polarized. They both hurt me badly: my father with abuse, and my mother with neglect.

My dad left my mom when I was about seven. He went to work overseas and I did not see him much for ten years. His departure, however, was a great relief. All I ever got from him was criticism, coldness, and belt whippings. Although my mother was neglectful, at least she did not consciously and deliberately inflict pain on me. She left me to myself with very little to do. Although I did not have much of a life, my father's leaving, in my opinion, marks my ascent from Hell to Limbo.

The pain I was more conscious of has to do with the people, such as teachers and classmates, whom I dealt with after my parents split up and my mom moved us to the town where I spent the rest of my childhood. In second grade I had a teacher who absolutely hated me. I had attention problems. I got bored with class and I spent most of the school day spacing out and daydreaming. Maybe my teacher felt ignored or slighted by my apparent lack of interest. I don't know. What I do know for certain is that she singled me out for some very harsh criticism, yelling at and embarrassing me. I think I was categorized as a hopelessly bad student or simply stupid and lazy. In any event, my second-grade teacher was my introduction to the public school system as I would know it. I was shy, introverted, and unable to stand up for myself. I did not know how to fight back—so I just took it, all of it. The majority of the class (the good boys and girls) wanted nothing to do with me. Except for the other outcasts, I was alone. This stigma stuck with me for the rest of my life. Worthless and creepy is how people treated me and that is how I felt inside.

My teachers scolded and humiliated me. The other kids picked on and bullied me, that's if they had anything to do with me at all. I felt I was inherently unacceptable, defective, unworthy. It was not okay to be who I was. Translation: I WAS BAD.

I went on through adolescence with this shit inside me. Although it was generally accepted that I was a smart kid, I simply could not bring home decent grades. I was lazy. I wasn't applying myself. I had a bad attitude. I was not living up to my potential. I was going to be a failure. I heard it all. I believed it all. Not surprisingly, I dropped out of high school after ninth grade.

When I was sixteen I had an epiphany. I suddenly realized something was terribly wrong with everything—not just me. My mom separated from her second husband because he was a drunk, like my father. Every man I had known was an alcoholic. I thought the smell of alcohol was just the way men smelled! It became so clear that Mom made a serious mistake which fucked up several years of her life and mine. Before her breakup, I had always trusted her judgment. Looking back, it occurred to me that I should never have trusted her judgment at all. I began to wonder what other things she screwed up. Suddenly the lights were on and I was waking up. Overnight, my world turned upside down.

I followed a trail of bibliographies in psychology books which eventually led me to *The New Primal Scream*. Halfway through the book I knew one way or another I was going to get Primal Therapy. I had been doing quite a bit of independent reading about psychology. Some of what I had read was intriguing; some was boring. But this book went straight for the jugular. It made everything else sound like total bullshit. Five years later at the age of twenty-two I had saved enough and moved to Venice, California, to begin my therapy.

What Feeling Feelings Has Done for Me

One of the first feelings I had in my intensive came out by my saying, "I'm a bad boy." Until I actually said those words outloud, I hadn't realized how much I believed them. It was a feeling I had fought away from consciousness my whole life. Feeling I was "bad" meant feeling worthless and unlovable. I felt unlovable because I was not loved—and it HURT!

I cried, feeling, "Daddy doesn't love me and I don't know what to do." This feeling came to a climax when I screamed in a recent session how much I hated my father for what he did to me. I kept yelling over and over, "You hurt me so bad!" until my voice gave out. It took everything I had to get it all out. I finished completely exhausted. But, it was deeply resolving for me. I felt such relief! The insight that came from it was that I did not have a daddy. Sure, I have his blood in me; but that is all he gave me, and begrudgingly at that. He did not do anything with me that fathers do with their sons. He did not want me. Now, I can give up the struggle to get my father's love. I don't have to struggle to make him love me. Indeed, I can give up the struggle to simply GET a father. I don't have to act out not having a daddy with my bosses and others. My reality is I didn't have a daddy and I never will. It is a shitty truth, but is *my* truth and I know I own it.

I have also felt a few things about how flat and boring my childhood was with my mother. Feeling the pain of her neglecting me is very hard. When someone is beating or abusing you it is easy to know what is wrong, but when your life is dull and unstimulating and it has always been that way, you don't realize what you are missing. It is very hard to pinpoint something so generalized. If there was never any water in the well to begin with, how can you miss it?

I came here with a head full of the Primal books, Primal Theory, Primal this, Primal that, etc. Looking back on it, "Primal Theory" was my religion. It kept my hope alive until I got here. For that, I am grateful. The hope Primal Therapy gave me kept me from falling apart. However, now I have lost this "religion." Religion is hope and hope isn't as big for me as it once was. Hope to me is looking toward the day when I don't have to suffer. My suffering isn't what it used to be. I have good days and I have really shitty days. If my pain comes up and I start feeling crazy I can feel it and move on or at least get some relief. Before, all I could do was suffer. Primal Theory means nothing to me now. My feelings are what matter to me. That is what Primal Therapy is. Primal Therapy is just a label. It means to me simply this: Living life with a commitment to my own feelings. That is what Primal Therapy helps me do. I don't care any longer about the day when my suffering will be eradicated or "cured." I believe what is best for me is to live in the moment and not worry about that magical day when I will be "cured." What is that word "cured" really saying about me, anyway? It says: there is something wrong with me that needs to be fixed; something about me is defective; that I am bad. The truth is there was nothing wrong with me to start with. I DESERVED to be loved, accepted, nurtured, listened to, and allowed to BE. For me, there is no more looking for the cure. I just want to FEEL, to get better, and to grow every day of my life. I want to live my life with passion, creativity, and enough courage to face my pain head-on. That is the way I feel it should have always been for me. Maybe when I was very young, I am not sure, I was actually on this path. If so, I lost the way. Facing my pain is allowing me to quit the battle against my feelings (myself) and helping guide me back to where I left off.

"Courage" is an important word. This therapy at times has been as easy for me as breathing. Other times it has been one of the hardest, most frightening, frustrating, draining, and physically demanding undertakings of my life. I remember times when I lay in group session, writhing, choking, gagging, and gasping for my first breath of life. There were times it got so severe, I got scared I might actually choke on the fluids my body was producing. For most of us, delving deep into the dark pits of our ear-liest memories means reexperiencing the complete and total abject terror of death. And wouldn't you know that's where the biggest payoff is. It seems unfair that I have to go through this twice in my life.

It IS unfair. But unfortunately that is the only way I know of to defeat repression and all that it entails, including its perpetuation of unresolved, unconscious pain. Before I entered therapy, I talked incessantly to my friends about Primal Therapy. A few asked, "Why would you put yourself through so much? Aren't there some things you shouldn't fuck with?" It is a great deal of agony that I will go through in the name of feeling. I suspect I have only scratched the surface of the suffering I will encounter. It is hard to put in words many of the things I have written about so that a person who lacks this kind of experience can understand. Feelings go so often into the realm of wordlessness. So I will leave it at this: Feeling feelings, feeling unfelt pains, confronting unmet needs and long-denied truths is at times indescribably torturous. It exposes my true self in its most vulnerable places. I have to face things that scare the shit out of me. I have to tell secrets about myself which I am deeply ashamed of. When I do though, I can't tell you how wonderful it feels! It isn't always that way, but every tear brings me a little closer to me. Why go through all of this pain and agony? Am I a masochist? No, I am not. All of this shit I crawl through is freeing me. I AM ALIVE! I AM LIVING! I AM GROWING AS A HUMAN BEING! Two years ago, I was dead inside. Worse yet, I only vaguely knew how deeply I was not living. And so, I can proclaim triumphantly: I was dead inside but now I can feel! That is what really counts.

NOTES

1. Ronald Melzack, *The Puzzle of Pain* (New York: BasicBooks, 1973).
2. Clonidine is an old high blood pressure medication. If we want to see the relationship between brainstem stimulation and blood pressure, it is there to see.
3. See: T. J. Sejnowski, "A High Point for Evolution," *Science* 283, no. 19, (February 1999): 1121.

4. Though there is research now to implicate genetics in certain forms of dyslexia and reading disabilities, for example.

5. "Study Links Bulimia to Chemical Malfunction in the Brain," *New York Times*, Science section, 16 February 1999, p. D8.

6. Ibid.

7. Personal communication, November 1998.

8. "Of Mice and Menace," *Los Angeles Times*, 11 February 1999, Science File, p. B2.

9. See G. Kempermann and Fred Gage, "New Nerve Cells for the Adult Brain," *Scientific American* 280, no. 5 (May 1999): 49.

10. Ibid., p. 48.

11. Steven Locke, *Science News*, 11 March 1978: 151.

12. Research carried out with St. Bartholomew's Hospital, London, and Open University, Milton Keynes, England.

13. Solomon Snyder, "Opiate Receptors and Internal Opiates," *Scientific American* 236, no. 3 (March 1977): 44–67.

14. Ibid., p. 49.

15. N. Ghanshyam Pandey et al., "Increased sup-3H-clonidine Binding in the Platelets of Patients with Depressive and Schizophrenic Disorders," *Psychiatric Research* 28 (April 1989): 73–88.

16. S. M. Pearl, S. D. Glick, and I. M. Maisonneuve, "Evidence for Roles of Kappa-Opioid and NMDA Receptors in the Mechanism of Action of Ibogaine," *Brain Research* 749, no. 2, 28 February 1997: 340–43. There are many other related studies by Pearl at UCLA Biomed Library.

17. See Arthur Janov, *Why You Get Sick and How You Get Well* (West Hollywood, Calif.: Dove Books, 1996), for an in-depth discussion of our brain research.

18. P. Levitt, B. Reinoso, and L. Jones, "The Critical Impact of Early Cellular Environment on Neuronal Development," *Preventive Medicine* 27, no. 2 (March–April 1998): 180–83.

19. Ibid.

20. Ibid.

21. See the works of Drs. Frederic Leboyer and Michel Odent on proper birth processes.

22. See Peter W. Nathanielsz, *Life in the Womb: The Origin of Health and Disease* (Ithaca, N.Y.: Promethean Press, 1999).

Part III

THE POWER OF LOVE

15

LOVE BY ANY OTHER NAME

W e have seen how fetal life can have lifelong consequences. I
call deprivations while living in the womb a lack of love. Now
let us see what love is above ground, in our life after birth. But let us be
clear that any continuous deprivation of basic need is a threat to love.
Put differently, the way we love children is by fulfilling their basic needs,
even before they become children.

In the new biological literature, love falls under many names. When
the moods of both the mother and father are attuned to those of the baby
it is one expression of love. A depressed and therefore uninterested
mother is not going to match the exuberant mood of her infant, leaving
the child feeling unattuned, and hence unloved.

Love has to do with fulfilling all the basic needs of the baby. Before
birth it means practicing good nutrition and abstaining from alcohol, cigarettes, or other drugs. During birth it means adequate oxygen and no
heavy anesthetics. After birth it means proper breastfeeding and holding
and touching with warmth. All of this will take place if the mother and
father can feel and can love. They will look at their baby lovingly in the
eye, nuzzle, cuddle, and protect it, keep the baby warm, talk to it in a
slow, measured, gentle way—all commonsense practices that automatically emanate from a feeling of love. How love is manifested is going to

differ with different people but the general principles are the same: you must hug and cuddle the baby and infant, protect her from danger, make her feel secure, match her moods so she feels understood, talk to her, not constantly demand that she perform for others ("How do you say . . . ?" "Let's hear you count," etc.). Parents shouldn't push development beyond what the baby wants to do; walk when it's time, not on a timetable of the parents, but at the same time expose her to optimum stimulation so that her abilities flower. Finally, spend time with the baby, look at her play and let her know that you are there. Be there when she is hurt and sympathize with her feelings when she skins her knee. Let her know you understand. If we can feel, then it all comes naturally.

If the father is anxious and brusque, he will talk in a rapid, high-pitched, irritated manner, and the baby will feel it. It will affect the baby's developing brain, inhibiting the production of repressive cells and altering the excitatory ones. A baby who is left to "cry it out" is not loved. No one cries for no reason. Crying means there is a history of pain somewhere, and if we cannot find out where it is, at least we can offer comfort. Doctors may tell the worried parent, "The baby is not wet, she seems comfortable, and really has no reason to cry." Not so. The reasons may lie in what happened before birth. Even in the womb she was a human being, had a brain, and could feel pain, and as we know now, can cry in the womb. She couldn't express her discomfort in words at that time, so she now expresses it in tears. Let us listen to our feelings and pick the baby up whenever she cries. Love your child and treat her as a feeling being from the start of life. It is not a "child," it is a human being.

HOW TO LOVE A FETUS

Love also means taking care of oneself during pregnancy, when the neurons in the fetus's brain are developing at an incredibly rapid rate. The mother must not do things that threaten that baby's development, such as taking alcohol and tranquilizers that will find their way into the baby's system. Love means wanting the baby, because mothers who do not want their child find that their children have more health problems, both physical and psychological, than other children. Above all, no smoking while pregnant. The fetus feels it and reacts to it in the womb. It can literally choke and gasp in the womb.

A smoking/drinking mother can damage the alerting centers of the brain of the fetus, centers activated by dopamine. Couple that with over-the-counter medication and poor nutrition and you have the makings of permanent dopamine deficiency in the offspring.

Animals cannot articulate a feeling of not being loved; instead, they act it out in hyperactivity, aggression, a lack of curiosity, an inability ro relate to other animals, and so forth. We act it out and also put a name to it. When my patients cry out during a feeling, they first scream, "Hold me! Be with with me." Their need eventually becomes more specific: "Look at me. Want me! Play with me." Finally, "Love me, please!" "Be happy to see me." That last one is so important. Parents take their children too often for granted. They are just "there" to be given orders.

These are the needs we hear daily. These are the pains we observe when they are not fulfilled. "Play with me," doesn't seem like such a pain but too often parents are too busy and too preoccupied to calmly spend time playing with the child. The parent is often too driven to be able to do that. All this is the real meaning of love. But it is not just what one does; it is who one is, a feeling being or not. A driven, tense, impatient person, or a calm, relaxed parent who can teach and listen to the child with patience and adoration. Even adoring parents can demand too much from a child. Children repeat the alphabet gladly because they get approval for it, but it is often better to get love just because they exist and not for their performance.

Love means optimum stimulation; not too much, not too little, but the right kind of stimulation. As we shall see later, the entire body and the brain do not develop effectively when there is massive emotional deprivation early in life or other kinds of trauma. Institutionalized children experience physical growth spurts when they are delivered to warm and accepting foster homes. Loving interaction with parents stimulates the hypothalamus, which in turn activates the pituitary gland to release growth hormone. Deprivation of love can stunt a child's growth. It is the body's way of saying, "I can't grow without love."

With early love, particularly in the first year-and-a-half of life, the system will tend not to be in an overexcited state and can better tolerate stimulation. Love during this period is crucial. This means holding the baby when it cries. If you have an adopted child who spent her first months in an orphanage, you can assume there will be later problems. Loving, adoptive parents can ameliorate the pain but cannot make it disappear. Remember, subcortical, lower-level brain systems evolve much earlier than cortical ones. Life has first been lived on those subcortical levels and these experiences are carried around on such levels long before there are words. We have found a way to access those levels and have learned what lies there.

Without love and stimulation we cannot have a normal brain or normal life. The prefrontal cortex and its associate, the orbitofrontal site, are incredibly self-deceptive. That is why a dentist can administer a placebo (a neutral, empty pill), tell the patient it is strong medicine that kills pain, and the patient does not feel the drill against the nerve. The frontal area denies us our own agonizing sensory experience. The tooth is in agony but "we" are not, "we" being the appreciative, comprehending cortex. If the idea were changed would the patient be in agony? Yes. If the dentist says, "This is going to hurt," the patient will grimace and double over. This is no more than to say that the cortex can be alienated from subcortical centers. It can have ideas that counter reality.

I have begun to discuss love and its essentials. I go on now to discuss what a lack of love does to the brain, specifically, the messenger system which transports feelings to our higher centers for understanding and awareness. I use the term "love," but I could just as easily avoid the term and call it need-fulfillment. "Love" is just shorthand for that. It is not a mystical notion. It is not something that exists in the ozone; rather, it is concrete and specific. What may seem to be difficult to pinpoint is the feeling of feeling. It is a quality not easily measurable. Nevertheless, I am going to try. Once we have a good idea of what love is we can make efforts to measure it. One can go through the motions of child care without feeling and the baby senses it because she is mostly a sensing system with a wide-open sensory window, more open than she will ever be again. I mentioned earlier how a concerned father asked all the right questions of his son, was quite concerned, but never touched him. The father could not as he was never touched in his life. The baby's sensory system picked it up and saved the need in pristine form until adolescence when the touch of an older man "felt right." Finally, the need was fulfilled, much too late, and the homosexuality was engrained. It would not have led to homosexuality early on had the father caressed his son. That early touch would point him toward heterosexuality. Later touch would not because it was long beyond the critical period and, as such, became symbolic fulfillment. It feels real to the person but it is still substitute fulfillment, fulfilling old need. I have treated several hundred homosexuals over the decades and this seems to be an unavoidable fact. I do not wish to simplify a complex question. But the above is one central element in the problem. Other elements, obviously, can be a fear of women, a hate of the opposite sex, and the like.

THE CHILD IS FATHER TO THE MAN

There are intangibles in child rearing because feelings are intangible. You can sense in others if their feelings are repressed, if they don't have access to them, but you cannot grab hold of a feeling and say, "Here it is!" It is important to know that how we treat our baby is crucial to the development of her brain. An inattentive, distracted mother may in turn imprint her child with that very same distractibility. The child, too, may become inattentive because he hurts due to the lack of his mother's attention. That hurt stimulates his cortex, overstimulating it so that concentration is out of the question. Thus we have a manic, hyper adult who has an impaired frontal cortex due to a mother who was manic and hyper and could not relax and stay with her young infant.

HOW DO YOU LOVE A BRAIN?

How do you love a brain? By fulfilling the functions that the brain processes. It really is about loving a person who carries that brain around. For example, the largest area of cortex is given over to touch. If we want that area of the brain to develop, we hug and caress the child. The baby needs to be taken into our arms. Animals who are blindfolded in the first months of life never develop visual brain pathways and are functionally blind thereafter. No amount of visual stimulation later on will make a difference. It's no different with love, except that when love is lacking early in life, we cannot "see" it in front of us.

Serious deprivation of human contact early on can damage us forever in terms of being able to sustain relationships. Lack of early emotional closeness can produce a psychopath. No matter how much love psychopaths receive as adults, in my clinical experience nothing changes them. They are long past the critical period when love would have mattered in the construction of the brain. They may look human, develop a kind of charm that seduces, but inside there is no human being there. Most therapies are defenseless against psychopaths.

A mother who drinks when a child is eight is not going to have the same impact as a mother who drinks while pregnant. That early drinking can produce childhood cancer and is a major cause of mental retardation. It can change the function of the baby's organ systems and heart rhythms. It can alter the body's vulnerability to high blood pressure later in life, and could eventually result in stroke in middle age if that high blood pressure (hypertension) goes on for a long time. Chronic alcohol intake in the mother decreases the amount of blood and oxygen going to the brain of the fetus. If the mother smokes at the same time there is even less oxygen available; subtle brain damage will settle in. Yesterday, I saw a photo in *VSD*, a French magazine, of a model who was announcing her pregnancy. She had a cigarette in her hand. If she only knew. The mother's smoking and drinking during pregnancy are already setting up a vulnerability of the fetus to a birth performed with anesthetic so that there is a double trauma of oxygen lack; the birth will be reacted to in terms of the already deficient oxygen reserves in the baby. Not only is there an oxygen lack due to drugs given the mother at birth but these kinds of traumas build on oxygen deficiency due to the mother's smoking.

If there is anything that emotional deprivation involves it is the lack of touch and caress very early on. When the baby is under stress from the lack of this stimulus, cortisol is released, and when this stress hormone is secreted over time it produces a toxic brain environment that can and does damage certain brain structures.

Cortisol is released into the system when love is lacking because the hormone is secreted as a reaction to pain. It warns of danger. We become alert and vigilant because needs are not being met, even when we are not aware that we even have needs. The vigilant system is the stress system as we prepare to fight an unseen enemy. To prevent the threat from entering conscious-awareness, certain structures in the brain secrete inhibitory neurochemicals to keep the message of pain from traversing the synapse. Lack of love also may damage the "pumping" capacity of key inhibitory neurotransmitters so that the person is thereafter under-funded, lacking the capacity to produce such inhibitors as serotonin to combat trauma. If the stress continues, it is because the danger is now inside us. With chronic cortisol output vigilance fails; there is less energy to combat stress and the system falls into a defeatist mode. The stress syndrome keeps us alert even when we are trying to fall asleep.

Many of my entering patients have uniformly high cortisol levels. Why are they so alert-stressed? They are in danger of feeling a lack of love, a fact whizzing around their lower brain sites. The brain system is constantly alert to a danger from decades ago. For the top-level frontal cortex to be aware of that pain is one thing; to be consciously aware (to have the cortex access deeper brain levels) is quite another. The latter spells pain.

We must bring that pain to the surface. If we don't integrate, we deteriorate. But if the message brings the worst of news—"I am not loved and never will be. It is all hopeless"—the system may instead deliver a false message—"They really love me but they can't show it." The message must be blocked because repression is designed to keep the frontal cortex from knowing the hopelessness of it all. Repression is another term for inhibition, the blocking of impulses and messages from deep in the brain. The system holds back this information automatically. Once the system really knows, it reacts! That reaction is what is dangerous, both for the body and for the brain. One thing the cortex can no longer do is pay attention: too many impulses or too strong an impulse arriving all at once at the frontal cortex scatters focus. Can all this happen because the infant was not touched and held sufficiently at six weeks? Yes, the child is vigilant against an understanding, a full comprehension of what happened to him in the first weeks and months of his life.

In our work, the patient may take months to become conscious of the message because of its devastating nature. Just isolating a patient for a few days before therapy causes the feeling to begin its journey from the lower depths to higher centers. Patients begin to cry in the hotel room for no reason or just feel overwhelmed. The messages are loosening up and rising. As the unconscious starts to become conscious, suffering intrudes. "I never realized how alone I was in my childhood," might be the complaint of the patient in the first sessions. "I've been fighting against that helpless feeling all of my life," is another lament. Until there is feeling, however, there is no real understanding; there is simply cortical awareness.

Chemicals such as serotonin and the endorphins, our body's self-produced morphine, help to create analgesia and block the message of hurt going to our conscious-awareness. The result is a paradox: The system goes on alert because of an absence of love, and stays permanently on alert because of the threat of the *awareness* of that missing love. Some patients simply cannot remember rejection by parents because there never was any, nothing that stood out that was different. There was just the everyday existence in a cold, sterile environment.

THE CHEMICALS OF REPRESSION

Love is not just recommended; it is the sine qua non of child development. Love makes the brain develop in positive ways. This cannot happen if total narcissism prevents the parent from giving his full attention to the baby. When the parent is more needy for attention than the infant, the latter suffers. A father who feels angry and jealous when he sees his wife with the baby is only doing more damage because she must abandon the baby to take care of the grown-up baby. He has leftover needs from his childhood that require soothing. A mother who feels she constantly needs to placate her angry, critical husband may be neglecting her baby. She is unable to protect her young child who desperately needs protection from the angry tone and irritability of the father. Too often, the mother is just another child in the home, feeling powerless to do anything against "daddy."

THE POWER OF LOVE

Love is the central ingredient in building a strong and resilient personality. It equips us with the mobilizing chemicals such as dopamine that allow us to be aggressive, to establish goals and pursue them, to stand up for ourselves and have the energy to accomplish things. It accounts for self-confidence, a "can-do" attitude. It prevents the need for drugs later on, such as cocaine, that do what dopamine should have done had there been adequate supplies; had there been adequate love. Most drug addiction, and the choice of drugs, is an attempt to normalize a system that is unbalanced. If the inhibitory/serotonin system is deficient then painkillers will be the later choice for addiction.

Emotional deprivation, lack of physical closeness, just after birth reduces the number of serotonin receptors, part of the gating system against pain. So pain stimulates the inhibitory system, while too much early pain cripples it. There is some research evidence that this may lead to introversion, an inability to express feelings, low self-esteem, and general lack of emotional control—in effect, permanent brain dysfunction.

The expression of emotional warmth from the caregiver over time inhibits the production of stress hormones in the baby. This makes the baby more emotionally solid. As a result, the child is not so easily overcome, does not overreact, and can handle more stress than children who did not have this early love. The child is not overcome by a homework assignment and can concentrate on her studies.

Emotional deprivation early on affects the right side of the brain—the emotional side—and can impair it for a lifetime. Because the right side of the brain—the side that governs our emotions and human interaction—is most affected by free-floating cortisol (the hormone secreted when we are stressed), it is the side that suffers the most damage from early stress. Thus, the right brain, being developed earlier than the left brain, absorbs the impact of preverbal, brainstem-targeted trauma, usually at birth or before.

When there is not enough dopamine secreted to keep the frontal cortex intact we become disorganized, suffer from attention deficit disorder (ADD), grow emotionally labile, and experience states of anxiety and panic. Small infants of depressed mothers, for example, show a right-side frontal asymmetry of the brain. One part of the brain is doing too much work, and it suffers. Intrauterine trauma has a devastating impact on brain development, particularly on the right side. This may be how later in life we become intellectuals, the left cortex concocting notions and ideas to combat feelings in the right. It is the right that contains much of our early lack of love. When there is a lack of love, and a depressed mother can often not be very giving, the right brain must work overtime to process the pain. It also may mean that the left-ideational side must later work harder to stem the pain and keep it out of awareness. The left side becomes overactive and, given certain life conditions, the person becomes "heady" or intellectual, lost in ideas and philosophy. Ideas and intellect become defenses against feeling.

There is also evidence of a lack of balance in dopamine in the amyg-dalae. Children who were not close to their parents in the first months of life have fewer dopamine receptors in the limbic area. Allan Schore espouses that nearly all later psychological pathology can be traced to early maternal deprivation after birth.

When love is not made available early in life, the system "shrinks" and, figuratively, does not develop the proper "love receptors." The capacity to receive and give love will be diminished for a lifetime. In this sense, love is not an abstraction but a literal neurochemical event. With love to a child, the inhibitory messenger serotonin proliferates and helps produce a feeling of ease and comfort. With hugs, dopamine increases. Dopamine is sometimes called the "feel good" brain chemical. These are the biochemicals of love. Or put differently, it is how love is transmitted physiologically. Later, we shall see how there are specific "hormones of love"; hormones that at certain levels help us be loving. When they are low we are less capable of either receiving or giving love. Most of us are addicted to love; our need for it. It takes the form of overeating or drinking but the real addiction is to ourselves, to the chemicals we produce in the brain that make us feel better when we get what we need.

In my clinical sessions I sometimes hold the hand of some of my more disturbed patients as they descend into early pain. I do what Prozac would do, but without the side effects. Also, I know when to let go so as not to drive the patient below the feeling zone, which would make her so comfortable and relaxed that she can't feel anymore. Many confrontation groups practice a "touchy-feely" style of "love" therapy; believing you can love pain away. Confrontational approaches ignore the critical period when love is absolutely crucial for brain development. One can have hugs and kisses from the age of ten on but that cannot fulfill the deprivation that occurred during the critical period just after birth.[1] Witness so many children who have lived in foster homes or who were adopted early in life; their pain remains. These are the adults who drink, smoke, need tranquilizers, and often do not sleep well. Their chemical gates are weak. They become "leaky" because of early deprivation. Tranquilizers are used too often in psychotherapy to bolster the gates while suppressing "Hold me, Momma!" "Be with me!" If patients or any of us can cry out our need it would lessen the necessity for tranquilizers. If we can feel, "Hold me, Daddy!" there is no longer the need to push back that need with drugs. How do we know? The observation of several hundred patients, many of whom were deeply into drugs, confirms this. Patients who feel these feelings to the depths of their souls are able to stop drugs. We have incidental corroboration of this point as a result of our research on salivary cortisol among our patients. After one year of therapy, levels were systematically lower, meaning that these individuals were under less stress. They no longer had a need to quell their tension with drugs. We have treated every kind of drug addiction, from heroin to glue sniffers, and have found the same result: no normal (or normalized) person wants to put mind-altering drugs into his system.

Because we can't feel what we can't feel we are not usually aware of the diminished capacity for love or feeling in general. We may confuse need for love because when we need desperately we imagine that anything resembling warmth can be love.

A patient of mine, an endocrinologist, lived in several foster homes. She eventually attended medical school and did well. But she had sleep problems and could not relax. Adults who were in foster care as children suffer more than others because they were neglected both before and after birth. The father most likely abandoned the mother, who may have been unable to cope, so she gave away her child. Whatever the reason, the end result is lack of love, resulting in a permanent defect in gating. This means deficiency in holding down feelings. Compounding the problem is that often the child is unwanted. That produces pain in the baby. The Finnish researcher A. Myhrman found that "unwantedness" felt about the unborn children by the pregnant mother may "operate directly or indirectly as a psychosocial stress during development, making more children liable to schizophrenia, or it may be a marker for behaviors associated with risk in either mother or the child.[2] Unwanted children can be affected by the mother's physiology and then later by the mother's attitude of neglect and indifference.[3] An *absence* of interest by the mother, in short, can be imprinted biochemically in the fetus; the feelings of rejection, felt by her even unconsciously, impact the fetus negatively. The mother is under stress from having to face having a baby without any help. Her stress hormones work on the fetus, and he, too, is vigilant. He can become a hyperactive baby who is unable to be cuddled.

Many births are viewed as "accidental" or "inconvenient," and too many parents are not happy to have a child. It has been found that an unwanted baby has many more health problems later on. Think of the implications: a mother's attitude while her baby is in the womb stays inside of the baby for the rest of his life and changes his neurophysiology. Not only is the pregnant woman under stress but it is often followed up by the mother's social attitude of neglect and indifference. The child, already, with a despairing, defeatest, down-regulated physiology, due to the anesthesia of the mother at birth, is born to a woman who is stressed and still depressed. She may be emotionally removed from the child at a time when he needs every bit of her attention for the development of his frontal cortex and limbic brain.

Two of my patients suffered from lifelong depression. Both of these women had been unwanted by their mothers. Both of their mothers were depressed for months during their pregnancies. The changes in their physiology could have invoked similar changes in the physiology of the fetuses and left the babies with depressive tendencies—tendencies to be internal, introspective, reflective, and moody—in other words, down-regulated. "What's the use?" these grown women would tell themselves. "I'm not going to try anymore. It's hopeless." Those thoughts are the representations in language of the feeling and sensations imprinted deeper in the brain. It is the language of neurophysiology, of sensations of despair and perhaps approaching death. They are the outgrowth or reflection of these early events. The *idea* of despair and defeat is the latest evolutionary development of a brain system hundreds of millions of years old.

The simple fact of a drinking mother-to-be who souses her baby's brain so that he is disoriented and confused, can leave him with the *physiologic* sensation of confusion. There is nothing the fetus can do to change the situation, except to tolerate it. It is as yet unarticulated. But when growing up in a household that is overbearing, where one really cannot change anything about one's life, the sensation and the feeling merge to form a powerful force. It can be triggered later on with the loss of a mate who leaves for someone else. The response may be total defeat: "There's nothing I can do about it." The consequence can be suicidal thoughts. The predominant weight of this is from an unarticulated brain-stem-originated trauma. Without the push from this old sensation there may be great unhappiness but not suicidal inclinations.

Why such a drastic response? The reason may lie in a near-death experience in the womb; of being strangled by the umbilical cord where death appeared to be the only way to end the agony. Death as a solution is imprinted. It may have then been reinforced by periods of neglect as a young child. Now, when the mate leaves, the old memory of being neglected or abandoned by one's mother kicks in.

The fear of abandonment this person felt could not be transmitted in pure form to the prefrontal cortex, particularly the left side, because of the level of pain involved and the gating system which blocked it. So when there is no longer access to our history we must believe that the reasons for our deep mood are in the present. We then cling for dear life to the departed. The neurotransmitters are spitting out inhibitory chemicals into the synapses, as are the excitatory catecholamines, both keeping the deep pain from connecting to the prefrontal cortex while intolerably agitating the system. Unable to connect, the feeling is symbolized in the association cortex. This leads to the correct feeling: "No one wants me anymore." Only the focus is wrong. To then go for help to a counselor who stays focused in the present compounds the problem by driving the person away from the context. So long as the focus is in the present the suicidal impulses will remain. They are not irrational; only the lack of context makes them appear to be.

This man's fear of abandonment could not be transmitted to the prefrontal cortex because he was experiencing the tremendous pain of loss. The limbic system neurotransmitters secrete inhibitory chemicals into the synapse to keep the message away from conscious-awareness. What may come up to awareness is the feeling of hopelessness. Unable to connect to the entire scene and its feelings, it is symbolized in the association cortex, leading to the perception that "no one wants me anymore." It is then acted out, either in depression or suicidal tendencies. It can also be acted out in clinging, dependent behavior to keep "no one wants me" away. All this just from being unwanted in the womb? It is possible because of the mother's physiology and also because the baby, after birth, will not be wanted. If the unwanted baby is put up for adoption and she stays several weeks unadopted that deep feeling will be reinforced.

THE TRAUMA OF BEING UNWANTED

In a study by Myhrman[4] children from unwanted pregnancies were revisited when they were age thirty. They were found to have "less favorable psycho-social adjustment."[5] A Finnish study of 11,000 individuals revealed that unwanted babies had a greater risk for becoming schizophrenic.[6] Researchers in Ireland found that when there were obstetric problems at birth, there was a much greater chance of the child becoming psychotic later on. More importantly, the authors stated that obstetric complications may be secondary to even earlier events, i.e., gestational events: "Increasing and converging evidence suggests that anomalies develop prenatally in schizophrenia. It is likely that those destined to become schizophrenic are already more fragile when labor starts."[7]

Sleep disturbances in one of my patients were caused by the imprint left by early lack of love. Amorphous as they are, these memories can be relived in a feeling. Afflictions such as hypothyroidism, in which thyroid output is chronically low, sometimes seem to normalize after a feeling. This tells us that setpoints for hormone secretion are set very early on during gestation. Trauma alters these setpoints in either up-regulation or down-regulation.

Tranquilizers can suppress the vigilance/energy-producing sources of imprinted trauma, reducing the release of cortisol and lowering blood pressure. The pain says, "Pay attention. Look alive! There's danger coming. Get ready!" And medication such as those that work on the brainstem structures dictate, "Be calm. No reason to get excited!" There is a reason but the alerting mechanisms have been dulled. Thus, the medication allows us to lie to ourselves. It lulls us into a false sense of calm

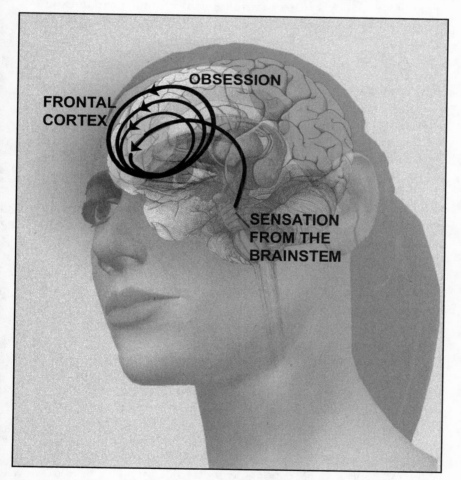

Fig. 11. Repressed feelings can drive the frontal cortex into obsessions and paranoid ideas.

when danger lurks; in this sense some of the tranquilizing medication is antisurvival. It lulls us into complacency when we should be alert. The problem is that a constant state of alert becomes the danger. The system will collapse with this chronic alarm state. We have to choose our enemy: either vigilant-mobilized or tranquil-immobilized. We will eventually be struck down by this unreality. Any chronic alterations in our systems can lead to disease; long-term high blood pressure can lead to a stroke later in life due to the same imprint behind both.

The danger, of course, is the memory. For if it is fully reacted in one experience of reliving, the system will be in danger; the brain and body cannot tolerate extended periods of stress hormone release, high blood pressure, or a rapidly beating heart. We should be alert and vigilant but when that state persists, it itself becomes a danger. Thus, a double bind. We need to be alert but when too alert for too long the system crumbles. We fall ill with high blood pressure or from excessive release of stress hormones, which among other things, can produce premature births.

An article in the 22 February 1999 *Los Angeles Times* discussed a new treatment for obsessive-compulsive disorder—surgery on part of the orbitofrontal cortex.[8] This psychosurgery is performed at Karolinska Hospital in Sweden with successful results, doctors claim. If the part of the brain that obsesses is removed, one no longer has the equipment to obsess. However, nothing has been done about whatever is generating those obsessions. I also question what the long-term effects of surgery will be on the brain's ability to think, plan, and integrate.

Surgery is a radical therapy that often can be avoided with deep-probing, feeling therapy. The brainstem-limbic pressure militating against the orbitofrontal cortex (OBFC) may well eventuate in obsessions. If we eliminate that pressure, I do not believe orbitofrontal cutting would be necessary. The surgeons in Sweden are treating a thought disorder as, literally, a thought disorder, which it is not. Because one has localized where the thoughts take place doesn't mean that removing the location will remove the thoughts. The imprint will just travel elsewhere.

Biology is never capricious. If your body contains an increased level of hydrochloric acid, apart from dietary considerations we need to know what produced this excess acid. It doesn't hypersecrete out of whimsy. The memories can be an accumulation of similar feelings ("I'm starving";

"I need my mother"; "Hold me"; "I'm being tortured in the birth canal").
Reactions are commensurate to the threat. We just need to find out what
the threat is.

Today's conventional psychotherapist inadvertently and mistakenly
reinforces the gating system of patients by using the tools of concern, listening, care, guidance, and advice. Therapy can become another act-out
for the patient who is unconsciously getting what he wants (symbolic fulfillment) instead of what he needs (feeling the *lack* of fulfillment as a
child). The implication is that you can have good intentions and love
neurosis away. If all those fail, the therapist uses the more direct means
of quelling need/pain by prescribing tranquilizers. A therapist who tries
to build a patient's self-esteem by telling her, "You really are capable, you
know," is actually encouraging the patient to block out her *real* feeling of
"I'm bad. People don't love me because I'm worthless." By trying to
"love" pain away by being "nice," the therapist is fighting reality. He is
functioning as the brain gate for the patient. In Primal Therapy, we want
to open the gate and let in love, beauty, and life! To do that we must
open the gate to real feelings of "No one loves me. I'm unlovable. It is all
so hopeless," etc.

Let us remember that any love outside the critical period is nice,
helpful, and relaxing, but cannot make permanent changes in the neurobiological system. We can get addicted to this kind of love—reassuring
warmth by a therapist—because it is always substitute fulfillment. The
patient must eventually feel the lack of love she underwent in childhood.
To receive warmth in the present is still to keep love out because repression
remains intact. It is the pain of feeling no love that lifts repression and will
let love in. Otherwise, to be loving, concerned, and focused only on the
patient is to give her what she needed in the past, not the present. Love
now, paradoxically, reinforces the gates and keeps "unloved" from being felt.

Of course, the patient feels better for a time and becomes addicted to
the therapist because she is getting what she needed long ago. If there
were any way that an imprint can be "erased" it would be in bringing the
trauma up to the prefrontal area for integration. Remember, it is the suffering component that is buried which keeps it "alive." Once the suffering is felt the trauma loses its force.

I'm always amused when I hear therapists talk about treating narcissistic patients while focusing solely and completely on them for each and every session. And so long as we focus on the narcissist he will love us, and think we are marvelous therapists. Every patient and person is a narcissist so long as he needs.

ON THE NATURE OF FEELING

Feeling is the ability to sense and experience all of ourself; it is the essence of being human. If we don't have a totally intact brain, we will not be capable of feeling 100 percent. Feeling means we are not walled off from accessing aspects of our brain, particularly those structures that provide the essence of feeling. Feeling, although not an idea, has ideational aspects. It can have a name—sad. But it can exist without a name. Feeling is not the discharge of energy through screaming or crying; that is the release of feeling without the connection to history and without the ideational counterpart. Access to feeling means access to all key levels of brain function, the ability to descend and experience what lies in the deepest reaches of the brain. We see through case histories what I mean. Blockages to feeling are the result of the repressive or inhibitory neurohormones. They are the response to the imprinted pain of lack of love or to physical trauma even before birth and, of course, afterward. It is the blocked energy of early trauma that militates to organ systems and creates havoc. "Hold me, Momma," is a need that can be walled off. Its energy can move to the circulation system, producing high blood pressure. Patients who feel that need to the depths of their soul find their blood pressure dropping to normal limits.

We need love to develop the brain and our lives, to learn, create, love others, and be healthy. Pain is a warning signal that the system is in danger. The less imprinted pain there is in the system the more access there will be to lower levels. And that access ultimately means harmony, balance, and ease. It means a life of calm and contentment, of joy, exuberance and, yes, even sadness, when called for. It means no more unexplained symptoms or behavior out of control. It means not to have to overeat despite our will; not to be driven to have constant sex, which can be little more than a drain for tension. It means not having to keep on the move with this plan or that, this meeting or that; not having to make phone calls to keep from feeling primal aloneless, and not having to move from one house to another or one job to another because standing still or in one place is anxiety producing. It means not being ridden with jealousy and envy; having a life of our own negates that. It means being able to produce without anxiety, to finish what we start, and to have tenacity for the difficult projects in life. It also means to be able to do nothing; just to "be," and be there for your child. Who you are is what matters.

"How-to" books can change what you do but not who you are. Children are sensing machines. They know before they have words who we are, whether they can express their anger in front of us, whether they can feel sad with us or joy, and above all, whether they can confide in us. With so many of my patients it is a given that when they were five or six that they could not confide in their parents. It just never occurred to them. They "sensed" it. They know without cerebral "knowing" if the parent is truly interested or not. They do not yet have the intellectual baggage to deceive themselves. Later on, self-deception becomes a key tool in going on with life despite internal pain.

If the parents do not show affection, the child acts on their feelings toward her without ever articulating them to herself. She stays out of her parents' way and begins to act shy and timid, as if no one is interested in her. She is acting-out what she has learned. This is not a set of false ideas she labors under; although the ideas may seem irrational, they are correct, just out of context. *No one was interested*, and that feeling becomes an imprint. Later, in therapy, that so-called irrationality should be put into historic context in order to make sense of it. The right brain already knows all this, but it doesn't have the sophisticated words to deliver the message to the left brain for expression.

Many of us go through childhood "knowing" something is wrong but not being able to articulate it. All we know is that we don't feel good. I never knew I was chronically anxious until the advent of antihistamines. I took two of them, and my mother had to call the doctor because I was soon troubled by a new affliction—relaxation. I had never experienced it before and was convinced I was truly sick. A little warmth from an outside stranger would have produced the same effect as the drug. Many children get "love" or approval for not expressing their need. Parents don't want to be bothered sometimes, so the child is rewarded for not asking for anything, staying quiet, playing by himself, and keeping out of the way. It is need turned inside out. Being good means not needing. There used to be the notion that constantly indulging a child's need would make her spoiled; she would demand more and more. It is quite the opposite. It is not indulging a need that matters; it is fulfilling it. Dialectically, once need is fulfilled there will be no more inordinate demands. No one wants more than they need, unless of course, they demand more to fill up an early lack. A child will want to be held just enough to fulfill his need and no more. After that, it is possibly the parent who needs to hug him too much, perhaps to make up for the parent's early lack of love.

Being healthy means needing. A child whines and expresses his needs in an inchoate way. The response by the parent may be, "stop whining and get on with your life." If his needs were fulfilled he could get on with life.

Nothing is quite as infinite as self-deception. It keeps us from knowing that parents cannot love, do not care, and are not interested. It is a survival measure, a necessary defense against reality. It is not necessarily a good thing to disabuse people of their illusions that can often be protective. Certainly, the delusions of a psychotic are protective.

Many parents feel they can't win. No matter how hard they try they can't get through to their children. Even if they are nurturing and loving, the child already may be blocked due to very early trauma, a trauma that possibly had nothing to do with the parents' behavior. Perhaps the mother had to be hospitalized for a time following the birth; the child may been left in the hands of others because the father had to return to work. In any case, the child was neglected, unloved, and feels unloved. He can't say his feelings but he can wet the bed or he can stutter or develop tics.

That early deprivation affects his thinking, spatial orientation, coordination, perception, ability to relate to and empathize with others, and a whole host of cognitive processes. Trauma prior to, during, and after birth are key events that have been neglected in the literature. For example, a number of studies reveal that twins separated at birth were found to have a surprising number of traits in common years later when they joined up again. The investigators alluded to genetics as the key factor. What they neglected to examine, however, is the crucial nine months of womblife the twins shared that shaped them irrevocably. Those nine months are more important than any other nine months in their lives. A trauma at age twelve is not going to change the brain extensively, but a trauma in the womb will.

When feeling pain the system is reacting. That reaction is what I call feeling. Feeling pain is *feeling*. Blocking it is not feeling. Most feelings in adulthood are built on need. The frustration from early deprivation may produce anger, but anger is not basic; need is. Patients go beyond their anger, after it is expressed, often violently striking out against the padded walls, to feel, "Give me a break. Say you like me. Stop criticizing my every move. Look at me! Hold me just once!" If you stop at the expression of anger there is no cure.

FEELINGS ARE US

Feelings remain stamped in us because they are part of our cytoarchitecture. *Feelings are us.* They remain so we can be whole again and be ourselves. That is the ultimate meaning of "finding yourself." If we discover we were unloved at age four, we are finding our true self. The aim in any therapy is to give the patient back her real self. No therapy can do more than that. The descent into the subconscious is, according to my patients, an incredible voyage as they explore the hidden recesses of the brain. It is a trip to reclaim aspects of a life put away for years.

The body is but a piece of a whole. When it suffers repression from *any source*, it shuts down, attempting to block any feeling inside, and that includes love. No amount of wanting or willpower changes that fact. Feeling unloved lifts repression and, above all, reduces the overload. This partially unlocks the gates so that love from others can be let in. *Once a person has been unloved over time by her parents early on, she always feels unloved somewhere in her system, conscious or not . . . and hurts. This feeling is what most people are tranquilizing with alcohol, overwork, and drugs.* Why do people drink even when they now have a loving family? History!

Without early love, an adult may resort to taking drugs such as Prozac to accomplish what that love should have done. Literally. Prozac ensures adequate serotonin in the synapse, exactly what early hugs would have done. Hugs avoid drugs. Loving eye contact and plenty of hugs and kisses in the first three years of life create a chemical bulwark that endures so that drugs are never necessary. Holding the hand of a patient in our therapy who is overloaded, fractured, and "all over the place" in her thoughts can bring the level of pain down to the feeling zone, a zone that has definite neurobiologic parameters. If she is held too long or too soon, she will find herself below the feeling zone (and the feeling will stay repressed). Touch serves the same function as administering a shot of Demerol, but it must be moderated: not strong enough to block feeling but strong enough to separate some of the catastrophic limbic pain from the brainstem.

We will never talk anyone out of need, and it is need that drives us. Need is the motor that pushes us into all kinds of imaginable and unimaginable outlets. Frustration of need can cause rage and that can result in mayhem over the slightest sign of not giving in to someone's demands. The husband wants the wife by his side at all times, wants her to obey and comply. If she doesn't he becomes furious. He has nothing that tells him that this is another person with needs of her own. He only acts out of need.

There is no basic need for fame or fortune or power. These are not hardwired needs; rather, they are symbolic derivatives of real need that come into play when basic need cannot be fulfilled. They may have the urgency of those real needs, though, because real needs have been funneled into them. To deal with symbolic needs is to be led down a false route, for they are merely conduits for real need. If we cannot get real love from parents we develop symbolic channels to get what looks like love from others. We overeat or get desperate in a restaurant if there is any delay in being served. It is not really a desperate need for food. It is a desperate need for love transformed.

NOTES

1. I would suggest a simple study of children raised in institutions or foster homes, and their longevity. Does early deprivation shorten lives and how?

2. A. Myhrman et al., "Unwantedness of a Pregnancy and Schizophrenia of a Child," *British Journal of Psychiatry* 169 (1996): 637–40.

3. Ibid.

4. See also L. Kubicka et al., "Children from Unwanted Pregnancies in Prague: Czech Republic Revisited at Age Thirty," *Acta Pschiatrica Scandinavica* 91 (1995): 361–69.

5. Myhrman et al., "Unwantedness of a Pregnancy and Schizophrenia of a Child."

6. T. Forsen et al., "A Coronary Heart Disease, Weight in Pregnancy and Birth Weight," *British Medical Journal* 315 (1997): 837–40.

7. E. O'Callaghan et al., "Season of Birth in Schizophrenia: Evidence for Confinement of an Excess of Winter Births to Patients without a Family History of Mental Disorder," *British Journal of Psychiatry* 158 (1991): 764–74.

8. Thomas H. Maugh II, "Obsessive Compulsives May Find Relief from Unlikely Source," *Los Angeles Times*, 22 February 1999, p. S1.

16

LACK OF OXYGEN
IS THE LACK OF LOVE

At UCLA Pulmonary Laboratory my staff and I filmed two patients in slow motion moving exactly like a salamander (in a birth reliving that was spontaneous and unexpected) for over half an hour each. I discussed birth and its reliving in chapter 12. It is only when a patient has been in the therapy some months that she can approach deep-lying imprints, particularly brainstem imprints, of hypoxia (diminished oxygen) at birth. Judging by the tremendous changes in my patients after their reliving episodes of birth (and it takes months or years of it) we can assume that the original trauma made significant changes in the neurophysiology of the person. Reliving birth never involves words; it includes fetal movements and positions, grunts and no cries and dolphinlike movements for more than an hour—something that the patient can never duplicate afterward without utter exhaustion. During the reliving the patient breathes very deeply for a long time, sometimes thirty minutes. In the ordinary course of events these patients would pass out. This is never the case in reliving. Never a moment of dizziness. I realize I am discussing events out of the norm in the psychological universe. It needs "getting used to." I therefore ask the reader to bear with me as I develop the case. Regarding the way my patients move during a Primal, it was evident that no person, not even themselves at a later

287

point, could duplicate their movements voluntarily, and certainly not for half an hour. They would have been exhausted. These patients were not. The more we understand about this the more we understand our phylogenetic development, and vice versa.

If in a session the patient is reliving a lack or lessened oxygen (anoxia or hypoxia, that he experienced at birth), his system is responding only to that past event. There is obviously plenty of oxygen in the therapy room. It is the same when we relive an early lack of love, even though we may be loved by our family in the present. In my syntax, inadequate oxygen at birth is a way of not loving. It causes pain and aborts development.

Pain is the constant companion of need. If the body needs oxygen and doesn't get it, it suffers. To deprive the newborn of oxygen is tantamount to depriving the two-year-old of hugs. Both are unfulfilled need and are therefore signs of lack of love. We call it love but what matters is that love is fulfilling basic need, no matter what name we give to it. If we starve a child we are clearly not loving her.

To find out what happened while you were being carried and at birth, you need to speak the language of the brainstem. In essence, you have to become a salamander again. This is not a figurative expression since many of my patients reliving birth do make salamander movements.

When threatened, the salamander runs away by instinct, not by thought processes or even feeling processes. To "cure" instinctual terror, manifested in anxiety and panic, we must address anxiety in its own language by tapping into the salamander brain where terror originates. This must be done not with words but with something more primitive: writhing, suffocating, coughing, arching of the back—all of the concomitant visceral reactions. It is the language of the old brain. The terror may seep up in disconnected fashion toward awareness in the form of anxiety attacks. It is a memory bereft of its context, which is often arcane, to say the least. The terror may be coming close to dying at birth. We have found a way to speak to that ancient brain; able to ask the right questions and get the right answers. We meet it on its own terms. We speak the language of movement; the language of visceral reactions, and then we can communicate with it.

A kind of salamander brain already is installed in our inner hard drive. We provide the software for accessing it. *Access* is a key term. It is a complicated matter requiring years of training for therapists to learn its techniques. Primal Therapy differs from all other therapies by taking into account the evolution of the brain. We begin the therapy in the present, focusing on the prefrontal cortex and current events. We then help the patient access her feelings located in the limbic system. Finally, we help the patient relive events long before feelings or thoughts—the brain-stem. If we are focusing on childhood we don't expect complicated syntax or the use of adult words. If it is early infancy we expect the cries about early scenes to sound like an infant and not an adult. There are many cues we use to guide the patient. It is all about feeling. Therapists do not use complicated phrases or words when addressing the patient approaching childhood memories. We note the signs—a change in breathing patterns, a catch in the throat, trembling, eyelid flutter, etc. Therapy rooms are fully padded and soundproof. The therapist sits on the mat behind the patient. Dialogue is kept to a minimum. The average session is two to three hours. The feelings of the patient determine when the session is over. It is not insight therapy. It is a matter of reliving events lodged in the brain long before insights were a neurological possibility. Therefore, insights follow feeling; they do not precede it. We must not skip neurologic steps in providing access as the rebirthers do, plunging patients deep into brainstem imprints long before they have access to higher level memories. The results are nearly always disastrous. We must respect the levels of brain function if we are to succeed in liberating suffering from the brain system.

Only history holds our truths. It is essential to travel into the past, into the far reaches of the brain, with the patient, back to the time when the frontal cortex was not fully functional. This cannot be accomplished through words and explanations. We cannot use the cortex to delve below it; there are no verbal means to arrive at preverbal events. If the patient only *talks* about his sensations ("I feel crushed. I feel suffocated. My stomach is churning. I feel pressure on my chest."), he will find no lasting relief from his pain. Sometimes just a push here, a physical pressure there is all that is needed to reawaken a specific early memory. This is no different than a patient describing an early emotional scene in order to fall into the old feeling. The language of the brainstem is instinct and sensation. We need to find a way to match the sensations the patient reports and then travel down those sensations to origins. It can be done.

I have discussed levels of brain function, and how our therapy follows the lead of evolution in addressing certain levels of brain function so that we do not plunge into brainstem imprinted events before the patient is ready. One way we know how disturbed a patient is, is through observing his initial primals. If he is showing signs of birth early in therapy we can almost be sure that his gating system separating the levels of consciousness is defective.

We will examine in the next chapter the hormones of love. We need optimum levels of certain hormones in order to love and to feel loved. There is no love without these hormones.

17

OXYTOCIN AND VASOPRESSIN
The Hormones of Love

(The two are in bed together)

She: Do you love me?

He: Of course I do.

She: How much?

He: A whole lot. Ouch! What are you doing?

She. I'm taking a blood sample to see how much you love me. I'll be right back.

(twenty minutes later)

She: Sorry. You don't love me as much as you think. Your oxytocin levels are low.

He: What?

She: Your cortex may be thinking you love me but your body is telling me something else.

He: What the hell is oxytocin? And by the way, what the hell is the cortex?

She: I'll let him tell you, but first let me give you this nasal spray of oxytocin. I think we can get closer.

He: No thanks.

She: Just a little sniff of love?

Oxytocin is a neurohormone that is possibly the hormone of love. In some respects oxytocin can be considered a neurotransmitter that binds to limbic/feeling centers in the brain. The importance of the inhibitory neurotransmitters such as serotonin to love become evident when we find that when two close talapoin monkeys who have been separated reunite, they groom each other with enthusiasm and their serotonin levels mount considerably.[1] Love calms and so do the neurochemicals that put down pain. The equation should read that, "Love suppresses pain through the release of certain neurotransmitters and relaxes us." Early love does that permanently.

When we miss someone it may well be that our serotonin supplies are lower due to the pain of separation. We are hooked onto the other and need that other person to normalize. That is how we can be addicted to someone else. When it is low there is less emotional attachment, less social behavior and caring, less touch and caress . . . in short, less love. When it is high there is relaxation, rest, growth, repair and healing, loving behavior, and feeling-attachment. It is found only in mammals. It may be that love and nurturing in whatever form was necessary throughout the history of organisms; critical brain development and evolution could not take place without it. When we consider the essential nature of humans we must take into account the role of love in development and evolution. Love is of the essence. Oxytocin, like hugs, calms. Oxytocin accelerates birth. A synthetic oxytocin (pitocin) is given to mothers who need stimulation for contractions at birth. What we shall learn later is that it has uses far beyond birth. It may well be that we can "inject love" or at least inject something that encourages it, that helps us attach to others and bond with partners; something that allows us to feel close to someone else, to feel and empathize with their feelings and pain.[2]

This is not as far-fetched as it may seem. Scientists recently took mice that were loners and injected a gene of vasopressin into them (discussed in full later). This was taken from a rodent known as the prairie vole, known to be gregarious and faithful to its mate. Result: the mice became more social, more caring about female partners, and spent more time with them. They were generally "nice to them."[3] There is a lesson there somewhere. Imagine its value for those on the verge of divorce, who go to a clinic for a shot, and the marriage becomes good again. Or for those jingoistic, bellicose souls who want to start wars, there may be a way to soften them down and make them caring.

Bonding is a strong emotional attachment that helps us want to be with one another, to help and protect one another, and to touch each other. Bonding is the most positive of human relationships, the most human and caring. Those who did not bond very early on with their parents may well be condemned to a lifetime of broken, fragile, tenuous, and truncated relationships. And it may be in large part due to deficits in oxytocin. And that may be due to tenuous, distant, alienated, and glacial relationships very early with one's parents. The question is which came first: the lowered oxytocin and then the inability to love and to bond, or the lack of love early on which lowered the setpoints of oxytocin? I would bet that pain comes first.

There was in Freud's time the notion of the repetition compulsion: the acting-out of childhood traumas over and over again in order to get love. He concocted a rather elaborate theory to explain it. But now it seems that when someone has not been close to either parent very early on he is deficient in oxytocin; that deficiency prohibits him from getting close to others. Put differently, if we see someone who cannot sustain long-term relationships, has one superficial relationship after another, and is stuck in a "repetition compulsion," we may postulate that he lacked close parental contact in infancy. That lack lowered his oxytocin levels so that now as an adult he does not have the chemical wherewithal to relate intimately with another human being.

We learn how to bond emotionally through early bonding, as simple as that sounds. It is not learning in the academic sense. It cannot be taught! And it certainly cannot be taught in later life. It is an emotional state transmitted through feelings that must take place very early in our lives. In certain mountain rodents such as the montane vole, a species of which lives an isolated life (as differentiated form the prairie vole), a shot of oxytocin encourages bonding and pairing with other voles. After repeated injections there is a long-acting antistress effect, a calming. Those humans who are able to bond to a support group have higher levels of oxytocin and have less reactivity to pain. Those who did not bond properly to their parents may be those whose relationships later on are sporadic, not because of their current relationships, but first and foremost because the biochemical equipment needed to attach to others is absent or diminished. Continued physical contact by the parent is essential for a child's well-being.

What Thomas Insel, neurobiologist with the Center for Behavioral Neuroscience at Emory University, has remarked is that, "Many of the affectional ties to the mother observed postnatally could be laid down by prenatal experience."[4] It underlines my point; even the sound of the mother's voice has had prenatal determinants. There is enough evidence now to show that the newborn's heart rate, body temperature, and respiration rate are governed by the mother; when she is maternal there is a positive affect on the baby and the setpoints of heart rate and blood pressure become normal. When she is not, it becomes negative and traumatic and we may find later on a tendency toward high blood pressure, for example, or cardiac problems. Her neglect changes the biochemistry of the baby, perhaps permanently.

The postnatal period is a simple extension of the prenatal one; loving feelings are transmitted to the fetus through the biochemistry and oxytocin levels of the carrying mother, and then later through the physical contact. The physiologic effects of the mother's caring on the infant are the same.[5]

We all have a positive need to bond. We are social animals. If we were not loved early on, looked at, touched, listened to, nuzzled, and adored, those biological changes, subtle though they may be, follow us throughout our lives until later when their continued force causes a breakdown in physical and mental systems. If the traumas of birth, prebirth (as for example, the mother's chronic depression), and early childhood are inundating the system, there will be an eventual breakdown of the serotonin and oxytocin systems. Supplies will be used up in the fight to keep pain down. The biochemicals such as serotonin and oxytocin will be used in the battle against emotional deprivation.

The avoidance of the conscious-awareness of agonizing feelings is what drives so many of us because we were not loved, no matter what we think now about our childhood. A therapist can ask us if we were loved, and we may insist, "Absolutely," while our oxytocin levels are far too low. And indeed, we may have been loved after birth but suffered severe traumas in the womb while we were being carried. The body and its physiology do not lie. If there were severe traumas or early lack of love it will show up in the imprint. That imprint is neurochemical. It is my guess that some mothers who need oxytocin to help out in the birth process may have had a history of pain that has lowered their levels so as to make giving birth difficult. Those mothers who give birth by cesarean have lower levels of oxytocin.

It isn't how many times you look at the baby, how many times you hold him, it is that intangible love you feel while doing it. It is never enough to hold the baby. There has to be a feeling underlying it. That feeling is made up of neurons and biochemicals. There have to be decent levels of the love chemicals and not too many stress chemicals in the system. Oxytocin in animals inhibits the secretion of stress hormones (glucocorticoids).[6] When the system is in a vigilant mode, the oxytocin levels drop and the anxiety system heightens. When we "love" there is obviously a chemical component; and it is entirely possible that the more intense the love feeling the higher the oxytocin level. And vice versa; the higher the oxytocin level the more love there is to give. There is a hidden implication in all this. Even though you swear you love someone, your biochemicals may limit you. They may indicate that your capacity for love is not what you think it is. The second lesson: stress and inner drive are inimical to love. Driven people are often not very loving; they've got places to go, things to do. Oxytocin release is an important aspect of serotonin secretion. They seem to work in harmony to help us repress feeling, specifically pain.[7]

It is the love of a mother to the baby that provides a secure platform from which the baby approaches life. She will be unafraid and curious, not afraid to explore and seek out. It is the substrate of fear that reduces curiosity and makes a baby phlegmatic and uninterested in her surroundings. When the protector, the parent, becomes the threat, as in incest, or in being an angry, irritable tyrant, there is no longer a secure base and the child is in a devastating position, with no one to turn to, no one to lean on, and no place to go with her feelings. She must repress.

In animals, when their bellies are stroked, there is more oxytocin and their blood pressure drops. Most importantly, there is a shift from sympathetic to parasympathetic dominance, as the relaxing, rest, and repair system takes over to promote survival and good health. It has long been thought that the alerting, vigilant, aggressive system, the sympathetic, was the survival mechanism because, with the help of vasopressin, it was on the watch for danger and could flee or fight it. Now it turns out that when the system is too vigilant it can shut down, and that shut-down system is ultimately about survival. Overstimulation, in short, is dangerous to the system. It can fragment the thinking apparatus resulting in distraction, loss of concentration and short attention span. We know that a lower body temperature, parasympathetically organized, helps to promote longevity; that is certainly one key sign of survival.

My first critical point: Early bonding, contact, touch, and attachment provide long-term calming effects. They provide, in my opinion, the ability to love later on. That includes feeling maternal in women, and being able to properly lactate and nurse their babies. Second, early social experiences that affect oxytocin levels, especially in the womb, constitute memories that endure and exert a force for the continued optimum levels of it. These memories reactivate the same physiologic processes as originally, and extend the original effects onward and forward. In short, the ability to love later in life is a neurophysiologic memory. If you were loved the memory is there. If not, you cannot love to the same degree. When there is too much early pain, and the original reaction is reduced oxytocin due to trauma, then that reduction may be reactivated at times such as childbirth and just after when it is sorely needed. You need a calm interior to feel loving. Early loving seems to produce long-term reductions in blood pressure and heart rate. This kind of person not only heals faster but grows to normal levels, to his genetic destination, whereas those chronically low in loving may not heal as well and may not grow in terms of their genetic destiny.

We now have some techniques for measuring how much someone has been loved in early childhood. Certainly, there is a reason why our entering patients have uniformly high stress hormone levels.[8] When we have been unloved as infants our systems are on the alert. It drives us toward fulfillment, even symbolic fulfillment, the applause of an audience, for example, or the acquisition of money. Deprived individuals, driven as they are, usually go for secondary goals having nothing to do with parental love. Food is a good example. Someone can be as obsessed about food as about sex. Both may derive from the more basic need for love. These are rerouted needs when love is and has been missing. The force of the obsession is still the need for parental love. The energy of that need is displaced. We cannot get enough because the fulfillment is temporary, a substitute for the real thing. No matter how much we get it cannot ever be enough. We are trying to right the system of its lacks. So we get massages and our oxytocin levels rise. In a few hours they drop again. We make a good business deal and levels go up and then down. Time to get more.

There is a neuroendocrine substratum or biochemical stratum that underlies our behavior and endocrine-hormone secretions. Oxytocin is part of this substratum, which results from positive, loving experiences early in life, and therefore helps direct the rest of our lives. It keeps us from killing ourselves working, keeping on the move, planning, doing, going, all because we are on the alert from not being loved early on; on the alert against the conscious-awareness of not being loved, something devastating for our mental integration. The imprint, "I am not wanted. I am not (never will be) loved. It is hopeless to try," is far too much for a baby to understand and accept. The drive for love is rerouted toward different kinds of fulfillment—symbolic ones, at the same time as the person's ability to give and receive love is reduced. Even in late adolescence it is too late to be loved as we needed as infants, the critical period having passed. The drive is therefore twofold: (1) to escape the knowledge of deprivation and its agony, and (2) to militate toward the fulfillment of secondary goals such as success. For those who were unloved, secondary drives seem absolutely natural. The need for success can easily replace the need for love.

Once unloved, the feeling and the related physiologic levels remain. So now there is a vicious cycle: feeling unloved makes one act in ways to be further alienated and unloved: failed relationships, marriages, etc., which make one finally despair of ever being loved. The consequence may be depression and suicidal thoughts and attempts. Why? Because the imprint "unloved" can make one exigent, irritable, aloof, distant, angry, cold, and unaffectionate. So the partner has had enough and leaves because she or he too has needs which are not being fulfilled.

Lack of love provokes not only stress but subsequently high degrees of repression. So we think we feel and love; but we cannot feel what we cannot feel; therefore our thoughts dictate and help us imagine we are feeling beings who love, when in fact we may be handicapped emotionally and are just acting-out our needs. Our capacity is compromised physiologically by insufficient love in our early lives. The brain-body-physiology carries on that memory, not only about our early lives but about the history of all human life. If the memory is of excess and chronic early pain, of being left to cry it out in the crib, of being constantly shouted at or neglected, oxytocin levels may be low. One reason is, among other things, that it is an antianxiety, antipain hormone whose supplies are limited. Diabolically, the supplies become exhausted when we suffer emotionally—precisely the time when we need them the most. Oxytocin receptors are found throughout the feeling-limbic system. The hypothalamus/pituitary sends oxytocin on its way to other key brain sites, importantly to the brainstem where very early trauma is imprinted. How well hormones function depends on their ability to connect or bind with their receptors. Receptors can be altered and/or redistributed, depending on the state of stress of the organism.

LOVE AND SURVIVAL

Love is not just the avoidance of pain. It is the key to survival. With the absence of love, when parents neglect a baby by not looking at her, not listening to or matching her moods (a depressed mother cannot be exuberant with her child, and the child soon learns that exuberance is *non grata*) there is pain; worse, there is the danger of the conscious-awareness of this pain, which threatens the integrity of the brain system, particularly the integrating neocortex. The brain and the body gear up constantly to keep that awareness at bay. That is what repression is: holding real feelings out of conscious-awareness. The system must be constantly mobilized to keep that repression going. And it enlists certain biochemicals to help out, such as oxytocin. When the pain is too great, too early, and continued over too long a period the repressive system breaks down and there are later anxiety and panic attacks. These attacks often mean that the repressive trauma-feeling is close to conscious-awareness, signaling danger.

One of the agents of that breakdown may be vasopressin. This neuro-hormone (also a neurotransmitter) is a close cousin to oxytocin and can bind to its receptors. It has to do more with arousal, aggression, and territoriality; guarding the homestead against invaders. Together with oxytocin they can retune some neural pathways that have gone astray due to stress, rebalancing the system. Vasopressin, as well as oxytocin, can be regulated by stress hormones. When vasopressin and oxytocin work together there can be enhanced social bonding.[9] It is also possible that vasopressin can override the abilities of oxytocin to calm the organism when stress is exceptionally high in childhood. I will discuss vasopressin later in this chapter.

With higher levels of oxytocin one heals faster; certainly, that is a survival measure. If we cannot heal from an infection, for example, we may die. So survival is not just about combatting or running from danger; not just about defense; it is approaching love. Survival is also about positive things.

There are psychopaths who look human but who never establish any kind of loving relationship with anyone. They leave a trail of human debris in their wake. These individuals relate only to acquire and only know how to manipulate. Their false charm sometimes allows them to get away with it. But they are victims of not enough humanity in childhood with their parents. Just below their seeming human charm lies an empty shell. You cannot be good to them because they cannot feel it. They just want more.

LOVE AND NURSING: THE TRANSMISSION OF LOVE THROUGH THE BREAST

Lactation is inhibited by stress, as are many of our natural functions: elimination, eating, sex, and others. It may be that early pain lowers and imprints this physiologic level of oxytocin, thus already predetermining whether a mother will have enough milk later on. It is the hormone prolactin that is responsible for the actual secretion or production of milk, while oxytocin is in charge of most ejaculations, including the "ejaculation" of mother's milk to the baby. Prolactin can be considered another hormone that contributes to maternal feelings. It is beyond the purview of this chapter to go into all of the related hormones. Suffice to know that they exist and have been well written about.[10]

Oxytocin injections facilitate the onset of maternal feelings. Of course, early parental love would obviate that necessity. Blocking of oxytocin stifles maternal behavior.[11] If you give a sheep this hormone she will adopt other infants for mothering. She becomes "earth mother," and is more apt to "love the whole world." Whereas without this hormone she tends to reject outsider babies. In rhesus monkeys who received oxytocin there was an increase in touching, lip smacking, and watching by mothers toward their infants. Primate research approaches human behavior and the human brain and is therefore a bit more important than rat studies.

If we prevent oxytocin production in a baby animal, preference and closeness to the mother does not occur. Bonding does not occur. When there is no closeness the baby suffers, perhaps for a lifetime. Attachment is a basic need. It is a two-way street: lowered oxytocin in the baby prevents him feeling close to his parent. He becomes a baby who does not adore being cuddled, who squirms when being held. When the mother gives birth her levels rise dramatically, offering her the wherewithal to love her baby deeply. Some of that is transmitted to the baby. The biochemistry is telling us that love is essential. In the womb it has already been transmitted by the fact of love for her baby. That love, even when the baby has not been born yet, has its chemical roots. Yes, the baby can feel loved in the womb. Not in the sense of comprehension, but of biology. That is why biology can speak volumes, even contradicting our thought processes, which come along much later to deny our internal reality. It seems that eventually we might be able to give someone a "shot of motherhood," and turn a nonmaternal type into a more loving, caring mother.

Can we really inject love? In animal studies, remember, they share most of the same hormones with humans. We can take virgin females, inject them with oxytocin, and within thirty minutes they become maternal. So, yes, we can inject love if we define it carefully. At the very least we can inject the qualities of love: attachment, touch, paying attention, protecting, and nurturing. The pathways of this love seem to stem from hypothalamic centers where so many of our feelings are organized. Much of this evidence has been confirmed in primate research.

When stress levels rise, however, there is often a drop in milk production. The system is geared for struggle and conflict rather than its natural functions. It may be that oxytocin is released when there is stress in order to help combat it; to help calm the individual and not be so overwhelmed. It joins other blocking agents such as serotonin to shut down pain. Injection of oxytocin can return milk production in mothers to normal levels. The evidence is building on the role of stress in the regulation of human milk production. It is not an extravagant extrapolation to think that long and enduring imprinted stress can prevent milk production entirely. Early pain lowers the physiologic level of oxytocin, thus already predetermining whether a mother will have enough milk later on or whether right then the baby will lack nurturing and closeness, all because his mother did not get the same nurturing and closeness as an infant. The simple fact that a mother was not nursed herself as a child may result in her inability to nurse twenty years later.[12] We can begin to understand some men's fixation with the breast, getting all excited when it comes into view. It may well be a throwback to some atavistic need to try to recuperate lost oxytocin supplies from infancy. In adulthood the early need becomes eroticized but it is still the basic need that excites, stimulates, and attracts.

Mother's milk contains high levels of oxytocin. That is one reason why breast milk is so important in nursing. It is sent directly to the suckling baby's brain for comfort and calm. When animals suckle they have higher levels of the hormone. It has been found that mothers who nurse are calmer, more social, handle stress and monotony better, and have more skin-to-skin experience with the baby. In one experiment, women were encouraged to place their babies at the breast right after birth. The earlier the contact the more physical the mother was later on with the newborn and talked more to them. There was, in short, more loving contact. Lactation and nursing is one expression of loving a baby. It is very clear that the best preventive of symptoms, mental and physical, is love and its hormones.

You may not be a good, loving mother when under chronic imprinted stress. You may not be a loving person when oxytocin levels have been exhausted in an internal combat of feelings versus repression. What I must stress over and over is that early love becomes a physiologic memory that endures which can later obviate symptoms, prevent anxiety, reduce phobias, and allow the person to love.

I am using the example of lactation to point out how most of our natural impulses can be blocked by a stressor; something so seemingly banal as hunger. Many of my patients who blocked their cries in the crib when no one came to feed them, now do not even know when they are hungry. It is only when hours later that they suddenly feel starved that they know that they should eat. Clearly, it is usually not *current* stress that does this since it is often a lifelong problem.

Lactation reduces obsessive symptoms in nursing mothers. It is clear that obsessive thoughts are defenses against pain and anxiety as thoughts attempt to absorb the rising energy of repressed feelings. These symptoms are driven by a hypervigilant state which mobilizes the cerebral cortex, the thinking brain, to concoct rituals and obsessive thoughts to block feelings. For example, latent fear, underground terror occasioned by angry and violent parents, can rise up and become the need to check the locks ten times a day in order to feel safe and not in fear. Any number of research studies show the calming effect of oxytocin.[13] Uvnas-Moberg has noted the enduring effects of several injections of this hormone in animals. Oxytocin levels may be affected by very early experience, even in the womb. It is, as far as we know, the key ingredient in bonding between two people.

Mothers who themselves were not loved in their childhood, whose parents hardly ever touched them, and who were left neglected most of the time may have less oxytocin secretion on their own. Their pain or imprinted stress may have prevented them from being maternal. They may believe that it is not a natural instinct for them because they don't feel like having babies and taking care of them. Their maternal instincts have been snuffed out by parental indifference and coldness early on. One research study I envision is to measure oxytocin levels in adult women who were bottle fed versus those who nursed at the breast. Second, I want to ascertain if the length of nursing time heightens oxytocin levels. Lastly, because I say that feeling unloved early on in a primal can help us accept love, we would want to measure oxytocin in our patients before therapy and after six months and one year. Levels should rise in our therapy.

Once a calm reaction is in place it cannot be reversed by chemicals that antagonize or reverse oxytocin. It is as if to say, once we are really loved, there is not a lot anyone can do later to undo it.

There's a good deal of research on panic and anxiety states. It is clear to me that if there were no prebirth and birth trauma, and much love after birth we would not see such states. It is so difficult to establish the line from trauma at birth to obsessiveness at age thirty-five. My patients do it for me. They relive early traumas and the symptoms leave.

THE LACK OF TOUCH EQUALS THE LACK OF LOVE

When babies are not held and caressed, if basic needs are not met, they are, by definition, under stress. The baby needs love as much as milk. When needs are neglected the baby's system sends out alarm signals of danger. One of these, as I have mentioned, is cortisol, the stress hormone. When suddenly love and touch are introduced to the baby, however, there is oxytocin release and a general calming reaction. One aspect of the alarm is that there may be a lifelong deficit in oxytocin if warmth and holding did not occur. Because earlier I redefined parental love as fulfilling basic need, we may be able to quantify it in the future by measuring oxytocin levels. A person can swear he was loved but his low levels may betray him. It would be a measure of therapeutic success, as well.

Are those who suffered incest early on very low as compared to control groups? Are those who suffered it at a very young age lower than others who underwent it in adolescence? It is not such a mystery (although it is often an intellectual conceit that nothing could be that simple) that a little love here and there could change the structure of the brain, stop later obsessive-compulsive behavior, anxiety, and depression! Love is not simple! Based on widespread emotional deprivation it seems to be the most difficult thing to do.

Whenever we see the word "stress" in the literature we must always emphasize that most stress is imprinted and can date back to our womb days. It is one reason why it is so hard to comprehend this notion. Of course, it is exacerbated by current stress, the loss of a mate or a job, financial worries, and the like. It is in my opinion one explanation why oxytocin levels may be chronically low in certain individuals; it is being utilized in the combat against the imprint.

The female prairie vole, when treated soon after birth with steroid/ stress hormones, had increased masculinization later on (mounting behavior of the female).[14] Most of us don't have to be injected with stress hormones; stress in the womb and just after birth will accomplish the same thing, and may indeed masculinize females, as I discussed earlier in this work. It is perhaps logical to think that an injection is something special, when in fact the exact same chemical process takes place naturally. We can inject oxytocin or we can massage the animal and produce increased oxytocin. We can stress a carrying mother or inject her with steroids. The psychological injection is precisely the same as from a needle. A mother can be kind and loving and raise the serotonin levels in her offspring so that she can better handle adversity, or a doctor can inject serotonin and produce a temporary calming that is no different from a loving look by a mother.

A mother can "inject" oxytocin into her baby through her milk. A chronically anxious mother may leave her offspring with low oxytocin levels who later may have trouble bonding and forming attachments. (This, obviously, is subject to research. I am raising possibilities.) This may ultimately mean failed relationships and failed marriage with suffering abandoned children, who bear the brunt of something that had its cause in the infancy of the mother.[15]

What neuroendocrine researcher Sue Carter has suggested is that oxytocin is affected "by the developmental history of an organism."[16] When there are high steroid levels in the womb due to the carrying mother's stress level, the whole development of the fetus can be altered, including the lowering of the levels of oxytocin. Then years later a mother has no milk for her newborn and no one can understand why. Or she insists on going right back to work after giving birth, rationalizing that her job is so important. She may not understand that her drive has inhibited her maternal, loving hormones from secreting, dictating her behavior to get back to work. Her attitudes, interests, and thoughts may be rationalizations for her physiologic hormone status. She hasn't the biochemical equipment to want to be maternal, and has not had that wherewithal since childhood. Her mother, not being maternal, has managed through her lack of physical contact with the baby to lower the maternal hormones in her daughter. If by chance this daughter has babies they will be left soon enough so that she can return to work. She will resent being a mother, and the children will feel it. Her lower oxytocin level may already be affecting the fetus in the womb. I would hypothesize that he may be born deficient in the love department. I have noted how womb trauma results in lowered serotonin levels. It is but a small leap to apply it to oxytocin. Of course, there are mothers who cannot part from their children. It is usually because they are trying to get love from them.

LOVE AND ADDICTION: ADDICTED TO LOVE

There is evidence that oxytocin and dopamine work together toward a feeling of well-being; in addiction, it is this feeling and hormone status that hooks one permanently on drugs; the dopamine potentiates the oxytocin by increasing its receptor binding. Oxytocin inhibits the development of tolerance to drugs such as morphine, and also prevents the withdrawal symptoms when one is taken off these drugs. Rats who were able to self-administer painkillers by pressing a lever did not do so when given oxytocin.[17] Otherwise said, a mother's love or its chemical analogue can prevent addiction. Love is the preferred method.

Painkilling (opiate) activity is increased when an animal is given oxytocin injections.[18] Oxytocin is a counterbalance to feeling unloved and being in pain. Rats given cocaine become compulsive sniffers. Oxytocin reduced that behavior. And with oxytocin those on drugs do not need more and more. Again, it is like a shot of love; it keeps one away from painkillers because one is less in pain, as with all of us who are truly loved. Addicts and alcoholics are trying to feel loved. It is the rush and feeling of warmth they experience when the drug or alcohol hits that drives them to take more and more. That warmth is like a mother's caress; they often describe it as a warmth that is completely relaxing.[19]

What I am discussing leaves a good deal for philosophers to ponder. Is the drug taker responsible for his actions? To say "no" means that none of us has free will; all of us are victims of our childhood. What I am saying is that "just say no" to a lifetime of emotional deprivation is not so easily done. And it is not just a matter of willpower. Of course, each of us is responsible for our actions, but we often need help. We must understand that someone deficient for a lifetime in pain-suppressors such as serotonin does need chemical help to normalize. Yes, there has to be something inside of him that makes him want to take his life in his hands. Not all of us have that strength or determination. It is sometimes not easy to be tolerant of weakness. If someone just came off the desert and was dying of thirst, he would want large quantities of water. The problem is that we cannot see the emotional desert that some of us have left in our childhood. How to draw the line between responsibility and being a victim is a constant philosophical-psychological problem.

The degree of addiction can often by measured by the severity of withdrawal symptoms once one is off drugs. Oxytocin attenuates these symptoms. Love will do it, as well, but not as quickly. A shot of oxytocin is like receiving a shot of a loving mother. Isn't that what heroin does? Momma in a syringe soothes, calms, and relaxes.

HOW ADDICTION GETS ITS START

Early trauma, prebirth or birth, has a lot to do with proper functioning of the cortical site. It is here that the seeds of drug addiction may be planted because of the dysregulation of the frontal cortex and its affect on the limbic and brainstem connections. These people have to constantly deal with their pain. If you break your leg and you take a strong painkiller, and then the leg heals, you may still need drugs. This is because the pain from which you are really suffering is hidden, lying in the antipodes of the brain system; a hurt perhaps forty-five years old. That pain still needs calming. That doesn't mean one is addicted. It's just that pain still exists but is not observed nor palpable. Until you take the drug you often don't know what you were missing. Methadone for heroin addicts in withdrawal or painkillers for those with anxiety slow down or block the transmission of the pain message. The message isn't obvious. It *is* when there is a broken leg, but less clear when there is a broken heart from early childhood. If our broken leg needs months to heal and we take pain pills while we are healing it is considered normal. There would be no diagnosis as "addicted" (with all the opprobrium attached to this label). It's odd, to have a pejorative label attached to us because we need to kill pain. But if we suffer from an agonizing imprint from infancy that is just as real and painful as a broken leg, we may be considered an addict. Why? Because we are soothing a hurt that happened at two weeks of age.

We are still in the frontier mentality of not complaining and toughing it out. After all, being addicted to painkillers means that someone is in pain or thinks he or she is in pain. It is not a criminal act. It is an act of survival. No one would put massive amounts of painkillers into his system if he did not have pain. With no imprinted pain massive doses of painkiller would be lethal.

Once arriving at adulthood love can no longer leave a lasting effect. That is, once low levels of oxytocin or high levels of stress hormones are registered early in life it is difficult to reestablish normal setpoints. The need for cocaine, for example, happens when dopamine levels are chronically exhausted; cocaine artificially increases dopamine in the synapses. One may get hooked on cocaine in order to feel more aggressive, have more pleasure and fun in life, feel greater self-confidence, and be able to confront others. Cocaine can do that but so can parental love. Cocaine makes one far less afraid—for the moment. That is one reason one has to go back again and again to it. It does not last; unlike mother love, which does. Mother and father are establishing the setpoints for their offspring for life. They cannot decide to love the child at the age of fourteen and make up a neglect at the age of one and two. It is already physiologic.

Why wouldn't deprived people want to hook onto drugs that produced such a wonderful feeling? All they are trying to do is normalize, to recreate what was and is missing from the earliest days of life. They want that warm and fuzzy feeling all over. They want to feel relaxed and comfortable in their skin. I seriously doubt that someone would get addicted who has normal levels of oxytocin and serotonin. I would suggest a research study on addicts for these levels. (I plan to do a research study on oxytocin levels before and after therapy among my patients.)

What do many New Age therapies do? They ease the addiction occasioned by early lack of love temporarily by elevating oxytocin levels and calming us. Massage, Rolfing, and mystical ideas are all part of it, as is the concerned, kind, interested look of a therapist. There is nothing wrong about feeling good, even temporarily. But we can become addicted to any of the therapies and therapists who help raise our oxytocin/dopamine levels. They make us feel better, for the moment.

For the treatment of addiction I would hope one day that there would be research into the use of oxytocin together with first-line, brainstem blockers such as clonidine and/or the antiseizure, antipain medication, tegretol. The combination, in my opinion, would be effective for addiction, anxiety, and panic attacks. While early pain may galvanize the system into hyperactivity, oxytocin is more associated with the opposite system, the parasympathetic hypoactivity. Primal therapy is basically a balancing act, making those who are hypo into a bit more hyper, and vice versa. We are doing what nature would have done had not trauma intervened.

VASOPRESSIN

As I stated, the autonomic nervous system that governs automatic functions is composed of two branches, the parasympathetic and the sympathetic. The first is given impetus by oxytocin, while the sympathetic is more involved with vasopressin. Some can call it "yin and yang," but I prefer "the dialectic," one of the key laws governing human development. There is a balance of the sympathetic and parasympathetic systems in all of us. Vasopressin has more aggressive features allowing us to be alert and on the watch for intruders. It is dominated by the sympathetic nervous system. Indeed, as I discussed earlier, we see that the birth trauma can occasion a predominance of one or the other system depending on the nature of the trauma, e.g., heavy anesthesia to the mother producing basically a parasympathetic imprint in the newborn. Both are methods of survival. But early trauma skews the balance between those systems—between oxytocin and vasopressin as one key element. It is when there is a sympathetic imprint that we often later find obsessive-compulsive behavior. And wouldn't you know it, there is a predominance of vasopressin in these disorders (as measured in cerebral-spinal fluid).[20]

Vasopressin helps male animals spend more time with their offspring. It makes for caring fathers. If we block vasopressin there is immediately less paternal behavior. Vasopressin injected directly into a section of the animal's brains increased paternal behavior on the part of male voles.

They couldn't be loving fathers without it. Vasopressin is a counterbalance to oxytocin, dealing with more aggression and territoriality in animals (directed by the sympathetic, alerting, driving, mobilizing nervous system). How you feel, your attitudes about love, parenting, bonding, in short, may well be dictated by your hormone state, and that may be dictated by the setpoints of your hormones from experiences going all the way back to the womb. You may change your attitudes through exhortation by others but you will not change your hormone state permanently. Both vasopressin and oxytocin are located on neurons; both seem to have a role in brain maturation. So when there is trauma early on, even in the womb, the maturation of the brain is interfered with. In the vernacular, "We don't have all our marbles." It is a different brain, thanks in part to these two neurohormones. It is crucial when synapses are being organized and neuronal networks fixed that there is a proper balance between these neurohormones to aid in this process.

Vasopressin and oxytocin are capable of altering the firing rate of even single neurons. Their deviations help to produce a different brain before the fetus sees the light of day. It is not impossible that the different brain is one less likely to feel and to make social contact later on. We may say, "He is a chip off the old block. He is exactly like his father, inside himself." Yet he may be that "chip" because the father was so inside himself that he could not reach out and be physical with his child, or because the mother's chronic depressive state while carrying had impacted the fetus adversely.

Vasopressin and oxytocin can be traced back millions of years in evolution. One might induce from this that love or attachment or bonding has always been important to living organisms and is the key to survival. It is no wonder that it is closely related to sex and reproduction. In sexual arousal vasopressin is at its peak, while oxytocin peaks during ejaculation. Vasopressin cells are concentrated in the amygdala, in the feeling centers of the brain. Sexual activity increases the oxytocin levels. Perhaps that is why after sex and strong physical attachment, as strong as we can get—being inside someone else's body—one wonders with the partner, "Do you really love me?" It is love that motivates us toward reproduction. When there is no attachment there is no love. When there is little oxytocin there is no attachment. When there is no love, survival is at stake. Sex and emotional attachment share some of the same under-lying hormones, not the least of which is oxytocin. It is therefore easily confused. Love makes us strong for our progeny. And you need sex to enhance love, and have progeny, and vice versa. It is the natural out-growth of love. What is also easily confused is love and need. Those who never had their needs fulfilled early on keep on looking for fulfillment believing it is love when someone is helping or protecting. So long as someone is needy she will confound that need with love.

Male rats treated with vasopressin during the first week of life were more aggressive later on to strangers who came close. Vasopressin, released when there is stress, can be combatted by oxytocin, which is strange since they are so close molecularly as to use the same receptors. It seems that they form a dialectic unity, part of some overall, larger system that governs both stress and relaxation responses. For feelings not only encompass these two neurohormones but belong to a cascade of reactions. That is why feel-ings can be measured along a whole panoply of hormone responses orga-nized by the hypothalamus, the pituitary, and other limbic structures.

Vasopressin takes part in partner preference and in some animals encourages the selection of specific female partners. It is one essential element in pair bonding in animals. It is also associated with testosterone which increases vasopressin levels. In some cases, vasopressin acts like a neurotransmitter.[21] It remains locked in synaptic vesicles and then is released into the circulation to exert effects on other neurons, which then either facilitate the transmission of messages (often of pain) or inhibit them.

It is never a good idea to focus on one hormone or one chemical and believe that "this is it." It is nearly always part of some grand system. The overall grand system in most cases is human feeling. I have noted earlier that clonidine (working on many structures, most importantly the brain-stem), when used in an experiment with my patients, was quite effective in calming anxiety states and aiding sleep, to say nothing of lowering the need for cigarettes by lowering brainstem agitation. Remember, many addictions, including tobacco, are driven by first-line imprints. It is the very early traumas that are imprinted in the brainstem and locus ceruleus that respond well to clonidine and secondarily to its cousin, oxytocin. Put another way, anxiety and post traumatic stress disorder (we are most of us suffering from this disorder if we underwent a trauma at birth or severe trauma and lack of love later on) may be in part due to lowered oxytocin levels. It has also been found that estrogen plays a major role in regulating the number of oxytocin receptors in some key nuclei of the brain. Clearly, oxytocin is not the whole story, but a very important part of it.

I submit that it is feeling that is the central organizing principle of human behavior. You can measure feeling in the brain, in human biochemistry, in mother's milk, in saliva, and in spinal taps. We can measure it in serotonin, oxytocin, vasopressin, and dopamine. Feelings are all-encompassing, and of course, love is the key feeling of human intercourse. It can be found everywhere in the system because feeling is everywhere. We are first and foremost feeling beings.

I have selected new research in biochemistry to discuss human behavior. I could have just as easily chosen other biochemicals. The hormone system interacts with so many other systems, first and foremost the brain and its development. If we are trying to find the overarching linchpin of what can go right or wrong with the brain we must ask where was the love or its lack. We can investigate biochemical changes for a lifetime and never arrive at a solution to why we are low or high in certain hormones, why we have high blood pressure or a rapid heartbeat. We cannot find solutions so long as we avoid inquiring into the kind of love there was or wasn't early on. We have not looked enough into love because it is a feeling, more difficult to quantify and measure; and for those cut off from feelings who operate on the cognitive level it is an alien universe. If we insert love and feeling into the equation we are going to be able to solve some of the critical biochemical problems of our day. Without love and feeling we shall remain adrift.

Notes

1. The work of Barry Keverne of Cambridge University.
2. Thomas Insel, "A Neurobiological Basis of Social Attachment," *American Journal of Psychiatry* 1554 (6 June 1997).
3. Emory University, Atlanta, as reported in "Gene Transplant Turns Mice into Social Creatures," *International Herald Tribune*, 20 August 1999.

4. Insel, "A Neurobiological Basis of Social Attachment," p. 732.

5. K. Uvnas-Moberg, "Oxytocin May Mediate the Benefits of Positive Social Interaction and Emotions," *Psychoneuroendocrinology* 23, no. 8 (1998): 825.

6. K. Uvnas-Moberg et al., "Oxytocin as a Possible Mediator of SSRI-induced Antidepressant Effects," *Psychopharmacology* 142, no. 1 (February 1999): 95–101.

7. Ibid.

8. Our 1984 research with St. Bartholomew's Hospital, London.

9. Uvnas-Moberg, "Oxytocin May Mediate the Benefits of Positive Social Interaction and Emotions," p. 825

10. See the work of Michel Odent, *Birth Reborn* (New York: Pantheon, 1984).

11. Insel, "A Neurobiological Basis of Social Attachment."

12. C. Carter, and M. Altemus, "Integrative Functions of Lactational Hormones in Social Behavior and Stress Management," *Annals of the New York Academy of Science.*

13. Uvnas-Moberg et al., "Oxytocin as a Possible Mediator of SSRI-Induced Anitdepressant Effects."

14. Thomas Insel has studied the prairie vole extensively. See "Voles are Addicted to Love," *Science News* 154 (5 December 1998), p. 367.

15. Carter and Altemus, "Integrative Functions of Lactational Hormones in Social Behavior and Stress Management."

16. G. L. Kovacs, Z. Sarnyai, and Gyula Szabo, "Oxytocin and Addiction: A Review," *Pyschoneuroendocrinology* 23, no. 8 (1998): 945–62.

17. Ibid.

18. Ibid.

19. Ibid.

20. K. Uvnas-Moberg, "Oxytocin Linked Antistress Effects: The Relaxation and Growth Response."

21. C. Barberis and Elaine Tribollet, "Vasopressin and Oxytocin Receptors in the Central Nervous System," *Critical Reviews in Neurobiology* 10, no. 1 (1996): 119–54.

18

ON SEXUALITY
AND HOMOSEXUALITY

A study of mothers of homosexual men found that two-thirds of the mothers versus one-third of mothers of heterosexual males were able to recall stressful events while pregnant. This, together with other similar studies, uncovered excessive trauma very early in the systems of those mothers whose offsprings were to become homosexual.[1] This is not a value judgment. It has been my clinical experience for many years that womblife is a true prelude to later personality, sex life and sexual orientation.[2] I term it "aberrant" because there is a basic deviation of the hormone system due to the mother's trauma.

My homosexual patients have told me time and again that they felt "different" from the ages of five and six on. They may be responding to basic alterations in biochemistry and nerve circuitry laid down in the first months of life after conception. These changes may set up tendencies toward aberrant behavior. Particularly when it is compounded by social circumstances, for example, an absent father or a tyrannical mother. If during pregnancy a mother is very anxious, that anxiety would be mediated by a number of hormone changes. This may later have a decided effect on sex hormone function of the offspring.[3]

Some years ago Gunther Dorner of the Institute for Endocrinology, Humboldt University, Germany, studied the connection between hormonal changes in the womb and sexual orientation later on.[4] If carrying mother rats did not get enough sex hormone, being artificially deprived, there was a permanent change in the fetal brain, specifically, the hypothalamus. He found that when the changes were radical enough homosexuality resulted in the offspring in some cases. What Dorner pointed out was that the later sexuality results from the stamping in, the imprint, of hormonal states. He points out that these alterations are written into the system permanently and will determine how a boy or girl will respond to hormonal changes in puberty.[5] Much of this makes sense since it is in the first two to three months of gestation that male/female differentiation takes place. If you seriously interfere with these hormone-based changes you can significantly change sexual orientation. It has been found, for example, that if you give rhesus monkey mothers extra male hormone while carrying, the female offspring will be more aggressive, play rough, and will tend to mount other monkeys. When it comes to humans it may be more complex but the basic principles are clear. Given this kind of hormonal base, together with an absent or abusive parent, there can be the makings for later homosexuality. The changes in the sex hormone levels can be altered by stress in the carrying mother which alters the setpoints thereafter. Homosexuality gets its start so early that it seems genetic. At the very least, it seems "natural" to the homosexual.

A study on the sexual problems of Americans was reported in the February 8, 1999, Los Angeles Times. It revealed that 80 million adult men and women have some kind of sexual dysfunction. Many women between the ages of eighteen and twenty-five have low libido, as do older men. What is important here is how deep and very early sex problems can be based. A smoking mother plus a heavily anesthetized birth can down-regulate the newborn, which eventually can mean a down-regulated sex drive, i.e., low libido.

The confluence of the three traumas—prebirth, birth, and immediate postbirth—produces an overwhelming strain on the heart in situations of fear and terror. A child may survive but become a bedwetter, awash in old, painful brainstem impulses. Sexual compulsion and aggressiveness is another result. Part of this problem is the compounding of impulses, and part may be the possible impairment of the frontal cortex due to the trauma in the womb. With less repressive cortical ability there is a loss of control. As soon as the child is asleep with defenses lowered, up comes the brainstem pressure and the outlet in wetting the bed. In adolescence it will turn into sexual hyperactivity, the penis as outlet for tension. If the childhood is deprived, then the hyperactivity may turn into uncontrolled sexual perversion. Now we may have a pedophile or rapist. The impulse is given uncontrollable force by the first-line imprint. Can one imagine how ineffective it is to do sexual counseling in cases of serious sexual problems? Someone who has arrested development, whose maturity stopped in puberty, will not respond to counseling, no matter how effective.

Peter Nathanielsz, who has written on fetal life, quotes a study on sexuality: "Researchers in California have shown that when male fetal rats develop in an environment of roughly half the usual amount of oxygen in the mother's blood for the last third of pregnancy, there are problems with sexual behavior when the rats grow up.[6] This is a very important study because it again points out that oxygen deprivation in the womb has an effect on later sexual functioning. In my opinion, it is not only oxygen deprivation; it can be any important trauma. Sexual functioning, in short, is affected by life in the womb. Further, if we are to really understand sexual problems we must look beyond the sexual domain.

Sex problems are not just sex problems. The body reacts in its entirety so that when there is repression of *any* kind of early pain there will be general repression, and that includes sex drive. The conversion of imprinted pain, as I have noted, into high or low sex drive takes place in the hypothalamus and other limbic structures.

LITTLE BOY LOST

A patient of mine lost his twin sister in an explosion when he was nine. The two had shared a close, warm relationship. The death was so sudden, so violent and unexpected, that the loss was imprinted unconsciously. In our session, immersed in his feeling, he begged his sister not to leave him. He realized that in every female relationship he had had up to that point, he was looking for his sister.

He was enjoying a good relationship with one woman until recently. One night, after much kissing and hugging, she took off her top and bra and pulled him onto the couch. He immediately went into a state of shock and disgust. His girlfriend's actions had taken him beyond the warmth and camaraderie he had shared with his sister. It turned out he had had a half dozen relationships that had failed when they threatened to turn sexual. His act-out was to seek female companionship and then reject it. He was still the little boy looking for his sister who comforted him when his mother was cruel. She was his complete refuge.

Anxiety is a signal that the original event or feeling is approaching consciousness. All systems immediately go on alert against conscious-awareness and against connection. Energy moves to the frontal area of the cortex to relay the danger, but the cortex can't hear the shattering message, and it is sent back to the brain's lower centers by the thalamus and hypothalamus to churn us up and alter our sexuality. Anxiety is a vague, unfocused symptom because the origins are. Originally, there was a bodily discomfort that the baby suffered long before he had the brain-power to even call it something. The current treatment for this is again a vague, global, unfocused therapy—a tranquilizer. It shuts down agitation in general. So here is one dilemma. The feeling is a total body reaction while the underlying force of terror is specific to an event or series of events. What we need to do is focus the vague symptom into something specific. It is my experience that anxiety is not a genetic legacy. It happens because of *experience*. We need to find out what that is. Otherwise we are force to try the shotgun approach using all sorts of globally acting nonspecific tranquilizers, and then hoping for the best. Anxiety is not a mystery; it's a memory!

Many people who had tyrannical fathers find that in the face of anger by someone else, an old anxiety creeps in that is totally out of keeping with the situation. The imprint of fear is triggered and the reaction is the inability to confront the person. It doesn't take many irritated shushes or angry looks from a parent to solidly cement a young child's fear into place. We as adults tend to forget that.

Why do we remain shut down, living in a gray world? We do so because the imprint lies in our neural underbrush, providing continuity to our deadness. Feeling the deadness makes us come alive because we are feeling. Too often we simply act "dead," which keeps us from feeling it.

RAGE AND THE IMPULSE-RIDDEN

Rage is an example of feelings that cannot simply be counseled away. In rage management, one learns how to keep oneself under control. But that cannot eradicate the imprinted rage. Rage management implies that rage is permanent and requires constant control. Rage doesn't have to be permanent. If the patient cannot pound the padded walls and scream and yell in historic context against a brutal, cruel father, or against the frustration at being blocked at birth, the rage is going to remain. Rage is not a business to be managed.

Studies have found that children with violent childhoods have a propensity toward violence later on in life. This may be due to the fact that early violence leaves a clear mark on the chemistry of the brain, one result being that the serotonin system becomes less effective. This impairs the repression of aggressive impulses.[7]

There are many studies showing low serotonin levels in a variety of categories of people: suicides, homicides, obsessives, and others. The researchers often then draw the conclusion that people are suicidal because they are low in serotonin due to a genetic imbalance. They then may prescribe pills that boost serotonin, believing that this rebalances the system, and is therefore the therapy of choice. What rebalances the system is addressing the early traumas that destabilized it in the first place.

Why does the imbalance continue for decades after an early emotional deprivation or trauma? Because of the imprint. Notice that it is the impulse-ridden person (low inhibitory neurotransmitter levels) who is involved in homicide and suicide. It is the first-line, brainstem unarticulated impulses which drive this behavior.

Individuals who have had birth trauma and later emotional deprivation both were found to be six times as prone to commit violent crime as those who did not have similar traumatic experiences. "Having one factor alone," study authors Adrian Raine, Patricia Brennan, and Sarnoff Mednick noted, "didn't increase the risk [of violent crime] very much but the two together seem almost like a chemical reaction."[8] This study suggests much about the relationship between compounded early trauma and later mental illness and antisocial behavior. It has been found that birth trauma coupled with early maternal rejection can lead to violent crime by the time the individual is eighteen years of age. But this was not the case in those who suffered maternal rejection without the birth trauma.[9] If we are looking for solutions to the high suicide and homicide rates, we'd better begin looking at our prebirth care and birth practices. Just improving that will change a great deal of unnecessary deaths in society. This is to say nothing about deaths from chronic drinking and smoking. Cigarettes are an excellent first-line blocker, aiding the secretion of endogenous painkillers.

The memory of a brainstem reaction such as deep or shallow breathing as a result of early anoxia is *itself* a brainstem reaction. That is the meaning of memory. The reactions take place where the memory was lodged, and the reactions endure and become lifelong patterns deriving from those lower structures. The body remembers in its own way, on its own level, just as the limbic system remembers in a feeling way.

To be clear, reactions of rapid heartbeat, for example, are the first-line component of a feeling. Presenting a report in school shouldn't produce 180 beats per minute heart rate, but the event it triggered off, terror at one day after birth being left alone, should. High blood pressure therefore may well be a memory of early trauma impressed into brainstem structures. Brainstem blockers normalize blood pressure. Rapid heartbeat, palpitations, and high blood pressure are all part of a memory; it is just missing its context. To treat this heart rate as the real disease is to miss the mark. Meanwhile, palliatives are used; all palliatives have one main characteristic: they must be repeated over and over.

If we have a fear of riding in an elevator, we should not be dissuaded from that fear; we should be persuaded to feel it in context. No great fear resides in the system without a reason. If we try to conquer it, we make it an enemy. It is a friend that tells us about a life lived, about experiences we have forgotten and pain we have buried. It is liberating. It holds the key to freedom. To find that key, we must first search through the archives of personal history and find out what it holds.

During a feeling, a patient suddenly grasped the hand of one of my therapists. The therapist withdrew his hand—a mistake, for even though the patient could not articulate it, she was feeling that, "If there is nothing to hang on to now, I will die." She needed that contact to assuage her utter terror.

Sleep apnea, in which breathing temporarily stops, is a possible response to experiencing anoxia (oxygen deprivation) at birth, as is a child holding his breath to try to get his way. History directs the need. Treating the patient in the here-and-now is not progressive because the patient is in the there-and-then. Only his symptoms are in the here-and-now.

In photos of a birth trauma (shown in a previous book by the author), the attending obstetrician's fingerprints actually have reappeared on the legs of a patient. The first time I saw this phenomenon I was as skeptical as I am sure many readers are now. But it happens and is not a chance occurrence. Such phenomena are the concomitants of memory. If the body suffered a twisted neck at birth, then the tendency to suffer neck symptoms may be carried for a lifetime. Carrying one's head at a tilt can be one lifelong result. Some of my male patients report a cutting feeling on the tip of their penis when they witness an accident or read about a knife attack. Circumcision may be the imprinted culprit here. No child should be circumcised (if at all) until he is grown enough to understand and want it. Hurting a baby for what he deems is no reason can be very traumatic. This played a role in one homosexual I treated. His penis was aggressed and, together with other reasons, turned him away from sex for a long time. He later took his circumcision as punishment for his sexual impulses.

All roads lead to pain. The goal of Primal Therapy is not pain, however. It is pleasure, contentment, and a good life. Pain is only the way in. One of my patients, Sarah, takes solace in knowing that relief lies on the other side of pain.

SARAH'S STORY

This morning I woke up around 4:45 A.M. with an anxiety attack. This has been happening almost daily for the past week. The feeling is one of being very, very scared. I have been experiencing it throughout my life, but I never knew what it was all about. I know now, and when I awaken with this terror, an internal dialogue immediately begins: "You know what this feeling is, Sarah. Your womb/birth memory is shooting through to consciousness. It's okay."

Knowing that makes a huge difference, because not knowing it was driving me insane. A feeling with a source I can deal with, but a feeling with no apparent source makes both the mind and the emotions crazy. The feeling starts as panic, then I become sick to my stomach. The waves of nausea continue. I have to get up and walk around before my body settles down and begins to shake this feeling off. If I stay with this feeling and don't get out of bed, it just intensifies. My upper shoulders and neck start to hurt, and then my face begins to have pain as well.

I know this feeling is a big one, and I'm not willing to experience it at home alone. I have had a strong suspicion lately that I am going to throw up when I finally do allow myself to feel this. It's not something I look forward to, but the relief it will bring me far outweighs any discomfort. Knowing this is what gives me the courage to go into the scariest of feelings. What is on the other side of these feelings is relief and freedom from them, something I have wanted all my life.

NOTES

1. See D. F. Swaab and M. A. Hoffman, "Sexual Differentiation of the Human Hypothalamus in Relation to Gender and Sexual Orientation," *Trends in Neurosciences* 18 (1995): 264–70.

2. G. Dorner et al., "Stressful Events in Prenatal Life of Bi- and Homosexual Men," *Experimental and Clinical Endocrinology* 81 (1983): 83–87.

3. I. L. Ward, "Prenatal Stress Feminizes and Demasculinizes the Behavior of Males," *Science* 175(1972): 82–84.

4. Ibid.

5. Dorner et al., "Stressful Events in Prenatal Life of Bi- and Homosexual Men."

6. See the original study: R. H. M. Hermans et al., "Altered Adult Sexual Behavior in the Male Rat Following Chronic Prenatal Hypoxia," *Neurotoxicology and Teratology* 15 (1993): 353–63.

7. See *Science News*, 27 June 1995.

8. A. Raine, P. Brennan, and S. A. Mednick, "Interaction between Birth Complications and Early Maternal Rejection in Predisposing Individuals to Adult Violence: Specificity to Serious, Early Onset Violence," *American Journal of Psychiatry* 154, no. 9 (September 1997): 1265–71.

9. Ibid.

19

WHAT'S LOVE GOT TO DO WITH IT?

History, history, history. Imprint, imprint, and love. How do you love a brain? You fulfill the basic needs of human beings and the brain will follow, as will the body; for love isn't just something we think about or words we utter. It lies in all of our tissues, hormones, and organ systems. The brain engineers love and spreads its joy everywhere in the system. It says, "Not too much of stress hormones," "Not too much of excitatory neurotransmitters," just enough to keep us alert and aware. With love, adequate oxygen at birth, great care by the mother during prebirth, holding, touching, caring, attunement, listening, praising, and encouraging, the system will right itself. If we want to avoid drug addiction and alcoholism later on we need a brain that represses effectively, and that means a loved brain. Serotonin is adequate when there is early love, and less than adequate when there isn't. We might be able to say no to drugs, but I don't think we can say no to our neurobiology.

We need a new orientation to love. It is not just words of endearment we need. We must not anesthetize the mother and therefore the newborn so that helplessness and hopelessness are stamped in for life, creating a deviated brain. We must mount a campaign against smoking and drinking while pregnant. The mother smokes, the fetus coughs. The mother drinks and the fetus gets drunk. Can you imagine what the fetus is undergoing, zonked, with no way to comprehend the assault? It is not an acci-dent that smoking pregnant women give birth to offspring who are often behavior problems and who do not learn well. It is because the brain is already compromised in these children.

There are the right-to-life people who want women who have been raped and/or who really don't want their babies, not to have the right to abortion. Yet, the research shows that unwanted children have much less of a chance to lead a normal life. That is what we are forcing on women: to give birth to mentally handicapped offspring. The right to life should mean the right to a normal, happy life. An unwanted child, for whatever reason, puts the mother under stress. Her cortisol levels are continually high. The result can be premature birth and all of those complications with inadequate development of the brain. Loving a baby means that his rights come first. If the carrying mother needs a drink she needs first to think of the effects on the fetus. If she is trying to diet to keep her figure, she needs to think about malnutrition for the fetus and how that will damage its brain. It is hard to put someone else first when we need so des-perately ourselves.

If we want to produce new human beings with a solid brain we need to change the birth practices in accordance with Drs. Leboyer and Odent. We need to take great care in prebirth and, of course, in the first months after birth. That is when the brain is forming new sypnases and dendrites; its communication system is developing that will allow the child to be more than competent in many spheres, physical, artistic, and intellectual. I have seen children born to mothers who are very careful and loving in prebirth, birth, and afterward. These children are different. They are alert, smart, physically advanced, not sick, not whiny, creative, warm, and cuddly. Who would want more than that? They have every chance in life, which is the reason for writing this book—to give society a chance to create a new kind of human being. It is not so difficult at all. It is the way to avoid later alcoholism and addiction, criminality and psy-chosis. It is a way to produce humans who care about their brothers and sisters in society.

I am impressed by the idea of how simple it is to accomplish what I am discussing. It is far easier than building prisons and mental hospitals to take care of the errors we have already made in child rearing. What most of us write about is how to fix the compensating mechanisms of early lack of love. We fix the migraines, the rapist, the drug addict and the voyeur, the hypertension and the teeth grinder, the anger out of control, and the depressive.

We need to start addressing causes before there is a deviated, abnormal brain system that forces deviated behavior. We need to understand the very deep, visceral roots of anxiety, that most primitive reaction that involves deep-lying sectors of the brain. We can try to combat it with exhortation, moralization, insight therapy or drugs, but wouldn't it be better to descend down to those deep levels and root out the cause of the anxiety? It can be done. First and foremost, we need to change our birth practices. Let us stop drugging mothers at birth. For all of my heavy-smoking patients birth trauma has been paramount. The same with the alcoholics.

Yesterday a TV crew interviewed some of my patients. They asked, "Isn't it scary to do what you are doing?" They said unanimously, no; it is scary not to do it because then it means chronic suffering. They all said they can't wait for their therapy sessions because it means relief.

I didn't concoct a theory about an imprint. I saw every day what the lack of love did to people, and how it stayed in their systems for forty or fifty years; how those early traumas are kept in pure form, untouched by decades of experience. I hear it every day in the cries of my patients who express their real needs to their parents, "Hold me. Want me. Listen to me. Praise me. Guide me. Be with me." What they cannot express in words they relive in inarticulated agony from preverbal pains. Their bodies express the anguish and malaise. We must reorient ourselves to how the body can express itself on its own terms. In high blood pressure, which says, "I am under pressure." In migraines, which say, "My blood vessels are constricting and dilating due to lack of oxygen at birth."

How do we change the early lack of love? I believe that the reliving of the agony portion allows the brain to rest and recoup. It seems logical, after seeing my advanced patients, that somehow the brain when not under a load of pain does very well. The brain may not recoup all of its early impairment but these individuals can lead a happy and productive life. We see by the case histories how they can eschew drugs and alcohol. We never address those problems in and of themselves. We address the pain; the rest follows. Yes, symptoms must be addressed but not as the ultimate therapy.

These are the critical concepts to embrace in addressing both physical and mental problems. Without them we are locked into a phenotypic, symptom-alleviating, appearance-only therapy, which at best is ephemeral. These therapies are holding actions only. In holding actions you have to keep beating back the early imprinted demons. By definition they cannot be long-lasting because the imprint is always there to remind the person of unfinished business. The imprint is a *survival* mechanism and *should* always be there. It allows us to go back in history to when we were not touched at six months or one year of age and retrieve and redo that history, crying out the need, reaching up to Mommy, pleading, begging (with the newly developed cortical brain), and overthrowing the repression of that need, a need that became pain because it went unfulfilled.

It is my assumption that when patients relive birth trauma they are also locking into the prebirth event and it may well be that the reliving encompasses both time periods. Each developing level of brain function encompasses the previous one. A hormone change in a depressed mother when the fetus is five months old may be compounded at birth with heavy anesthesia, which is dealt with by a slightly more sophisticated and developed brain system. Both events and many more will down-regulate the infant permanently. We must never think that because there are no words for very early pain, it cannot be coded and stored—and remembered on its own level of consciousness. We may have to wait decades to put a label on feelings, but it will happen.

It's the old philosophic question: Are we happy if we think we are? Are we cured if we think we are? No! We are cured when the body makes its statement. It speaks its own language in chemicals; they are also "us." We are not just a cortical brain. If there are high levels of stress hormones in a person the body is saying, "No, you are not well."

One original reason for the development of the frontal cortex was to keep uncomfortable truth far away. If we recognize the coding and storing of feeling we can begin to understand why we are the way we are. If we learn to follow the evolution of the brain in our therapy we will get much further on. The field of psychotherapy has largely ignored the imprint and evolution, hence the emphasis on the present, on behavior and on symptoms.

If the oxygen experiments at UCLA serve no other purpose they should offer strong evidence of the resilience and enduring power of early memory. Further, it means we have to take another look at recovered memory. There are ways to verify it. Let us not make our patients suffer even more by not believing their stories of abuse. That's not therapy; that's moralizing. It is not a matter of our personal beliefs. It is our job to search out historical reality, wherever it may lead. Therapists can say that a patient is dissembling, making up trauma, being hysterical, etc. But until therapists have deep access they cannot judge the veracity of the patient. Meanwhile, they may be doing a great disservice to the patient by such judgmental attitudes. Remember, veracity results from reliving, not recounting. Reliving produces the exact earlier vital signs as occurred during the trauma.

There is one important way we know that a reliving episode is accurate and that imprints exist. Once one is totally in a memory, body and soul, and one relives a lowering of oxygen supplies at birth, the system acts as though there is this enormous need for oxygen and accepts deep, heavy breathing without hyperventilation symptoms. But when one *recalls* the lack of oxygen and then voluntarily breathes rapidly and deep, the result is hyperventilation syndrome. That is why total memory heals and recall, even with tears, does not. It is the difference between crying about and crying inside the memory.

I have seen (and we have filmed) the lower brain levels at work many times in other ways. A patient during a session will vibrate his feet at over 100 rapid movements per minute for thirty-five minutes, something he couldn't begin to duplicate by any act of will later on. But, you say, it is the same as hypnosis. It is. Hypnosis is tapping into lower levels by suggesting us away from cortical critical thought. In our sessions the body is on automatic and reacts instinctively. If not, what I have just described cannot happen. What drove that vibration? It was very early terror, which he could feel only when he descended down to brainstem memories of terror at birth.

Are we basically angry, raging monsters, or are we kind and generous pussycats? We are neither and both. We are born with capacities that date back millions of years. If the system is loved and not traumatized, it will be kind and generous and not hateful and aggressive. If a young child is constantly frustrated, she is going to be an angry child and adult. The child is responding to hurt, and it would be the ultimate denial to pretend she has not been hurt.

Connection is healing. The wound we are healing is the lack of love. The method of healing is to experience this lack consciously. The moment we are hurt the system rushes in to heal. If we are cut, the epidermal growth factor is produced to help healing. When we are hurt emotionally, first the forces of repression rush in to keep us calm and functioning. Then the imprinted pain is constantly trying to connect with frontal consciousness so as to heal. The system knows that is what it takes to heal. All of our measurements show that connection heals, whether of permanent drops in blood pressure or the permanent lowering of stress hormones. Pain is a blessing. When felt, it sets in motion the forces of healing. *To feel love, you first have to feel unloved.* This opens up the system so that it can now receive love.

It seems paradoxical, but feeling unloved lets in love and warmth because it finally removes the pain-repression and lets in feeling. Otherwise, that unloved feeling suffuses everything else. An unreturned phone call is a trigger that brings on strange ideas: "She doesn't want to talk to me. She must not like me."

All psychological embellishments are extrapolations urged on by the imprinted feeling. It prevents one from reasoning that the call was not returned simply because the person was busy. That is because one cannot "see" the other person; one is too enmeshed in one's own need. If we already feel, "No one wants me," then it is easy to misinterpret a phone call in terms of that feeling. If we try to convince someone that "people really want him," we are fighting reality. Let's not focus on straightening out ideas; let's concentrate on what made those ideas go awry.

If we are dealing with a wound from the age of one week when there was little frontal cortex to understand anything, why would we use the later developing cortex to comprehend and try to heal it? It is true that information from the primitive brain is passed along in ontogeny to higher brain levels and then elaborated, but we must not confuse that elaboration with the source of the hurt. No level of brain tissue can do the work of another. We don't ask the brainstem to do calculus. Let us not ask the frontal cortex to feel and understand feelings all by itself.

I insist that inside most deviant behaviors and symptoms is a core of primal pains, and it doesn't matter whether it involves a lack of touch early on, circumcision, later being criticized, humiliated, denigrated, or being ignored by one's parents. It is all processed as pain. That is why drugs work on such a broad spectrum of symptoms. Take a tranquilizer and we can sleep better, avoid migraines, hold down acting out, stop feeling anxious, be less aggressive, be less depressed, stop bedwetting and premature ejaculation, stop using alcohol and taking drugs. *One specific pain pill can accomplish this universal task.* In short, pain is pain no matter what label we pin on it. It is not I who insist on this. It is what we find in each and every patient from twenty-four different countries who express their needs and pain without any direction from us. If nothing else, phantom limb pain, hurting from a foot amputated two years before, shows that we can hurt from a *memory!*

Unconsciousness is part of our genetic legacy that we transmit from generation to generation. We come equipped with the mechanisms to mercifully remain unconscious. Freud called it neurosis. It is no more than being unconscious. The neurotransmitters are the mechanism for the unconscious. That is why they exist; the most merciful of human processes. We cannot make anyone conscious, although we can make them aware. Consciousness cannot be manipulated and cannot be arrived at by any act of will. Awareness can.

Once the patient is consciously aware we don't have to teach integration or give her lessons in life. Once there is integration we must trust the patient in her own self-determination to make her own life. Therapists don't have to be omniscient or omnipotent. To tell people how to live presumes that we know better than they. Once liberated from their past they can make their own way.

Being smart doesn't mean we haven't made a mess of our lives. I believe patients will know well enough once they are integrated and are no longer being driven by unconscious forces. Self-determination is paramount. People need emotional counseling, by and large, when they don't feel. It is the reason for all those "how-to" books in psychology. And we see how limited those books are. In the final analysis, the person usually reverts to habitual behavior patterns.

Feeling human beings treat children and friends with empathy and kindness, all hostility having been removed; they treat themselves well, no longer having to suppress feelings with cigarettes and drink; and they treat the environment well, being in touch with their own nature, which allows them to appreciate nature.

It's not just a matter of thinking healthy thoughts; we need a healthy brain. An unloved brain is not healthy. It's not just cells we are discussing; they are part of a human being. And it's not just dopamine or serotonin that is in question. It means that on every level love determines how we are formed and our later personality. A deficit of a hormone during gestation can mean a deficit in the baby forever. Of course we can single out this chemical or that, this hormone or that, and find deficits in certain syndromes. But that doesn't necessarily mean the lack is the *cause* of the affliction. It is often a concomitant.

Madonna said it in her song "Drowned World": "I traded fame for love." She was discussing what she gave up for love. She found fame a poor substitute. "It's like a drug. It's so heady it sweeps you off your feet," she said in a March 1, 1998, cover story interview in the *London Sunday Times*. It is not *like* a drug. It is a drug! It covers not being loved. The trouble is we need more and more. "Suddenly, you're in a stadium with a hundred thousand people screaming your name and you've never felt so lonely." Who could say it better?

20

PSYCHOTHERAPY AND THE BRAIN
Getting the Brain Well

The goal in Primal Therapy is to produce feeling beings. To do so, we must trust biology. The biologic system is excruciatingly and inexorably rational. No patient reliving birth has any use of her arms or legs. We also must trust the patient, whose biologic system knows what should happen next. That system is governed by the imprint. We run around all of our lives trying to catch up with the imprint; alas, we never do. It rules. A father who is busy at work because he has to be busy, to keep on the run because of his own pain, is not going to be the attentive father a young child needs. He says he has to make a living for his family but too often it is a rationalization. And the baby's stress level rises because he needs a daddy. And he is going to grow up and keep on the run because his chronically high stress level forces him to. If we have high stress hormone levels and we do not act-out and keep on the run, then the pressure travels inside and we are candidates for a heart attack or stroke. Death awaits no matter which way we turn . . . outside or inside. I have discussed the "appointment in Sumara." Feelings are that appointment. Wherever we turn, wherever we flee, they are waiting. We ignore them, they make us sick. We drug them, they come back in force the minute we stop. We act them out until we drop. There is no surcease, no respite, no pity. The pained system is fascist, never letting up, never getting needs fulfilled except symbolically, dominating everything and every relationship, allowing no alternatives and no escape. It is a prison we construct for ourselves to keep strange feelings and needs out and pain in.

During a feeling the frontal cortex recedes as lower-level processes take over. Before that happens the brain is in a frenzy of activity as more and more neurons are recruited for the fray against the imprint. The recruitment of extra brain cells is what drives up the amplitude of the brain waves. We see that the amplitude mounts radically when a patient is on the verge of a feeling; when a feeling is pushing hard to enter conscious-awareness. After a connected feeling the amplitude drops equally radically. It is one more check on connection, a true feeling. Now instead of reacting by running from the imprint, one can embrace it, feel it, and above all, *react* to it.

Reactivity is central, because full reactivity was blocked and rerouted at the time of the trauma. If the event, say, watching your father and mother bicker constantly, made you feel unsafe, then feeling it over months and months in therapy will be necessary to allow a complete reaction to it. The feeling might be that at any moment the family would fall apart and there would no longer be a home with parents for the child. The person grows up insecure and frightened. He is waiting for the cataclysmic event—the divorce—the end of the family. In too many cases this is exactly what happens with devastating effects. And for the father who constantly threatens to leave the mother, "I won't have my daddy any more." The person grows up afraid of life and especially of death because he never had anyone to soothe and calm him, to encourage, support, and protect. He grew up naked before life; no scaffolding of love to insulate him, no early love to build a frontal cortex that could face life, integrate, and feel feelings and get along with others.

We can no longer neglect prebirth events because if we want to understand personality development we must focus on where it developed. Our brain cells are engaged in the Darwinian survival of the fittest; the strongest and most needed survive. That is why I believe that over millions of years the human brain is very effective, and all other things being equal, it should function properly. The strongest neurons have survived, and the most effective internally produced painkillers have also survived. As time went on and traumas impacted the human system the receptors became more and more refined. They are effective even before birth, and are found even in the placenta. This is why I tend not to place such heavy emphasis on heredity. There are plenty of reasons for deviated behaviors and symptoms given the various traumas we undergo beginning in the womb. I mentioned before, quoting Peter Nathanielsz, that those born with large placentas are more prone to high blood pressure, and possible stroke later in life. The placenta, like everything else in the human system, tends to compensate when there are below-optimal conditions during gestation. It grows large to make up for such things as poor nutrition.

Another reason the placenta grows is to work harder to break down prolonged secretion of stress hormones by the fetus. Unfortunately, there comes a point when stress overtaxes the compensatory mechanisms. The placenta is not just a sac; it is a living thing that produces painkillers. Yes, the fetus needs to kill pain even when it looks like a protoplasmic blob, and even though it has no words to articulate anything.

Deficient oxygen tends to weaken the blood vessels. This seemingly minute difficulty in the womb can become serious diabetes or cardiac problem later in life. Let us not forget that the placenta is the chief conveyor of oxygen for the fetus. A smoking and/or drinking mother produces low oxygen levels for her fetus; the placenta compensates by growing to provide more. The kidneys and liver may suffer, albeit slightly, as the system tries to supply oxygen to the brain of the fetus. It won't be slight later on as more trauma in life compounds the slight crack in the system.

When there is this kind of trauma, the lack of oxygen, the fetus produces stress hormones to galvanize it for danger. Prolonged secretion of cortisol, however, can account for high blood pressure later on.[1] This is why I note elsewhere that the making of early strokes (due to high blood pressure) happens in the womb.

Whether one is fat or not can also depend not only on heredity (although, I do not negate its effects) but on how well nourished the mother is during and after gestation. If she is undernourished during the first half of pregnancy there is a greater chance that her offspring will be obese later in life.[2] The system in these cases seems to be trying to make up for deficits in the womb throughout later life. The setpoints for the feeling of fullness in this case had been set before the middle of pregnancy. If the lungs are not properly developed in the womb, it can set the stage for chronic airflow obstruction throughout one's life.

Malnutrition during pregnancy may well decrease the offspring's life span, but if the infant is undernourished *after* birth it will not decrease longevity. We see over and over again that trauma alters setpoints in the womb that are not easily overcome, if at all. Trauma after birth may have enduring effects but not with such profound effects as womblife experiences. We must never forget the critical period. All the above emphasize that, in my clinical opinion, and based on much new research, many of the difficulties and afflictions we grown-ups have can result from prenatal influences.

Let us not forget the dialectic principles that govern biology. We speed up a carrying baby with coffee and anxiety and it grows up wanting downers to feel normal. We suppress a fetus with drugs and alcohol and it grows up wanting speed, coffee, sugar, and maybe cocaine. Our bodies spend a lifetime trying to make up for what happened in the womb. Setpoints are altered forever. We need thyroid hormone at forty to make up for a mother's lowered thyroid while pregnant. And we know that when she was under stress her thyroid (and that of the baby) was compromised. Thyroid hormone is essential for the care and feeding of the neurons and their dendritic connections. Even though the fetus starts to produce its own thyroid hormone at about the fourth month, the mother's thyroid production also enters the fetal system and influences its output. When the mother's level is very low the child can be born with mental retardation; the neurons are simply not adequate for the task. What are any of us trying to do by taking drugs . . . tranquilizers, thyroid hormone, insulin, heroin, pills to lower blood pressure and slow the heart, and vasoconstrictors for migraine? We are trying to normalize.[3]

The drugs we now use to control addiction and alcoholism often are those same serotonin-enhancing drugs such as Prozac, Zoloft, and Paxil. What is the addict trying to do? He or she is trying to normalize—bring the levels of internally produced painkillers up to optimum so that the lack of early love is not felt. With drugs the body is duped into thinking for a short time that it is loved, for that is what comfort does; it makes us feel all warm and cuddly inside. And what are physicians doing prescribing these same drugs for everything from depression to anxiety, from bulimia to suicidal tendencies? Trying to normalize the patient's system, whether they do it consciously or not. So here is the dilemma: very early trauma impairs the serotonin system, the very system we need to suppress that trauma. Someone who had a rather loving childhood but a terrible prebirth and birth may still be able to gather up resources to put down pain. But when you compound prebirth and birth trauma with emotional emptiness and rejection in early childhood, then you have an accumulation of pain that overtaxes the inhibitory system.

If we wonder why there is criminality and why so many criminals are on drugs we need to look to early deprivation and locked-in pain. So many of our prisons are taken up with housing drug addicts; those who should be treated for their lack of love. For those who prey on addicts and make a business of selling drugs it is another matter. Counseling addicts can be of help only after the pain is attended to. Killing pain is always the priority for those who were deprived of love early on. They can swear they will give up drugs, give up trying unconsciously to normalize their system, but physiology rules; the frontal cortex follows and does not precede—just like it did in evolution—brainstem first, limbic system second, and frontal cortex last. We must work with evolution, not against it.

If we think of the cost to society of criminals, for example, we find that half the women in U.S. prisons (it is reported[4]), are victims of physical or sexual abuse in their childhood. Many of their crimes were violent in nature, having experienced violence against themselves early in life. These women have a much greater likelihood of using drugs and alcohol. I am convinced that we can treat these victims and help them eschew violence, not by exhortation but by scientific psychotherapy, letting out rage and *need in context*, in a soundproof padded room. We have treated some one hundred incest cases, and we see the terrible destruction it creates. Drug addiction is the least of it; there are the crimes that this addiction forces the person to commit. There is something that can be done about all this, reliving the crimes against the person's humanity perpetrated by parents. The feelings carry the patient to where and when she must go.

Why would anyone want to feel agony? "Let sleeping dogs lie," is the oft-heard motto. We must feel it because on one level of the brain we're feeling it *all the time*—we are just not aware of it; and the damage it is doing will continue. We are "denormalized," and we are constantly playing "catch-up." The brainstem will go on pumping out excitatory chemicals to keep us revved up and on the go all of our lives. We then go to a doctor for this or that symptom—the high blood pressure, pedophilia, colitis, and compulsive gambling. Rather, we go to several different specialists who may all treat us in the same way. They often give us tranquilizers in the unconscious understanding that pain underlies all of those symptoms.

Because we have many more limbic pathways going to the frontal cortex than coming from it, feelings are far more influential on thought than thought is on feelings, as we might expect from evolution. A person needs to lose control completely in a controlled situation so that he is immersed in feelings. The brain will then learn self-control. It has less to control. (Before I had pads on the walls I had many holes.) The person needs to lose control *in context*.

When we go to the memory, very early memory, of daddy being out of control, screaming all of the time, the rage follows. We must travel to the baby brain that feels the rage, not to the adult frontal cortex that appreciates how the baby feels. We need to know the boundaries of our rage because so many of us fear ourselves and what we might do when we lose control. Better to lose control in a padded room where we learn what those boundaries are.

Memory is never approximate; it is exact. Too often, as I have witnessed over and over, rage begins at birth with the twisting and turning, the forceps yanking at the newborn. We don't have to theorize about this rage. We witness it every day. Never do my therapists encourage rage or tell the patients they are full of rage. Only in context will the patient express exactly the rage impressed in the system. When she does it at the behest of a therapist it is bound to be inexact.

Many therapists tell their patients, "Let the little child in you come out," "Tell your daddy you hate him," and so forth. There is no little child inside. There are only memories that need to connect. The great error of what I call mock therapists is to dictate where the patient has to go: "Tell your mother that she hurt you!" "Scream out your anger at your father!"

Dictating indicates a lack of trust and takes power away from the patient. That is why my therapy is not called Primal Scream Therapy. It is Primal Therapy. No one is ever told to scream.

A proper therapy takes time. That is why weekend seminars of reliving are dangerous. It is also why taking drugs to try to get there faster is a serious mistake. The pain exists on a timetable; we must respect biologic parameters if we are to be successful. That is precisely why screaming, hitting mattresses, expressing rage are absolutely useless without the early context. That connection is a sine qua non.

In some respects current conventional psychotherapy is an unconscious pact between doctor and patient implying that the doctor will know more about the patient than she herself. This is particularly true when the doctor is interested in the patient, warm, concerned, protective, and friendly—all the things the parents weren't. That is very relieving but we have to keep on going to therapy for years because it is only that . . . palliative and addictive. The patient thinks it's the insights that are helping. They only help a bit. It is the kind and concerned doctor that makes a difference. If it were the insights alone that help, a robot could produce them. It's the warmth and concern that goes along with them. He's the masseur of the aching ego. He is offering what we want, not what we need. What we need is need—old, infancy need, from older brain structures. There is a second-line limbic system relationship going on in conventional therapy that is essentially an act-out by the patient. She is being brilliant, having insights, and meanwhile being soothed and getting what she needs at age two. Too late. That is why it is addictive. It is short-lived and she has to keep on going back. It is still an act-out, whether in a therapeutic situation or not. In the first several years of life whatever happens becomes our fault because there is no other frame of reference to understand things.

The relationship between patient and therapist counts; it should be warm and supportive, but like the announcers at a tennis match, we should remember that the game is down there on the court and not in the booth. Brilliance is not called for. Empathy is. The insights the patient needs are already there in the frontal cortex. It doesn't need another frontal cortex to help out. The insight given by a genius will not penetrate the amygdala or the medulla, or the locus ceruleus, or the hypothalamus, or the thalamus. We can't convince or dissuade the amygdala. It is absolutely indifferent. No advice, counsel, or exhortation will make any difference. It knows what feelings it holds and is telling no one. What counseling will do is rearrange the frontal cortex so as to make the person feel more comfortable by hiding crucial information in the amygdala and hippocampus.

Conventional therapy is ahistoric and largely bereft of feeling, avoiding the very essence of our humanity. Yes, some dynamic therapies do explore history but not with the old historic brain that cries like a three year old from a three-year-old brain. *They cry like the adults they are; not the deprived child they were—and still are inside.* It is why therapists have not seen the depth of feeling in their patients. We are not trying to produce simply smarter people; we want to produce more comfortable, happier, feeling ones; those who no longer suffer from inexplicable symptoms or compulsive behavior.

If we can get over dealing with presenting symptoms as though they were the problem, we could then travel deeper in the brain and arrive at places we never dreamed existed. One also needs a dark, quiet, padded room to enhance the possibilities of going deeper, and of course, the proper techniques.[5] Not to deal with internal imprints is to bandage over a wound and then let it fester while we continue to believe that something has been done to treat the problem. The human brain in terms of our therapy is not such a mystery. It keeps our history safely hidden until we are able to retrieve it. That is its wonderful function.

A therapist can tell us that we are wonderful, worthy, important, etc. But that's not where worthlessness lies, and that's not where the need lies. The amygdala is insisting that we are not wonderful because our parents let us know that by their behavior of distance and indifference toward us, by ignoring us, never asking our opinion or even what we wanted to eat. It comes from years of hardly ever having eye contact with our parents. That is the predominant reality impressed into the brain system that was vulnerable in infancy and childhood, inflicted perhaps during a critical period. The critical period is over; the deed is done. The child needed his parents as a baby to be praising, encouraging, and loving—meaning plenty of touch. The amygdala holds that truth in its repository, never to be convinced otherwise. Never! It can't hear! It can only be temporarily strangled by ideas. Babies have to be held close from the first minute of their lives to six years later, night and day; not every minute but based on the need of the baby.

In the case of a woman whose mother had tuberculosis, love never happened; hence the feeling she carried of being unworthy and unimportant—not worth anyone's kindness. It is not just an *idea* of low self-esteem; it was in the blood system and in the brain cells. Neglect at two weeks made her feel unimportant and unworthy of attention.

There is an article in the *New York Times* which indicates that for professionals most current psychotherapy is short-term.[6] Long-term therapy is suspect, even considered unethical. This is by fiat of the new ego psychology to accommodate insurance companies who do not want to pay for long-term therapy. Implicit in all this is that the field has abandoned profound change in favor of counseling-style therapy. The deep, dynamic Freudian therapy has largely been out of favor lately when it comes to profound change. Because deep, dynamic therapy couldn't do it, due to faulty theory (in my estimation), long-term deep analysis has been left behind. It is not the problem of deep digging in the psyche that is at fault. It is the incorrect way of doing it. We should dig deep when necessary, once we have some idea of how to go about it. And we shouldn't rely on therapeutic ideas that are one hundred years old. Would any other branch of medicine stay stuck in techniques a century old? Not likely. We would have to go back to leeching patients. It should be obvious that deep change, the alteration of ingrained behavior, cannot be gotten rid of in a few sessions, yet in France the Lacanian method tries to do just that.[7]

Why has psychotherapy gone so astray? Because emotions and repression are involved that prevent highly educated practitioners from seeing the value of feeling; and because the early Freudian ideas had such a stranglehold on psychotherapy that it has been very hard to shake. Lastly, there wasn't enough neurologic information to inform us that we must take the brain into account when practicing psychotherapy. Too many therapies consider abreaction—i.e., getting angry at another group-therapy member, expressing love to another—as therapy. If the feeling is not in historic context, it is not curative and not therapy. It may be helpful, but then, so is voodoo. No one can get well without the help of history. I say this for both physical and mental ailments. Yes, we can treat cancer successfully. But until we see the awesome pressure of first-line pain we can never understand how cells can deteriorate and lose their integrity.

Neither directed daydreaming nor imagining therapy can take us where we need to go. It is a consciously willful act under the direction of someone else instead of following the dictates of our own nervous system. We can imagine or believe that we are relaxed, floating on a cloud all day long and still have anxiety churning below in the brainstem and limbic system. It is, by definition, a delusion. We don't need delusions for the treatment of serious pain.

Why must our nervous system dictate? Because it is dictating all of the time. Imagining therapy, whatever the name, is a mind game, not directed toward the reality of neurologic imprints, but curiously, away from them; only history is curative. We can imagine that the elevator is not a fearful space but a place of calm and peace, of floating on a lake while being whisked upward; but the brainstem is saying, "That is a terrifying space because it provokes the old fear in the incubator."

Anytime the power of therapy resides outside ourselves it cannot succeed. Guidance yes. Counseling yes. But not deep therapy. The power is already inside of us; all we have to do is tap into it. Whatever we have to learn is already inscribed in brain circuits. The slogan, "Power to the people!" should be taken literally. The patient decides when to come, when to leave for the day, and when to leave therapy permanently. He has the insights after feeling. He is the smart one, the one who is making major discoveries. His curiosity has been awakened.

The idea of the danger in opening up the psyche is too ingrained in us since the admonitions of Freud. I have found it to be the opposite. Opening up the psyche to all levels of brain function is the only way to eliminate ingrained patterns or symptoms. Insight is not going to get the job done. Our pain isn't built on lack of insights, and adding insights to the mix doesn't accomplish anything except to offer justifications for behavior to the patient, hence stronger defenses. Insights without prior feeling are pure guesswork. Imagine me trying to tell you what is lodged in your amygdala when even you don't know, and it's *your* amygdala.

The reason that psychotherapy is part of the problem rather than part of the solution is that it removes the patient's subconscious from his prefrontal conscious and treats the cortical "mind" as though it were something distinct from the rest of the body. The psyche is treated as though it were something floating in space to be reshaped and reconstructed. It is not *mental illness!* It is not *psycho*therapy we need. It is an experiential therapy. Pain is in the blood, tissues, brain, and muscles. It is in immune cells and hormones. It is everywhere and nowhere. It cannot be pinned down to one place because it is pandemic. We can treat the blood, the brain, the muscles, and the immune system separately, but until we treat the human being as something whole those measures are bound to fail.

Can a therapy help if we believe in it? Yes. Many things can help, not the least of which is religion. Does a placebo negate the efficacity of specific tranquilizing therapies if people get better on a placebo? A placebo can get us better because it provokes the secretion of the same chemicals as those contained in the tranquilizers. There are many roads to Rome. Just because we get better on a placebo doesn't mean that the medication isn't valid. It just means that beliefs and the hope they implied help the secretion of internal tranquilizers.

Without the cornerstone of need no therapy can produce any permanent change. To treat compensating mechanisms is to reform. It deals with the system as it is and changes the deformations occasioned by it. We need a revolution; we need to change the system, then health will flow naturally. I believe we have found the orchestrator of all the compensations, the brain system from which it all flows. We will need to compensate until each person finds the conductor. It is all about making up for a big hole of unfulfilled need.

Are we basically angry, raging monsters, or are we kind and generous pussycats? We are neither and both. We are born with capacities that date back millions of years. If the system is loved and not traumatized, it will be kind and generous and not hateful and aggressive. If a young child is constantly frustrated, she is going to be an angry child and adult. The child is responding to hurt, and it would be the ultimate denial to pretend she has not been hurt.

Does fetal memory exist? Yes, in terms of neurochemistry. Do we have a memory of all that? Yes, but in terms of neurochemical alterations, not in terms of scenes, words, or feelings. The lower brain system is constantly remembering. All we need to do is tap into that system. The human brain in terms of our therapy is not such a mystery. It keeps our history safely hidden until we are able to retrieve it. That is its wonderful function.

Sigmund Freud believed that the way to the unconscious was through words, as in free association. It is not. We cannot *think* our way to health. The way to the feeling level is through *feelings*; the way to the instinctual sensation level is through pure *sensations*. We must ask each level to contribute toward connection. That is what makes us whole. And ultimately, that is what gives us our selves back. We can find ourself but we must look in the most unlikely of places. Isn't it a paradox—constantly to elude the one thing that can liberate us?

As I stated in the introduction, we need to sail into uncharted waters, to set our compass for an extraordinary trip into the dark morass of the unconscious, to travel down to the lowest reaches of the brain. When we arrive, we will find it is not so dark after all. It is full of light and relaxation as we liberate all of those hidden memories. I believe I have charted part of the way. The rest is up to science. On this trip we have learned what we missed in life and what to do with our own children to avoid those mistakes. We can create new human beings. We have the choice, and we have the mechanisms to do it. All it spells out over and again is love.

Notes

1. Peter W. Nathanielsz, *Life in the Womb: The Origin of Health and Disease* (Ithaca, N.Y.: Promethean Press, 1999), pp. 146–47.
2. R. S. Strauss, "Effects of the Intrauterine Environment on Childhood Growth," *British Medical Bulletin* 53, no. 1 (January 1997): 81–95.
3. See Nathanielsz, *Life in the Womb*, for a fuller discussion.
4. "Half of Women in Prison Systems Were Victims of Abuse, Report Says," *Los Angeles Times*, 12 April 1999.
5. We offer training to all mental-health professionals.
6. "How Much Therapy Is Enough?" *New York Times*, 24 November 1998.

7. Henri Lacan, now deceased, held sway in the 1980s in France with his rapid analysis. A few sessions is all he would allow.

GLOSSARY OF TERMS

ACETYLCHOLINE. An important neurotransmitter in the cerebral cortex, also involved in the transmission of impulses from nerve cells to smooth and cardiac muscles and to certain glands, and from motor nerve cells to skeletal muscles.

ADRENALINE. A sympathetic ("fight-or-flight") nervous system hormone made by the adrenal glands; also called *epinephrine*.

AMYGDALA. Almond-shaped bodies at the front of the hippocampus in the temporal lobes which scan sensory input; when a threat is detected, the amygdala alerts consciousness and focuses the attention on it while preparing the body for fight or flight via the hypothalamus. The amygdala is functional from birth and involved in all memories to do with fear, terror, and rage. The amygdala is responsible for the feeling of feeling.

ANOXIA. The absence of oxygen. *See* **Hypoxia**.

ANTIPODES. Literally: any two places on opposite sides of the Earth; metaphorically: remote, difficult-to-reach parts of the brain harboring unexpected memories.

APPERCEPTION. The process of understanding in which newly observed qualities of an object or event are related to past perceptions and memories of it.

ATHEROSCLEROSIS. A disorder of the blood vessels in which fatty deposits called *plaque* build up on the arterial surface, narrowing them until there may be angina (if the coronary arteries are involved) or Transient Ischemic Attacks (mini-strokes) if cerebral arteries are affected. Should the artery be blocked by constriction, a blood clot, or plaque, heart attack, stroke, or phlebitis may ensue.

AUTONOMIC NERVOUS SYSTEM. Unconscious bodily control is mediated by the two arms of the autonomic nervous system, the alerting, fight-or-flight Sympathetic nervous system and the rest-and-repair Parasympathetic nervous system. During sleep and inactivity, the parasympathetic arm is dominant, and its primary neurotransmitter, serotonin, is plentiful. During wakefulness and excitement, the sympathetic arm is dominant and its primary neurotransmitter, norepinephrine, is ascendant.

AXON TERMINAL. *See* **Synapse**.

BREECH POSITION. Birth presentation in which the buttocks of the fetus engage the pelvis instead of the head. Breech delivery exposes the fetus to the risk of anoxia.

CATECHOLAMINES. The neurotransmitters derived from the amino acid tyrosine: epinephrine, norepinephrine, and dopamine. These are the excitatory neurotransmitters.

COLLAGEN. Connective tissue composed largely of albumin which forms a part of cartilage and bone.

COMPOUNDING. The process in which a later trauma elaborates an earlier trauma.

CORTICOSTERONE. A hormone produced by the adrenal glands which, like cortisone, helps the body adapt to stress, whether psychological or because of physical injury.

CORTISOL. A hormone secreted by the adrenal glands which prepares the system to handle stress, either psychological or because of physical injury.

CYTOARCHITECTURE. The specific arrangement of cells in tissue; often used to refer to the arrangement of nerve cells in the brain, especially in the cerebral cortex.

DOPAMINE. A neurotransmitter formed in the substantia nigra of the brainstem (and distributed throughout the brain via the axons of the substantia nigra cells) whose activity has much to do with our alertness and pleasure. All addictive substances provoke the secretion of dopamine.

ENDOGENOUS. Originating within an organ or organism.

ENURESIS. Bed-wetting.

GATE THEORY. The idea that there are "gates" in the brain which control the flow of information and provide the mechanism for psychological repression. Although such gates have not been found, the existence of endorphin receptors along the pathways of sensory signal processing in the brain suggest that our endogenous opioids may form one type of gate in the brain.

GLUCOCORTICOIDS. Corticosterone, cortisol, and cortisone are glucocorticoids, hormones which are secreted by the adrenal glands; these hormones mostly affect the protein and carbohydrate mechanisms of the body in times of stress.

HIPPOCAMPUS. A fold of cortex on the inner surface of the temporal lobe with a crosssection shaped like a sea horse, the hippocampus is involved in the laying down of contextual memory, meaning that it helps in the formation of memories of events in context. The hippocampus matures at about three years of age which may account for the difficulty we experience recalling events from before this time. This is an ancient structure, but not as ancient as the amygdala, which is functional before birth.

HOLOTROPIC BREATHING. A therapeutic modality propounded by Stanislav Grof in which accelerated breathing is combined with music in quiet setting, promoting a "nonordinary state of consciousness which activates the natural inner healing process of the individual's psyche."

HOMEOSTATIC REGULATION. The close control exercised by the body over physiological parameters such as body temperature and blood pressure. By analogy, a thermostat provides "homeostatic regulation" of the temperature in a house.

HYPOTHALAMUS. Situated below the thalamus, the hypothalamus is the brain's center for homeostasis, meaning the control of temperature, blood pressure, and so forth. It has close connections with the limbic system, especially the amygdala, and the pituitary gland. It is the final common pathway by which feelings are translated into bodily symptoms.

HYPOXIA. A deficiency of oxygen in the tissues of the body.

LOCUS CERULEUS. Literally "the blue place," this brainstem structure is the site where norepinephrine is made. Axons from the locus ceruleus distribute norepinephrine to limbic and subcortical structures in the brain. It is known as the terror center of the brain.

LYMPHOCYTES. The lymphocytes are produced primarily by the lymphoid tissues of the body—the spleen and lymph nodes. Their chief functions are (1) to migrate into the connective tissue and help build antibodies against bacteria and viruses, and (2) to differentiate between what is "self" and what is "foreign."

NEURON. Neurons are the cells which form the basic unit of the brain and nervous system. Each consists of a cell body with projecting dendrites which bring messages to the cell from other neurons, and an axon which transmits the output of the neuron to other neurons. Axons may be several feet long, or as short as a few millimeters. Neurons communicate at synapses, tiny gaps between dendrites and axons or between axons and cell bodies; a neuron may synapse with thousands of other neurons, so the brain is a neural network of almost unimaginable complexity. The nerve impulse which travels along dendrites and axons is both a chemical transaction and an electrical "wave of depolarization," while the message which passes across the synapse is in the form of a neurotransmitter such as serotonin or norepinephrine.

NEURONAL LOOP. Innumerable neuronal loops are formed by the interlocking networks of dendrites and axons throughout the brain. Repressed memories may reverberate in certain of these, altering physiological parameters while never reaching consciousness. Thus, there may be a feeling of unease without an apparent specific cause. Such unease may be the sensate portion of a repressed trauma.

NEUROPEPTIDES. Small proteins such as the endorphins, insulin, and oxytocin (which induces labor contractions, among its many functions), convey information between the cells of the body. Over one hundred of these proteins have been found to have receptors in the brain, and these have become known as the *neuropeptides*.

NEUROTRANSMITTERS. These brain chemicals permit neurons to communicate with each other by carrying the nerve impulse across the synapse, the tiny gap between the axon of one neuron and the dendrite or cell body of the next. Some, like dopamine and norepinephrine, are excitatory and tend to make the following neuron more likely to fire, while others such as serotonin are inhibitory.

NORADRENALINE. An excitatory neurotransmitter of the catecholamine family, also known as *norepinephrine*.

NOREPINEPHRINE. An excitatory neurotransmitter of the catecholamine family. Brain norepinephrine levels peak during the afternoon when serotonin levels are at their lowest, and are lowest during the night when serotonin is highest.

ONTOGENY. The course of development of an individual organism. "Ontogeny recapitulates phylogeny" means the developing fetus passes through the stages of the evolution of the species.

OPIOIDS. Any of a family of painkilling peptides. Morphine (made from poppies) and the endorphins, our endogenous (homemade) morphine-like molecules are examples.

ORBITOFRONTAL CORTEX. That part of the cortex above and between the orbits of the eyes where feelings are thought to meet reason.

OXYTOCIN. A neuropeptide which causes both labor contractions and the uterine contractions of orgasm when produced by the ovaries. In the brain, oxytocin made by the hypothalamus apparently promotes maternal behavior, and, in the male, helps sustain long-term monogamous relationships.

PALPITATIONS. Uncontrolled irregular or rapid heartbeat; often a symptom of anxiety.

PARAHIPPOCAMPUS. A transitional region of the temporal lobe adjacent to the hippocampus whose function it is to correlate input from cortical areas which process sensory input. This structure encodes memories for permanent storage.

PARASYMPATHETIC NERVOUS SYSTEM. *See* **Autonomic nervous system**.

PHYLOGENY. The evolutionary development of a species of plant or animal. "Ontogeny recapitulates phylogeny" means the developing fetus passes through the stages of the evolution of the species.

PITUITARY GLAND. Situated above the roof of the mouth, the pituitary is a ductless gland connected to and controlled by the hypothalamus above it. The pituitary controls the secretions of many key hormones as commanded by the hypothalamus.

PREFRONTAL CORTEX. The forward part of the frontal cortex. This part of the cortex is responsible for the integration of feelings, ambition, planning, and abstract thought.

PRIMAL. A deep-feeling event in which repressed memories are brought to consciousness; a reliving of imprinted memory.

PRUNING. The process of consolidation taking place in the first months of life in which neural pathways that are used the most are reinforced while the neurons that receive little stimulation die off.

RETICULAR ACTIVATING SYSTEM (RAS). A brainstem structure which samples the activity of the cortex and amount of sensory input, and adjusts the alertness of the brain accordingly.

REVERBERATING CIRCUIT. As the memory of a trauma approaches consciousness, neurochemicals are secreted to repress it and so protect the integrity of consciousness, but not before it has affected the physiology by (for example) raising the blood pressure. But, inevitably, some life experience will once more trigger the memory, and it will once more begin to rise toward consciousness so that the repressive process repeats itself. In this way, the memory of trauma reverberates beneath consciousness.

SEROTONIN. A calming neurotransmitter opposed by excitatory norepinephrine in the limbic system. Brain serotonin levels peak during sleep. Serotonin is a key inhibitory neurohormone.

STEROID. Hormonal steroids are synthesized from cholesterol in the body in the adrenal cortex, testes, ovaries, and placenta. While the sex hormones are necessary for reproduction, the adrenocortical hormones from the adrenal glands are necessary for life to continue. The glucocorticoids (e.g., cortisone) affect carbohydrate and protein metabolism, while the mineralocorticoids such as aldosterone principally regulate salt and water balance.

SYMPATHETIC NERVOUS SYSTEM. *See* **Autonomic nervous system.**

TACHYCARDIA. Excessively rapid heartbeat.

TEMPORAL LOBES. The lobes of the brain on each side, above and inward of the ears. The temporal lobes are home to the hippocampus and amygdala.

THALAMUS. All sensory input to, and motor output from, the brain pass through these "relay stations" at the top of the brainstem to and from the cortex. It is known as the switchboard of the brain. The thalamus is particularly vulnerable to anoxia at birth, and the death of cells at this time will later result in an impoverished cortex.

TITRATE. In chemistry: to add the exact amount of a standard solution necessary to react fully with a solution of unknown concentration. Applied to the feeling process, a skilled therapist "titrates" the amount of feeling that can be felt and integrated by a patient in a session.

VALENCE. Describes the strength or power of a repressed feeling, A strong, early feeling is said to have high valence.

VASOPRESSIN. A pituitary neuropeptide responsible for, among other things, controlling the production of urine. In the brain, it seems to be connected with the feeling of goodwill toward fellow humans. Vasopressin is responsible for paternal feelings from a father to his offspring while oxytocin does the same for a mother.

WARNING!

M ost of the clinics advertising today, despite their claims, have no connection with me. I recognize the great need for therapeutic help. To that end I have begun a training center. My hope is that these individuals, who come from many countries of the world, will be able to practice soon, and perhaps by publication date I will have graduates to recommend. We are taking applications now for our continuous training program, hoping to expand the Primal network as much as possible.

I must point out that I did not invent feelings. They have existed throughout the millennia. I have found a way to retrieve them once they have gone underground. In the absence of a formal therapy there is a good deal that can be done. An understanding and sympathetic friend is no doubt a good place to start. With him or her one can let down, cry, even scream, even if the friend isn't sure what it is all about. A little previous explanation would be helpful, but a good friend isn't going to be judgmental or critical. He or she will be content to "be there" for you. Just talking to a friend about one's feelings, without screaming or deep crying, is also an important step. Anything on the way to expression is a bonus.

There are those who have no understanding friends. That does not preclude crying and screaming by oneself, at least letting the pressure out.

It is, after all, feeling that we are after, and there is no monopoly on that. Of course, the best possible alternative is a skilled therapist. Rut there are not enough to go around, so we shall have to improvise.

It is not a bad thing simply to be aware that there is such a thing as feelings, and hopefully, what those feelings might be. There are many people who still don't realize that it is feelings that propel us; guide us; cause our symptoms, nightmares, and physical ailments.

There are those who are concerned because I do not place enough emphasis on value systems, not enough weight to cognitive aspects, nor to the spiritual. It is my belief that value systems derive directly out of feeling without having to be taught as such. For example, someone who has felt her childhood needs can sense what her own child needs. The mother doesn't need a list of values of what to do about child rearing. She doesn't need to be taught to pick up a crying child, to hold and soothe a child who has fallen down. She doesn't need to learn about the value of listening to a child's feelings, having already felt deep need to be listened to.

A spouse doesn't need to learn about the value of tenderness in a marriage—something so absolutely basic. I'm not denying values, nor awareness, nor certain ideologies. What I have found, however, is that they seem a logical evolution in those who feel. I'm therefore not advocating a bunch of decorticates roving around, mindless and helpless. On the contrary, teaching values is what is desperately needed for those who do not feel, who cannot sympathize, empathize, and understand naturally. Too many of us lead lives of quiet desperation, of broken dreams and secret compromises. We have compromised ourselves to make it through life. We can go back to that self that has been compromised.

What could be more spiritual than valuing human life and the human spirit? For those who are deeply repressed, the value of human life is not so evident. No feeling person could travel thousands of miles, while in a special uniform, to kill a stranger based only on some abstractions, such as "honor." In the same way, a person who has felt his own nature deeply and has discovered its profound beauty could not destroy nature around him for the sake of profits. One doesn't have to be educated to respect nature: it is inherent in the respect for one's own nature.

Values are the later development by the cerebral cortex all too often replacing feelings. Feelings came first. Values are inherent in them. We value life and everything associated with making it good and decent because we have felt the life inside of us and it is wonderful.

PRIMAL THERAPY IS NOT "PRIMAL SCREAM" THERAPY

Primal Therapy is not just making people scream. It is the title of a book. It was never "Primal Scream Therapy." Those who read the book knew that the scream is what some people do when they hurt. Others simply sob or cry. It was the hurt that we were after, not mechanical exercises such as pounding walls and yelling, "Mama." This therapy has changed what was essentially an art form into a science.

There are many hundreds of professionals practicing something they call Primal Therapy without a day's training. Many unsuspecting patients have been seriously damaged, thinking that they were getting proper Primal Therapy. I must emphasize that this therapy is dangerous in untrained hands. It's important to verify by contacting us.

Of the hundreds of clinics in the world using my name and falsely claiming to have been trained by me, I have never seen the therapy practiced correctly. We spend about a third of our time treating patients who come from mock primal therapists.

For years a good part of our budget went for research. I was hopeful that other clinical centers would continue Primal research, but such has not been the case.

I cannot honestly recommend any center doing Primal Therapy now as I am no longer associated with any of them other than The Primal Center in Venice, California, U.S.A. What has compounded the problem is that some therapists have had a smattering of training by me and gone on to practice.

I'd like to offer Primal Therapy to the world. Primal Therapy works. The patients know it. And I hope by this book to make it known to suffering humanity.

INDEX